The Fraunhofer IESE Series on Software and Systems Engineering

Series Editors

Dieter Rombach
Peter Liggesmeyer

T0254101

Editorial Board

W. Rance Cleaveland II
Reinhold E. Achatz
Helmut Krcmar

Jürgen Münch • Ove Armbrust •
Martin Kowalczyk • Martín Soto

Software Process Definition and Management

 Springer

Jürgen Münch
University of Helsinki
Department of Computer Science
Helsinki
Finland

Ove Armbrust
Alpine Electronics Research of America
Torrance, CA
USA

Martin Kowalczyk
Fraunhofer IESE
Kaiserslautern
Germany

Martín Soto
eleven GmbH
Berlin
Germany

ISBN 978-3-642-42842-5   ISBN 978-3-642-24291-5 (eBook)
DOI 10.1007/978-3-642-24291-5
Springer Heidelberg New York Dordrecht London

ACM Codes: D.2, K.6

© Springer-Verlag Berlin Heidelberg 2012
Softcover reprint of the hardcover 1st edition 2012
This work is subject to copyright. All rights are reserved by the Publisher, whether the whole or part of the material is concerned, specifically the rights of translation, reprinting, reuse of illustrations, recitation, broadcasting, reproduction on microfilms or in any other physical way, and transmission or information storage and retrieval, electronic adaptation, computer software, or by similar or dissimilar methodology now known or hereafter developed. Exempted from this legal reservation are brief excerpts in connection with reviews or scholarly analysis or material supplied specifically for the purpose of being entered and executed on a computer system, for exclusive use by the purchaser of the work. Duplication of this publication or parts thereof is permitted only under the provisions of the Copyright Law of the Publisher's location, in its current version, and permission for use must always be obtained from Springer. Permissions for use may be obtained through RightsLink at the Copyright Clearance Center. Violations are liable to prosecution under the respective Copyright Law.
The use of general descriptive names, registered names, trademarks, service marks, etc. in this publication does not imply, even in the absence of a specific statement, that such names are exempt from the relevant protective laws and regulations and therefore free for general use.
While the advice and information in this book are believed to be true and accurate at the date of publication, neither the authors nor the editors nor the publisher can accept any legal responsibility for any errors or omissions that may be made. The publisher makes no warranty, express or implied, with respect to the material contained herein.

Printed on acid-free paper

Springer is part of Springer Science+Business Media (www.springer.com)

Foreword

One of the most significant contributions of the agile methods community has been to put to rest the mistaken belief that there could be a one-size-fits-all software process by which all software systems could be developed. The agilists not only produced a family of process models that were clearly different from the traditional single-pass, sequential, requirements-first models, and their attendant baggage, but also they provided evidence of their successful application, often in situations in which the traditional approaches had failed. Further, they were willing to admit that their methods were not a panacea for all projects. For example, agilist Kent Beck stated in his pioneering 1999 book, Extreme Programming Explained, that "Size clearly matters. You probably couldn't run an XP project with a hundred programmers. Not fifty. Nor twenty, probably. Ten is definitely doable." (As an example of the pace of process technology, an increasing number of organizations have successfully evolved Architected Agile processes using a combination of architecting, XP practices, and a Scrum-of-Scrums approach to scale up to about 100-person teams—but not further to date).

Once one accepts that multiple types of processes are going to be needed for different project situations, a whole new field of questions arises. What are the process driver factors that lead projects toward more agile, more plan-driven, more risk- and value-based, or other methods? How does the existence of large, cost-effective, but often incompatible COTS products or cloud services affect a project's processes? What sort of processes best fit a project that must provide high levels of confidentiality, integrity, and availability assurance while being rapidly adaptable to high rates of change? How do factors such as corporate or national cultures affect a project's choice of processes? How does a project cope with the need to integrate different process models being used in different parts of the project? How does an organization evolve from an opportunistic quick-to-market process as a startup, to a high-assurance process once the product has a large customer base to satisfy? How does an organization evaluate the maturity and domain of applicability of new process approaches?

The number, variety, and importance of such process questions have caused many organizations to appreciate the need for a much broader and adaptable approach to software processes, including standards groups, professional societies, the Software Engineering Institute, and some government organizations. But there is a large amount of inertia to overcome, in terms of traditional standards, guidelines, contracting mechanisms, entrenched bureaucracies, and course curricula. Thus, there is a great need for well-organized guidance about the properties and areas of strength and weakness of various classes of software and system development and life cycle processes.

This book provides a major step forward in providing such guidance. It is written by authors with a wide variety of experience in commercial, industrial, government, and entrepreneurial software processes. It provides an organized approach for addressing the questions above, and numerous other questions, by describing and distinguishing among various classes of process technology such as prescriptive and descriptive processes, process modeling and simulation languages and tools, experimental and observational process evaluation approaches, and process improvement approaches.

Following the Osterweil "Software processes are software too" insight about the duality between software products and processes, the book addresses software process counterparts to software product technologies such as software process requirements engineering, architecting, developing, evolving, execution control, validation and verification, and asset reusability. It provides good illustrative examples of their use, well-worked-out definitions of process terms, and question-and-answer assignments for use in teaching software process engineering to students or practitioners.

As a bottom line, this book has arrived at an opportune time to help many classes of software-reliant people and organizations learn how to cope with a multiparadigm software process world. These include software-reliant enterprise managers and their staffs; software-intensive project managers, systems engineers, and developers; academic faculty researchers and teachers; and a growing body of next-generation software process engineers. If you fit into any of these classes, I believe that you will benefit greatly from reading this book and having it around for future reference.

Los Angeles, CA, USA   Barry Boehm

Preface

The concept of processes is at the heart of software and systems engineering. Software process models integrate software engineering methods and techniques and are the basis for managing large-scale software and IT projects. High product quality routinely results from high process quality. Process management deals with getting and maintaining control over processes and their evolution.

Who Should Read this Book?

This book is aimed at students in undergraduate and graduate courses, at practitioners who are interested in process definition and management for developing, maintaining, and operating software-intensive systems and services, and at researchers. Readers of this book should have basic familiarity with software development.

1. *Students.* The book can be used in general software engineering courses, in specialized process management courses, or in courses such as software project management, software quality management, software process improvement, or software measurement. The book may also be interesting for students who want to get a focused introduction to software process management, but would rather avoid general software engineering textbooks that typically present comprehensive process models with canned technology or nonintegrated development techniques.
2. *Practitioners such as project managers, process engineers, or consultants.* Practitioners may find the book useful as general reading in order to become familiar with the topic, for updating their knowledge, for understanding the relationships between process management and other aspects of their daily work, and for better assessing the relevance of the topic. Besides project managers, the book is especially relevant for process engineers, consultants, software engineers, SEPG members, members of process improvement groups,

heads of software development departments, quality managers, project planners, and coaches.

3. *Researchers.* Although the maturity of software process management practices in industry has increased and the state of software process research has advanced, the field is still quite immature. Students, practitioners, as well as researchers should be aware of the limitations of existing process management technologies, know the deficiencies of existing process models, and understand unsolved problems in the field. There is still a long road ahead toward mature software process management. We challenge software process researchers to address the vision that by using an appropriate combination of process and product engineering techniques, value creation for customers, adherence to cost and schedule constraints, and the fulfillment of quality requirements can be guaranteed on the basis of empirical facts.

Why a Textbook on Process Definition and Management?

One might argue that there are already many textbooks that include descriptions of software process models. The answer is "yes, but." Becoming acquainted with existing software process models is not enough. It is tremendously important to understand how to select, define, manage, deploy, evaluate, and systematically evolve software process models so that they appropriately address the problems, applications, and environments to which they are applied. Providing basic knowledge for these important tasks is the main goal of this textbook. There are many reasons that argue for a software process textbook:

Industry is in search of software process management capabilities. The emergence of new job profiles in the software domain (such as the agile coach, Scrum Master, process engineer, or offshore development coordinator), the lean and agile transformation of many organizations, and the establishment of so-called Software Engineering Process Groups emphasize the industry's need for employees with software-specific process management capabilities. Most of today's products and services are based to a significant degree on software and are the results of large-scale development programs. The success of such programs heavily depends on process management capabilities, because they typically require the coordination of hundreds or thousands of developers across different disciplines. Additionally, software and system development is usually distributed across different sites and time zones. To make things even more complex, technical and business environments as well as project goals often change during project execution, and an organization has to react to this in a controlled manner. The situation is similarly complex for operation and maintenance projects. Can such endeavors be mastered by using nothing but the appropriate software development and quality assurance techniques? The answer is "no, not at all." Analyses of large-scale development programs have shown that, with few exceptions, the reasons for the failure of such programs were not technical [1]. They almost always fail due to management problems. Due to the fact that process models glue together all activities, products, and resources, the relevance of process models for project management and especially for the success of large-scale software development programs is enormous. This need for process management capabilities is contrasted by the typical capabilities of young software engineering professionals. Such first-time employees are usually skillful with respect to software techniques such as coding or testing, but only have a marginal command of process management knowledge. This book provides basic building blocks of process management, such as process modeling or improvement, in order to lay a solid foundation for successful, sustainable processes.

Professional software engineers must fulfill process obligations. The duties of professional software engineers with respect to adherence to process models are becoming increasingly important. In order to illustrate this, let us compare a program that is developed by a student and a program that is developed by a software organization: Student programs usually solve small problems and are built to demonstrate that they work. If a student program fails, the consequences are limited. The student might not see the advantages of following a defined process because he does not coordinate his tasks with others and defects can be fixed without further consequences. If we consider the development of a software program by professional developers in a company, the situation is quite different: Each developer's personal work needs to be coordinated with the work of others; there is a customer paying for it, and the customer's business might depend on the resulting software. Thus, quality requirements are very important and the effects of potential failures are more serious or not tolerable at all. This means that there is often no way to avoid the definition, deployment, and control of high-quality development, operation, and maintenance processes. It is not sufficient anymore that a developer or a development team is convinced that specific quality requirements are fulfilled. Other parties such as customers also need to be convinced. Adherence to state-of-the-art processes and process management practices plays a crucial role when it comes to convincing others or even proving to them that quality requirements are fulfilled. This book explains different approaches to process improvement and conformance in order to support practitioners with respect to fulfilling process obligations.

Applicable knowledge from other disciplines is missing. Knowledge from other disciplines such as production engineering or business process management has only limited applicability for the software domain. One main reason is that production and business processes are typically repetitive processes in the sense that the same, well-understood process is enacted again and again with no or only minor variations. Quality assurance, for instance, is typically treated in production engineering and business management as the planning and deployment of a stable production or business process. Quality requirements can be fulfilled under given organizational constraints by just repeating this process. The situation is significantly different in software engineering: Software development is always the creation of an individual product. Therefore, process management cannot be based on the paradigm of repeatable processes. Quality cannot be achieved by just repeating processes. In the software domain, process and quality models need to be adaptable to individual development projects. There are no software development processes that fit for all types of projects or development environments. Consequently, approaches and techniques from production engineering or business process management (such as Statistical Process Control) cannot be transferred without difficulties. Sometimes they are useful when adapted appropriately. People who only have a production engineering or economic science background lack important capabilities for managing software projects and software processes. Software-specific process management capabilities are needed. This book introduces proven software-specific approaches to process management in order to support software engineers in their projects.

How Is the Book Organized?

Process management can be roughly divided into three areas: activities, infrastructure, and models (Fig. 1). Process management activities (left column in Fig. 1) can be seen as central: They consume, create, or modify different kinds of models (bottom part of Fig. 1), and are supported by a process management infrastructure (right column of Fig. 1).

The rationale for structuring the book is as follows (see middle part of Fig. 1): The basic concepts are given at the beginning. Afterward, existing representative process models are presented in order to give the reader an idea of what kinds of models exist and what they look like. A description of how to create individual models follows, and the necessary means for creating models (i.e., notations and tools) are described. Finally, different possible usage scenarios for process management are given (i.e., process improvement, empirical studies, and software process simulation).

Many books present practices, individual process models, or process standards in rich detail. However, there is often no description of how to customize these process models to a specific environment in a systematic way, information about the effects in specific project environments is not provided, and underlying assumptions are not true for many real situations (e.g., the assumption that development is performed in a colocated manner). As a consequence, project managers do not learn enough to assess the suitability of the presented models with respect to their own project goals and environments. Process engineers do not learn enough about how to customize or design appropriate models. In this textbook, we aim at providing knowledge that enables readers to develop useful process models that are suitable for their own purposes. In other words, the emphasis is not on working with given process models but on developing useful process models. Therefore, this textbook includes aspects such as descriptive modeling, continuous improvement, empirical studies, simulation, and measurement.

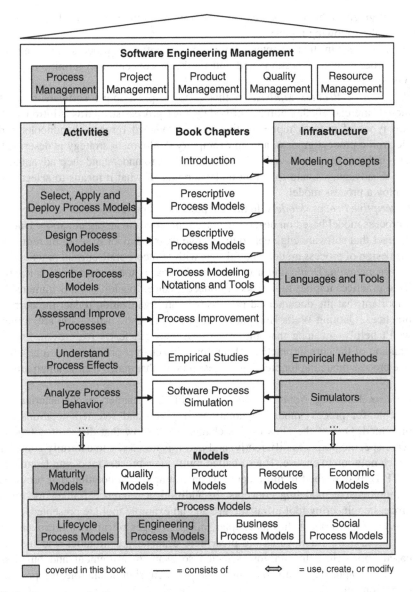

Fig. 1 Structuring of software process management

Reading. Although the chapters are self-contained, we recommend reading the book in a sequential order. Each book chapter starts with a short summary and a description of the chapter objectives. For each chapter, literature references, associated exercises, and sample solutions are given. The exercises aim at repeating and refining the material. They help the reader to get a better understanding and think about the contents from different perspectives. In addition, a glossary and an index are given so that the book can also be used as a reference book. The chapters focus on the following topics:

Introduction. In this chapter, the need for software process management and process models is motivated and the basic concepts and terminology are presented.

Prescriptive Process Models. In this chapter, prescriptive software process models are classified, a number of widely used process standards is introduced, two types of process representations are introduced (process handbooks and electronic process guides), and an exemplary deployment strategy is described. This helps to get an overview of existing models, to understand their advantages and disadvantages, and to get an understanding of what it means to select and deploy a process model.

Descriptive Process Models. In this chapter, a method is described for designing a process model based on observing current practices in an organization. Due to the fact that software engineers only change their behavior in small increments, the design of process models should start with or incorporate current practices of an organization. Deploying a process model that is too distant from currently lived practices implies high risks of nonacceptance. In addition, it is immensely important that the documented processes in an organization reflect the current practices. Quoting Watts Humphrey, "if you don't know where you are, a map won't help"—meaning that improving processes efficiently requires an understanding of the current practices. Therefore, this chapter puts a focus on descriptive process modeling for creating process models that match their counterparts in reality.

Process Modeling Notations and Tools. In this chapter, a characterization scheme for process modeling notations is given and selected notations are presented. One of the aims of this chapter is to show that different notations serve specific purposes differently, and that it is necessary to carefully consider which notation to choose. The so-called multi-view process modeling language, MVP-L, is described in more detail as an example of a notation that provides comprehensive modeling concepts. In addition, a reference framework for a process engineering tool infrastructure and an example tool are presented.

Process Improvement. In this chapter, different types of process improvement and assessment frameworks are presented, especially continuous and model-based approaches. In addition, selected software measurement and business alignment approaches are presented due to their significant role for process improvement.

Empirical Studies. In this chapter, a brief overview is given on how to determine the effects of a process model in a concrete environment. Such effects can be, for instance, the reliability of a developed code module, the defect detection rate of an inspection process, or the effort distribution of a life cycle process model. Software processes are, to a large extent, human-based and consequently non-deterministic. In addition, they are heavily context-dependent, i.e., their effects vary with the development environment. Therefore, empirical studies of different types are needed to understand and determine the effects of processes and to analyze risks when changing processes or introducing new ones.

Process Simulation. In this chapter, process simulation is introduced as a means for analyzing process dynamics. It is shown how simulation models can be created and how they can be combined with empirical studies to accelerate process understanding and improvement. In addition, a library of existing model components ready for reuse is introduced.

What Are the Benefits for the Reader?

Readers will gain knowledge and skills for designing, creating, analyzing, and applying software and systems development processes. In particular, the essential learning objectives of the book are:

- Understanding the importance of software processes and software process improvement
- Becoming acquainted with industrial software and system development processes and process standards
- Understanding the advantages and disadvantages of different process management techniques and process modeling notations
- Getting basic knowledge for modeling and analyzing software and system development processes
- Being aware of process management activities in software-related organizations

After studying the book's contents, readers will be able to contribute to process management activities, especially to applying common methods and notations for process modeling, designing software development processes, defining process improvement goals, selecting software process improvement approaches, participating in improvement programs, increasing process maturity, assessing processes, and evaluating processes by performing empirical studies.

Who Are the Authors?

The foci of this book were selected based on the comprehensive process management and software engineering experience of the authors. Although this book is intended as a general introduction to software process definition and management, it places an emphasis on specific areas, whereas others might highlight different aspects. The authors of this book have defined many organizational process standards, were involved in a multitude of industrial software process improvement programs, and have conducted many empirical studies of different types. They have produced national and international process standards for organizations such as the European Space Agency (ESA), the Japan Aerospace Exploration Agency (JAXA), and other governmental authorities. Some of the authors defined process assessment models and acted as certified process assessors for different schemes such as ISO/IEC 15504. Research-wise, the authors have developed, deployed, and evaluated a multitude of process management methods, techniques, and tools, including technologies for multi-view process modeling, process scoping, process tailoring, process compliance management, process visualization, and process evolution. All authors can draw on several years of experience as members of a process management division at a leading institute for applied research and technology transfer. They have helped many companies worldwide to improve their software development processes and their software process management. The authors also have significant experience in teaching software process management, be it by giving lectures at a university, in-house tutorials, or public seminars. The material presented in this book has been used, for instance, many times in a graduate process modeling course at the University of Kaiserslautern, Germany, and in a course of an accredited international distance education master program. One of the authors held several management positions in the area of process management, including being the head of a process engineering and technology group, the head of a process and measurement department, and the head of a process management division. In addition, the authors have served the scientific community in several ways such as co-organizing and contributing to the International Conference on Software and System Process (ICSSP), the International Conference on Product Focused Software Development and Process Improvement (PROFES), and the International Symposium on Empirical Software Engineering and Measurement (ESEM).

Helsinki, Finland
Torrance, CA, USA
Kaiserslautern, Germany
Berlin, Germany

Jürgen Münch
Ove Armbrust
Martin Kowalczyk
Martín Soto

Reference

[1] Humphrey WS, Konrad MD, Over JW, Peterson WC (2007) Future directions in process improvement. Crosstalk J 20(2):17–22

Acknowledgments

We appreciate the encouragement of Dieter Rombach and William E. Riddle to work in the area of software process management. Their way of thinking significantly influenced our approach to process engineering.

Our special thanks go to Barry Boehm, Thomas Bauer, Sören Kemmann, and Bastian Zimmer as well as many other individuals who gave us valuable review comments. We would also like to thank Sonnhild Namingha for proofreading the book.

This textbook integrates previous work by the authors (such as authored or coauthored articles, reports, or studies) and work of others. In cases where the authors intentionally reference material from others, the authors tried to cite this correctly and completely. The provided references can be used for a deeper or more comprehensive introduction to the respective topic.

We wish you interesting and enjoyable reading. We hope that you will benefit from this textbook and that you will be able to make use of the values of software process management—as an important step toward professional software and systems development.

Contents

Chapter 1
Introduction

This chapter motivates the need for defining and managing software process models. Basic concepts and terminology are presented. Figure 1.1 displays the chapter structure.

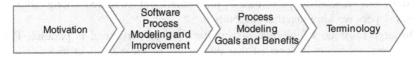

Fig. 1.1 Chapter structure

1.1 Objectives of This Chapter

After reading this chapter, you should be able to:

- Understand the reasons why software processes are important for software development projects and organizational learning
- Name the different goals of software process modeling
- Appreciate the need for software process modeling, process management, and process improvement in organizations that are developing, operating, or maintaining software-based systems or services
- Explain the basic terms

1.2 Motivation

Nowadays, the business of many companies and organizations is essentially based on software. Software-intensive systems, such as automotive or telecommunication systems, and services, such as financial services, increasingly depend on software. Software adds significant value to many products and services and allows for

J. Münch et al., *Software Process Definition and Management*,
The Fraunhofer Series on Software and Systems Engineering,
DOI 10.1007/978-3-642-24291-5_1, © Springer-Verlag Berlin Heidelberg 2012

competitive differentiation in the market. The increasing importance of software as well as new software development paradigms such as model-driven or lean software development and future software-based applications impose many challenges and demands on software development, operation, and maintenance. In the following, several reasons are given for why organizations should place an emphasis on process management.

Typically, software and software-intensive systems are developed with hundreds or thousands of people in teams. They perform a multitude of different activities, so-called processes. Systematic coordination and cooperation mechanisms are needed in order to successfully create customer value and fulfill project goals under given project constraints such as budget limitations or deadlines. Descriptions of processes, so-called process models, are a necessary means for coordinating such endeavors. Process models can be used to define work procedures, prescribe the interfaces between tasks, support the organization of work products, or support the management of necessary resources. Team-based development has several characteristics that are challenging to deal with when conducting projects. Some typical characteristics are:

- Many activities are not performed by individuals, but are shared among different developers working together smoothly.
- In large projects, a multitude of activities can be performed in parallel. This requires good coordination so that the results of these tasks fit together in a planned way.
- There are many relationships between activities. Documents or code, for instance, can be exchanged between activities or may be used jointly by different activities. In addition, temporal dependencies may exist between activities.
- Many activities need to be synchronized so that they contribute to overall project goals. In systems engineering, for instance, software engineering processes often need to be synchronized with processes from mechanical and electrical engineering.
- As software development is a largely human-based activity, building teams is an important issue. Teamwork involves, for instance, selecting a team, harmonizing the contributions of individual members, integrating different skills and interests, and solving conflicts. Clear responsibilities can help to overcome problems with team development.
- Managing human-based processes requires great leadership skills. One of the main tasks is to motivate people to contribute to common goals.
- Besides product requirements, project managers have to consider process requirements when performing projects and leading teams. Examples of process requirements include adherence to process standards or required productivity.

Software and systems development is being increasingly performed concurrently in different countries with many customer–supplier relationships along the development chain. Outsourcing, offshoring, and nearshoring are aggravating this trend. Global software development is close to becoming the norm. Motivators for globally distributed software development are [1]:

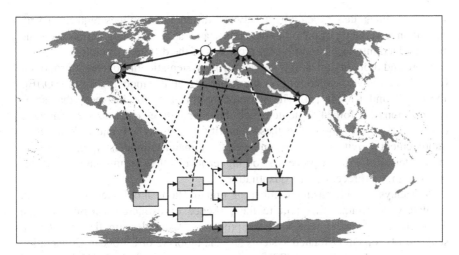

Fig. 1.2 Distribution of software engineering tasks to different sites

- Limited trained workforce in technologies that are required to build today's complex systems
- Differences in development cost that favor geographical dispersal of teams
- A "shift"-based work system facilitated by time zone differences allowing for shorter times to market
- Advances in infrastructure (e.g., availability of Internet bandwidth and software development and integration tools)
- A desire to be "close" to a local market

It is inherently more difficult to coordinate projects where teams are physically distributed than projects with colocated teams. This is mainly due to the lack of implicit knowledge shared among developers who work in colocated environments. In addition, different cultures significantly aggravate the coordination of large software development projects and lead to manifold new coordination mechanisms. Supporting such distributed development requires well-understood and accurately implemented process interfaces and process synchronization. In addition, tasks need to be distributed among different sites (Fig. 1.2).

Large systems usually consist of components from different disciplines (e.g., electrical engineering, mechanical engineering, software engineering). In addition, software-based systems penetrate more and more areas of our daily life, which means that these systems must be easy to use for nonexperts. Hence, disciplines such as sociology and psychology are getting increasingly relevant for software development. In consequence, specialists from many disciplines have to work together when developing, maintaining, or operating software-based systems and services. Historically, software engineering has, to a large extent, evolved separately from other disciplines. Other disciplines have developed their own terminology, methods, techniques, tools, culture, and way of solving problems.

Therefore, integrated development between different disciplines requires a very careful understanding of the other disciplines and, as a minimum, harmonized and synchronized interfaces between the processes of the different disciplines.

More and more organizations are deploying systematic improvement programs. Often they follow so-called process capability or maturity models such as ISO/IEC 15504 [2] and CMMI [3]. The reasons for this are, for instance, that some organizations are forced to demonstrate their capabilities (such as for winning a bid) or that organizations use these maturity models as a framework for their improvement activities. At a certain level, these maturity models typically require the existence of explicit processes; on higher levels, they require capabilities for managing these processes in a quantitative way.

Nowadays, an increasing number of organizations are forced to adhere to regulatory constraints that require the presence of explicit processes and the demonstration of adherence to those processes. Examples are the IEC 61508 standard [4] for safety-related systems and the tailoring of European Cooperation for Space Standardization (ECSS) software engineering standards [5] for ground segments [6] at European Space Agency (ESA).

One of today's most important challenges is that software is taking over more and more critical functionality. Therefore, software failures have a large potential for causing economic or even physical harm. Software is currently becoming the major source of critical system failures. This implies that the software included in many systems and services needs to be developed, operated, and maintained in such a way that critical qualities such as reliability, safety, security, privacy, or robustness can be assured at acceptable levels. Since many important critical product requirements cannot be fulfilled by features added to a system already developed, these requirements have to be considered systematically throughout the entire development process. As a consequence, activities regarding the assurance of these desired qualities need to be integrated into the overall development process, understood with respect to their effects on the resulting system, and adhered to during project performance.

Market dynamics require an organization to adapt better and faster to changes in the development environment, and to enforce innovations. Advanced process management is required to support assessing the impact of process changes and the flexible adaptation of processes.

All these challenges and demands on software development, operation, and maintenance require a significant transition from craft-based software development to more engineering-style software development. This addresses especially the following principles:

- Planning is based on experience
- Project execution is goal- and value-oriented and adheres to defined processes
- Projects are traceable and controllable
- Relevant process effects are predictable
- Learning and improvement cycles are established

These principles are widely accepted and established in traditional disciplines such as production engineering or mechanical engineering. In applying these principles to software engineering, one needs to consider the specifics of software (e.g., software is developed rather than produced; the effects of techniques depend on the development environment; software development involves many creative activities; data is less frequent and mostly of a nonparametric nature).

There are several approaches to applying engineering principles to software development that aim at so-called disciplined software development, including the problem-oriented Quality Improvement Paradigm (QIP) [7] and the solution-oriented Capability Maturity Model Integration (CMMI) [3]. According to Rombach et al. [8], essential elements of these frameworks are:

- With respect to processes: defined processes, prediction models (with respect to effort, schedule, quality), analytical and constructive quality assurance processes throughout the whole lifecycle, understanding of the context-dependent aspects of key methods and techniques
- With respect to products: adequate documentation, traceable documentation, evolvable architecture
- With respect to management: adequate workforce capabilities and staffing, sufficient continuing education and training, guaranteeing the sustainability of core competencies
- With respect to organizational improvement: traceable quality guidelines, comprehensive configuration management, learning organization

Understanding and gaining intellectual control over processes is a prerequisite for managing, controlling, and optimizing the development and evolution of software-intensive systems and services. This implies the establishment of advanced process management capabilities and an adequate understanding of the impact of processes on the generated products, services, and business values in different situations.

Due to the importance of software process models, organizations should have adequate process management capabilities in place to define, use, and evolve process models. Insufficient process management can lead to serious failures, including inefficient productivity, increased time to market, and decreased workforce motivation. If no adequate process management is established, this typically causes problems such as

- Unnecessary rework
- Deviations from plan are detected too late
- Confusion regarding roles and responsibilities
- Documents cannot be found when needed because they are not associated with process steps
- Variations in process execution
- Permanently incomplete and inconsistent process documentation

- Deferred certification because appropriate process documentation cannot be produced promptly
- Performance inefficiency (due to "unfit for purpose" processes)
- Uncertain execution and dependence on individual efforts (due to vague and incomplete process descriptions)
- Inefficient division of work and double work (due to poorly defined interfaces)

Hence, the typical question is no longer if process management is necessary, but how to define and implement a strategy for introducing advanced process management step by step and how to evaluate its success.

1.3   Software Process Modeling and Improvement

Following Osterweil [9], process models can be seen as generalized solution specifications that can be instantiated to perform concrete activities: While a process is a vehicle for solving problems and achieving development goals, a process model is a specification on how this is done. Process models can be used for different purposes, e.g., for coordinating, synchronizing, monitoring, and improving software development, maintenance, and operation activities.

There is no set of ideal process models that can be used for the development or evolution of software-intensive systems and services. The suitability of a process model heavily depends on the so-called context of a project, i.e., the characteristics of a development environment and the goals of a project. The effectiveness of a specific testing process, for instance, can highly depend on context characteristics, like the required reliability level of the test object, the experience of the test team, the budget for testing, the application domain, and other factors.

Choosing appropriate process models and tailoring them for a specific project and development environment is important and requires sufficient understanding of the effects of the processes in this very environment. This, in turn, requires an understanding of the cause-effect relationship between processes and products under typical conditions of the development environment. Therefore, development organizations should invest effort into determining the effects of processes in their own environment. Empirical studies and simulation are means to gaining such knowledge.

The need for software process improvement (SPI) is being widely recognized nowadays. Due to the fact that software development processes are usually human-based and depend on the development context, changes to these processes typically cause significant costs and should be considered carefully. Alternative improvement options need to be evaluated with respect to their implementation cost and their potential impact on business goals.

The field of software process modeling, analysis, and evolution is also an important research area. This is especially motivated by the following:

– Software engineering methods, techniques, and tools are being used in processes (i.e., the processes form the prerequisites for their successful use). Hence, research on methods, techniques, and tools requires an understanding of how they are being used. Appropriate processes are a critical success factor for gaining benefits from research results. Researchers who are not familiar with processes in which their research results are being used will likely fail to produce beneficial results.
– Processes need to be investigated in order to identify and assess strengths and weaknesses and to identify and evaluate improvements. Due to the fact that many processes are human-based activities, their behavior is nondeterministic, and the effects of processes need to be studied empirically for specific contexts.
– There are still many problems and challenges related to process management that lead to fundamental research questions (e.g., how to support the replanning of human-based processes, how to provide process models for reuse, how to define the degree of allowed flexibility).

1.4 Process Modeling Goals and Benefits

Software process modeling supports a wide range of objectives. Based on Curtis et al. [10], the following basic objectives for software process modeling can be observed:

– Facilitate human understanding and communication
– Support process improvement
– Support process management
– Provide automated guidance in performing process
– Provide automated execution support

Among others, the following benefits are expected from systematic process modeling:

– Better transparency of software engineering activities
– Reduced complexity of large development efforts
– The ability to perform process measurement (i.e., process models that are used in practice are a prerequisite for process measurement and, in consequence, for process improvement)
– The ability to undergo process assessments (i.e., explicitly defined process models are a prerequisite for demonstrating process maturity)
– Predictability with respect to the process characteristics and the characteristics of the results is only achievable with explicit models (i.e., enabling predictability for characteristics such as consumed effort, completion date, or reliability of a produced software component requires the existence of explicit process models, although this is not enough and other models are needed, too)

1.5 Terminology

Compared to other engineering disciplines, software engineering and especially software process modeling is quite a young discipline. Currently, a mature or standardized terminology does not exist. Besides the newness of the domain, this is mainly caused by the parallel emergence of different process notations and influences from different other domains such as business process modeling or programming notations.

In practice, organizations often use different terms for similar constructs (e.g., activity, task, work assignment, work package, step, . . .), or people mix terms that describe models with terms that describe real objects (e.g., using the term "software process" instead of "software process model"). Often the domain is unspecified (e.g., using the term "process" instead of "software process"). However, a common understanding of terms does exist. In the case of imprecise usage of terms, the semantics can often be determined by the context.

In the following, we present a terminology that can be considered as a kind of common sense in the process modeling community. This terminology is mainly based on [10–12], and to a minor degree on [9, 13] and [14], as well as on other publicly available sources.

> A *software process* is a goal-oriented activity in the context of engineering-style software development.

Examples are the creation of a product (e.g., coding of system component no. 15 in project Alpha at company ACSoft), testing of a system, measurement of a code module, planning of a project, or packaging of experience for reuse in future projects.

Typical characteristics of software processes are:

– They are enacted in the real world
– They usually transform one or more input products into one or more output products by consuming further products (e.g., guidelines)
– They can be performed by humans ("enactment") or machines ("execution") or both together
– They can be refined by subprocesses, each of which can also be refined

Often, software processes are also called "software development processes". We recommend using the term software process because (a) many processes are not directly related to development (such as maintenance processes), and (b) software processes are also relevant in areas where not only software is produced (e.g., when building software-based systems).

In this book, if the context is clear, the term "process" is used instead of "software process."

> A *project* is a unique endeavor, which is limited by a start date and an end date and should achieve a goal.

It should be recognized that permanent or routine activities are not projects.

> A *project phase* (short: phase) is a collection of logically separated project activities, usually culminating in the completion of a major deliverable or the achievement of a major milestone.

Typical characteristics of project phases are:

- Phases are mainly completed sequentially, but can overlap in some project situations
- Phases can be subdivided into subphases
- Unlike a process, a phase is always defined by a start date and an end date. If this period is finished, the phase is finished. Typically, processes can be activated multiple times
- Typical examples of phases are the elaboration phase, the construction phase, or the transition phase. Phases are usually used when looking at a project from a management perspective

A major reason why it is important to differentiate between a process and a project phase is that there are two essentially different views on projects: a management view and an engineering view. Management often needs a period-based view on activities because investors, investments, dividends, revenue calculations, and financial plans are typically period based. Engineers usually need a product-based view on activities, i.e., a view on activities that describe in a goal-oriented way the steps needed to create, maintain, or operate a product or service.

It should be recognized that a project phase can be only performed once. If a requirements definition phase has been declared completed, it cannot be enacted again, even if there are still requirements engineering activities to be done. A process, however, can be reenacted. If, for instance, requirements defects were detected during a design review, a requirements engineering process can be reenacted in order to remove the defects (Fig. 1.3).

> A *model* is an abstract and simplifying representation of an object or phenomenon of the real world.

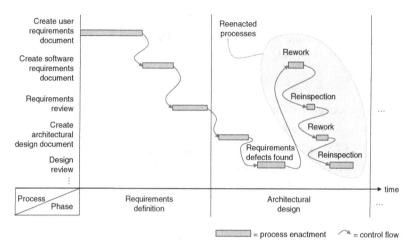

Fig. 1.3 Process vs. phase

Typical characteristics of models are:

– They describe only those aspects of the object or phenomenon that are (believed to be) relevant for the understanding and intended usage of the model
– They encapsulate experience and allow for an explicit representation of experience
– They can be created for different purposes such as planning, control, or prediction
– They have their own lifecycle, i.e., they can be specified, built, implemented, analyzed, used, assessed, evolved, or rejected

The frequently quoted phrase "Essentially, all models are wrong, but some are useful," attributed to the statistician George Edward Pelham Box, highlights that a model only represents a limited number of real-world aspects and details. The challenge lies in capturing sufficient real-world aspects and details in a model so that the model can be used for its purpose.

A *software process model* (short: process model) is a model of a software process.

A software process model is a description of a software process. Process models are often used as a means for problem solving. The specification of the enactment of a software process by a process model is comparable to the specification of baking a cake using a recipe. Process models can be represented by using different notations (e.g., graphical, natural language, machine-readable notations).

A process model can describe a process on different levels of abstraction (e.g., lifecycle process level, engineering process level, atomic step level).

The main elements of process models are:

- A description of an identifiable activity or a group of activities
- A description of the product flow (i.e., input and output products for activities)
- A description of the control flow between processes (i.e., the enactment or execution sequence)
- A description of a refinement (i.e., the definition of a hierarchy of processes)
- A description of the relationships to techniques, methods, tools
- A description of the relationship to roles

Other process-related definitions or statements are:

> *Process:* A set of partially ordered steps intended to reach a goal [12].
>
> *Process description:* While a process is a vehicle for doing a job, a process description is a specification of how the job is to be done. Thus, cookbook recipes are process descriptions, while preparing a recipe is a process [9].
>
> *Process model:* A software process model reflects an organization's know-how regarding software development. Software engineering know-how has to be developed and maintained. Practical experience has shown the need for modeling software engineering entities (especially processes), measuring those entities, reusing the models, and improving the models [8].

Often, only selected elements are shown in graphical representations of process models. Figure 1.4, for instance, shows only activities, artifacts, and the product flow, while Fig. 1.5 also shows the control flow and the relationships to roles.

In the following, further basic terms are defined:

> An *atomic process* (synonym: process step) is a process that does not allow further structuring in the form of subprocesses.
>
> *Process enactment* is the performance of process steps undertaken to reach a given goal. The process performer (i.e., "agent") can be a human or a machine. In case of a machine, the term "process execution" is usually used.
>
> A *process definition* is a description of a process that is enactable.

Process scripts and process programs are specializations of process definitions:

> A *process script* is a description of a process that is suitable for interpretation by humans. A process script should be tailored to the needs of the process performer.
>   *(continued)*

A *process program* is a description of a process that can be interpreted by machines.

A *process schema* (synonym: process metamodel, process architecture) is a conceptual framework for the consistent description of process models and their relationships. A process schema describes, on the one hand, building blocks and their relationships that form a process model, and, on the other hand, constraints on their composition.

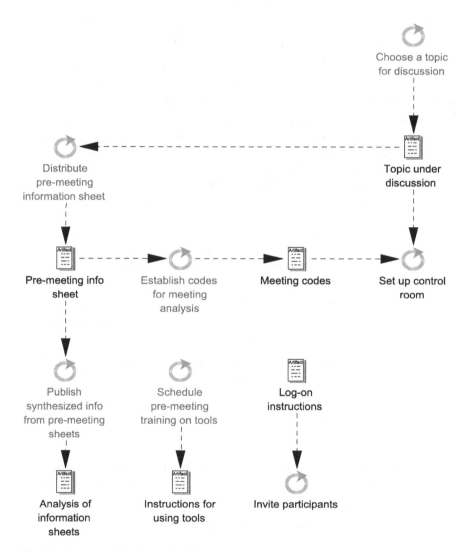

Fig. 1.4 Process model with product flow

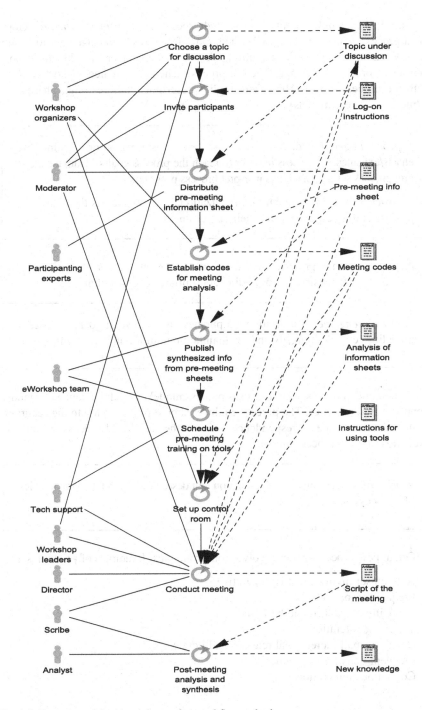

Fig. 1.5 Process model with product and control flow and roles

Until now, a single commonly accepted process schema for software development processes has not been established. Only few process management tools are flexible enough to cope with multiple process schemata or are able to import individual process schemata. Often, a process schema is created ad hoc together with the process model. This often implies description failures (e.g., phases are refined by process models).

A *process agent* (synonym: *process performer*) is a person or machine that enacts/executes the process in order to reach the process goal(s). Humans interpret process scripts, machines interpret process programs.

A *process owner* is a human or organizational entity that sets the goals of a process and is responsible for their achievement.

A process owner provides resources for the enactment or execution of the process and is responsible for providing appropriate process definitions.

A *process engineer* is a person who pursues one or several goals of process modeling (e.g., defining, extending, maintaining, improving process models).

To that end, a process engineer uses process models, which he defines, extends, improves, and manages. The process engineer should pay attention to the accuracy of the model, i.e., the correspondence between the real-world process enactment/execution and the process model.

A *principle* is a policy or mode of action that describes important characteristics of a process model.

Often, new process models evolve from principles. Examples of principles are:

- Active user involvement is imperative
- Frequent inspection
- Work in progress should be limited
- Timeboxed iterations
- Develop small incremental releases and iterate
- Frequent delivery of product
- Continuous integration

- Colocation
- Common coding guidelines
- Self-organizing teams
- Daily meeting

A principle is not a process or a process model, but a process or a process model can capture one or more principles. Principles should be adapted to contexts (e.g., by using experimentation) and integrated into process models. Sometimes the term "practice" is used as a synonym for principle, e.g., the principle "continuous integration" is often referred to as an XP practice.

A *product* is each artifact that is consumed or produced in the context of engineering-style software development.

Products can be refined by other products. Examples of products are:

- Source code
- Specification document
- Problem description
- Configuration data
- Component design
- Test case
- Test result
- Project plan

A *product model* is a description of a product or a class of products.

Usually, software product models consist of a description of the information units of a software product (e.g., functional requirements, nonfunctional requirements, design decisions) and a structure for arranging the information units (e.g., a table of contents for a requirements document).

The *product flow* consists of the relationships between products and processes that describe the access mode to the products.

The following access modes are typically defined:

- Produce (write)
- Consume (read)
- Modify (read/write)

> A *role* is a set of processes belonging together that are assigned to one or several agents. A role combines the functional responsibility for the enactment of a process.

Examples of technical development roles are: requirements engineer, designer (architecture), designer (data/algorithms), programmer, inspector, system integration engineer, and tester.

Examples of organizational and management-oriented roles are project planner, project manager, product manager, and quality engineer.

Like a process, a role is an abstraction. A role groups competencies (i.e., knowledge and rights). Several different types of relationships between roles and agents can be defined, especially 1:1 (e.g., the tester is Mr. Miller), m:1 (e.g., Mr. Miller plays both the role of the requirements engineer and the role of the code inspector), 1:n (the role of the project manager is shared by Mr. Miller and Ms. Scott), m:n (a mixture of the previous cases). It is important that the relationship between a role and an agent is explicitly defined. This is typically done during project planning, resource planning, and replanning.

A role is typically described as a specific view on the process by:

– The activities the role is involved in (described independently of the person)
– The documents that are consumed or produced in these activities
– The level of involvement of a role in an activity
– The requirements for playing a role (e.g., qualifications)

Figure 1.6 shows an example of the activities and the product flows that relate to the role module developer.

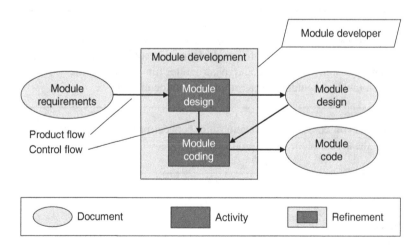

Fig. 1.6 Role example

Benefits of the role concept are:

- Activities and responsibilities of persons involved in a project can be clearly defined
- Transparency supports communication and cooperation between roles
- Necessary competencies are clearly defined
- Project planning is simplified
- Resources for a project or an organization can be specified independently of available personnel
- Role bottlenecks can already be determined at an early stage during project planning

The relationship between roles and process models can be qualified: For instance, a role can perform a process or a role needs to be informed when a process is performed or completed. Often, a so-called "Responsibility Assignment Matrix" (RAM) is used to qualify the relationship between roles and processes.

Finally, we define the term project plan, which integrates and instantiates several of the concepts presented above:

A *project plan* is a specification of the necessary resources for the execution of a process definition, the relationships between these resources and processes, the produced products including the product flows, and restrictions of any type concerning the execution of the process.

References

1. Sangwan R, Bass M, Mullick N, Paulish DJ, Kazmeier J (2007) Global software development handbook. Auerbach Publications, Boca Raton, FL
2. International Organization for Standardization (2006) ISO/IEC 15504:2004, 'Information technology—Process assessment'. ISO/IEC, Geneva, Switzerland
3. Carnegie Mellon Software Engineering Institute (2010) Capability maturity model integration 1.3. http://www.sei.cmu.edu/cmmi/. Accessed 9 Jun 2011
4. International Electrotechnical Commission (2005) IEC 61508, 'Functional safety of electrical/electronic/programmable electronic safety-related systems'. IEC, Geneva, Switzerland
5. European Cooperation for Space Standardization (2009) Collaboration Website of the European Cooperation for Space Standardization. http://www.ecss.nl/. Accessed 9 Jun 2011
6. ESA Board for Software Standardisation and Control (BSSC) (2005) Tailoring of ECSS software engineering standards for ground segments in ESA. http://www.esa.int/TEC/Software_engineering_and_standardisation/TECT5CUXBQE_0.html. Accessed 9 Jun 2011
7. Basili VR, Caldiera G, Rombach HD (1994) The experience factory. Wiley, New York
8. Rombach HD, Münch J, Ocampo A, Humphrey WS, Burton D (2008) Teaching disciplined software development. Int J Syst Software 81(5):747–763. doi:10.1016/j.jss.2007.06.004
9. Osterweil LJ (1987) Software processes are software too. In: Proceedings of the 9th international conference on software engineering (ICSE 1987), Monterey, CA, pp 2–13
10. Curtis B, Kellner MI, Over J (1992) Process modeling. Commun ACM 35(9):75–90. doi:10.1145/130994.130998

11. Rombach HD, Verlage M (1995) Directions in software process research. In: Zelkowitz MV (ed) Advances in computers 41. Academic Press, Boston, MA
12. Feiler PH, Humphrey WS (1993) software process development and enactment: concepts and definitions. In: Proceedings of the 2nd international conference on the software process (ICSP 2), Berlin, Germany, February 1993, pp 28–40
13. Heidrich J, Münch J, Riddle W, Rombach D (2006) People-oriented capture, display, and use of process information. In: New trends in software process modeling, vol 18, Series on software engineering and knowledge engineering. World Scientific, Singapore, pp 121–179
14. Cugola G, Ghezzi C (1998) Software processes: a retrospective and a path to the future. Software Process Improve Pract 4(3):101–123. doi:10.1002/(SICI)1099-1670(199809) 4:3<101::AID-SPIP103>3.0.CO;2-K

Chapter 2
Prescriptive Process Models

This chapter introduces prescriptive process models as a means of instructing an organization on how to achieve its business, software development, and improvement goals. It is structured into four main parts. First, two major classes of prescriptive process models are distinguished: lifecycle models and engineering models. These classes are described and discussed with respect to their advantages and challenges. Second, a number of widely used process standards are introduced to give an impression of the material the software industry is currently working with. Since these standards are not intended or fit for direct application, they must be amended and transformed into more user-friendly representations. Hence, the third part introduces two types of representations: process handbooks and electronic process guides (EPGs). Finally, it is typically not sufficient to prepare and publish a process handbook or EPG: Any new or changed process must be deployed in a systematic manner, to cause as little unnecessary pain for the organization as possible. The fourth part of this chapter thus discusses the deployment of a prescriptive process model to an organization. Figure 2.1 displays the chapter structure.

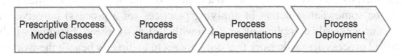

Fig. 2.1 Chapter structure

2.1 Objectives of This Chapter

After reading this chapter, you should be able to:

- Distinguish prescriptive and descriptive process models
- Explain the relationship between product and process
- Explain the prerequisites for applying prescriptive process models
- Name and explain different lifecycle process models

J. Münch et al., *Software Process Definition and Management*,
The Fraunhofer Series on Software and Systems Engineering,
DOI 10.1007/978-3-642-24291-5_2, © Springer-Verlag Berlin Heidelberg 2012

– Name and explain some widely used process standards
– Develop a process handbook for a specific target audience
– Support the deployment of a prescriptive process model to an organization

2.2 Introduction

This section distinguishes prescriptive from descriptive process models and discusses their relationship. It further defines the product–process relationship as a central basis for all process modeling activities. Finally, prerequisites for applying a prescriptive process model are discussed.

2.2.1 Prescriptive vs. Descriptive Models

One can distinguish two main types of process models: *prescriptive* and *descriptive* process models. Both types may exist in parallel in a software organization, often in several instances. They do not necessarily differ in content, but rather in their intended purpose: *Prescriptive* process models tell us how something should be done, whereas *descriptive* process models describe how something is done in reality.

This constitutes a major difference. Whereas a *descriptive* process model is created by observing the processes actually performed, a *prescriptive* process model typically aims to address all relevant issues of developing a piece of software. It is therefore often based on an ideal model of software development, for example, a set of best practices that should be applied in projects in order to yield their benefits.

This fact, by its very nature, leads to a number of conflicts. Human beings often tend to be somewhat reluctant in applying practices (or a process) perceived as boring, unnecessarily complicated, or laden with useless overhead. Especially if the prescribed process demands work that does not seem to directly benefit the working person itself, or only little so, it is often hard to persuade this person to do work perceived as unnecessary.

Hence, the problem is not only to construct a prescriptive process model, but also to get people to follow it as intended. In fact, the latter is more difficult than the former, but often neglected. A *descriptive* process model describes what people do every day—which means that it reflects current practices. A *prescriptive* model tells people to do (some) things differently, which means that they need to change their behavior. Getting people to change their behavior is one of the most difficult tasks in software engineering, so the successful deployment of a prescriptive process model is difficult, too: Deploying a prescriptive process model means changing people's behavior!

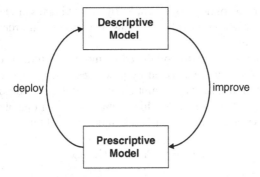

Fig. 2.2 The relationship between descriptive and prescriptive process models

Typically, descriptive and prescriptive models follow each other in a cycle. Often, the current processes are modeled and transferred into a descriptive process model. Using this model, problems are identified and mitigated by changes to the process model, often using additional external knowledge such as best practices. This model then becomes a prescriptive process model, effectively instructing people to do things differently than before. When the changed process is fully integrated into people's daily work, the process model becomes descriptive again, and another improvement cycle can start. Figure 2.2 displays this circle.

2.2.2 The Product–Process Relationship

The problems addressed by process changes are typically properties of the software product or the project that produces or modifies the product. For example, the product might not provide the required amount of throughput to satisfy its requirements, or it may be finished later than planned. Another typical problem is cost overrun. In any of these cases, a problem was detected with the product, and one should aim at solving this problem by changing the process. This is feasible because of the relationship between the process and quality aspects of the products. This relationship can be described according to the process–product relationship model from Rombach [1]:

$$Q \approx f \text{ (Process, Context)}$$

Q here means some quality aspect of the product, for example, reliability or cost of construction. This quality aspect is determined by a function of both process and context, such as a model-based testing (process) in the automotive domain, where the experience level of the testers is low and the programming language is C (context). So, in order to improve the reliability of a specific product, changing the context might be an option, for example, by improving tester experience. If this cannot be done, it might be possible to adjust the process, in order to cope better with inexperienced testers.

Besides quality aspects of the produced or modified product, other important properties of a project can be affected by processes. Such properties may be, for instance, the duration or effort consumption of a process. In addition, services can be considered as the object being developed, maintained, or operated by a process. Therefore, the function f can be described in more general terms as

$$\text{Goal} \approx f \text{ (Process, Context)}$$

Here, the goal can be any relevant product, service, or project property that can be affected by the process in the specific context.

Software engineering research is still quite immature in determining the function f (which is actually an empirical relation), because the methods and processes are not yet well understood and thus not completely manageable [1]. *Well understood* means that the effects of methods and processes on goal properties (such as product quality, cost, time) in varying contexts (e.g., different lifecycle models, personnel experience, or tool support) are known. *Manageable* means that for a given project context, processes can be chosen so that they guarantee the expected effects (such as product qualities).

Due to the relevance of cognitive laws for human-based processes, f (i.e., the relationship symbolized by $\approx$) is nondeterministic and can only be determined empirically. This implies that process and context must be described as precisely as possible, and that the respective goal properties need to be defined so that they are measurable.

The impact of changes to the process or context can then be determined through (combinations of) empirical studies of different types (e.g., qualitative or quantitative studies, controlled experiments or case studies, real studies or simulations). The results obtained in such studies can be used to create prescriptive process models that are proven to be beneficial in certain contexts and thus guarantee specific product qualities. Note that due to these circumstances, process changes only rarely result in major product quality improvement within a short period of time—in reality, process improvement (and thus, product quality improvement) is a mid- to long-term effort. Hence, process changes will yield most of their benefits in the long run.

2.2.3 *Prerequisites*

In order to apply any prescriptive process model, a number of prerequisites should be fulfilled. If one or more of the following prerequisites are not fulfilled, the effects of applying the prescriptive process model may be unpredictable. This means that in the optimal case, it may work exactly as intended. However, it is more likely that it does not work as planned, leading to worse results than planned, possibly even worse than before it was applied—which means that the new prescriptive model is likely to be rejected.

The prerequisites that should be fulfilled when applying a prescriptive process model include, but are not limited to:

The scope of validity should be known. It should be known which context(s) and goal(s) the process model is valid for. Context comprises factors such as domain characteristics (e.g., aerospace: highly safety critical, with products being used for decades), organizational characteristics (e.g., large organizations with low employee turnover), project characteristics (e.g., long-term projects with distributed development), and others. Goals comprise, for example, the reduction of cycle time or the improvement of code quality. A prescriptive model may have been applied successfully in a large aerospace organization with long-term projects and low employee turnover, leading to a significant reduction in cycle time. Applying the same model in a small Web application development organization with short-term projects and high employee turnover and the goal of improving code quality is likely to not achieve this goal, because the model was never intended for this context and goal.

The impact of a process should be known. It should also be known what the effects of the process described by the prescriptive process model are for a specific context. Effects may be, for example, the reduction of cycle time by 30% or the reduction of design defects by 20%. The specific context may be a large aerospace organization with long-term and distributed projects and low employee turnover. Applying the same process as prescribed by this specific process model in the same or a similar context is likely to have a similar impact. If the impact of a prescriptive process model is unknown, applying it leads to unpredictable results. Knowledge of this kind is usually specific for an application domain or organization and thus must be obtained in the respective setting.

The degree of confidence should be known. Furthermore, it should be known to what degree of confidence the process described by the prescriptive process model has been evaluated in a specific context. For example, the reports on the impact of a specific process may stem from a single application in a specific context—in this case, the degree of confidence is rather low, since other factors may have played a significant role, but were not recorded. On the other hand, if a specific process has been applied in a multitude of similar contexts, with the desired effects reported in all or most cases, the degree of confidence is rather high, because it is very unlikely that other factors were responsible, but not recorded, in all the success cases.

The process should be tailorable. Finally, it should be possible to adapt the process described by the prescriptive process model to specific project goals and contexts. Since the context for which a process model has been developed rarely presents a perfect match for the context it is supposed to be applied in next, and since goals may also differ, it should be possible to adapt the process and its corresponding model to the new context. For example, if in the original context, employee turnover was low, but in the new context, it is high, the process must be adapted to cope with this, e.g., by increasing the (written) documentation of project information. Obviously, there must be sufficient knowledge about the effects of the process changes in order to retain the validity of the process model for the changed context.

2.3   Prescriptive Process Model Classes

This section introduces two types of process models that can be distinguished: lifecycle models and engineering models.

The first subsection discusses important classes of lifecycle models such as the waterfall model, the iterative enhancement model, the prototyping model, the spiral model, and the incremental commitment spiral model (ICSM). Two example lifecycle models often found in industry that adopt these general concepts, the Unified Process and the IBM Cleanroom Process, are explained. The second subsection discusses engineering process models such as a process model for statistical testing, a process model for hybrid cost estimation, and the Extreme Programming process model.

Lifecycle process models capture the complete lifecycle of a software product. Typically, they abstract from a number of details, and instead provide a broader view on the process (focus on "what," not on "how").

Engineering process models describe (possibly in very much detail) a fraction of the complete software lifecycle process, for example a specific type of inspection. Engineering process models can be very detailed, often not only describing "what" to do, but also explaining "how" to do it.

2.3.1   Lifecycle Process Models

Lifecycle process models, as opposed to engineering process models, typically cover the complete lifecycle of a software product or a large fraction of it. This means that they often cover quite a lot of ground, which in turn generally leads to a high level of abstraction. Therefore, lifecycle process models typically tell the software engineer "what" to do, and in what sequence, but not "how" to do it. They usually do not recommend (or prescribe) any specific method or technique, but rather demand that something needs to be done "effectively," meaning that whatever method is applied, it must yield the expected result(s). For example, a lifecycle process model may demand that traceability be established between requirements and components, but it will not prescribe how this should be achieved (with or without a tool, how many traceability links are expected, etc.)—this can (and must) be determined by the process engineers at the respective organization.

The following subsections introduce some common classes of lifecycle process models. The main principles of these classes can be found in many existing lifecycle process models, two of which will be introduced in Sect. 2.3.1.6.

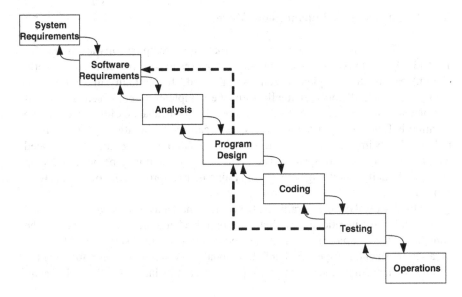

Fig. 2.3 Waterfall model as described by Royce, with iterations

2.3.1.1   The Waterfall Model

One of the best-known lifecycle models is the waterfall model. It was first formally described by Winston Royce in 1970 [2], although Royce did not name it waterfall model. The idea behind the waterfall model is the sequential creation of products on different levels of abstraction (e.g., precede code by design, precede design by requirements) and integration in reverse direction. The strict sequence can be weakened by controlled iterations. Figure 2.3 displays the original model, with envisioned iterative interactions between various activities (continuous arrows). However, Royce also noted that this kind of interaction is not likely to be confined to successive steps, but may rather jump from testing to program design and back to software requirements (dotted arrows).

Adhering to the sequential order of the activities is extremely hard to achieve, even if interaction with the immediate neighboring activities is allowed. Necessary prerequisites to applying a prototyping approach include being familiar with the domain, methods, techniques, tools, engineering processes and having a very good understanding of the requirements. The requirements themselves must be stable, and one must possess high capabilities for effort estimation.

Advantages. Typically, waterfall-like projects face only few problems during integration. Version and configuration management is also simplified.

Challenges. Unexpected requirements or context changes pose high risks. Gaining experience and learning during a project is difficult. Fixed delivery deadlines are risky for waterfall projects. The documentation created is often voluminous and heavyweight. The waterfall approach does not scale very well for large projects and long cycle times.

The waterfall process model is often referenced, but rarely applied in its strict form.

2.3.1.2 The Iterative Enhancement Model

Basili and Turner described an iterative approach to developing software systems in 1975 [3]. The iterative enhancement model proposes to first implement a (properly chosen) part of the complete system, and then add functionality in a number of iterations, which all together finally form the complete system. Each iteration is completed in a waterfall-like style, i.e., a requirements analysis for the respective iteration is followed by designing the system part of the iteration, which is again followed by its implementation, and so on. The result of each iteration is integrated with the already existing system. The focus of an iteration may be on introducing new functionality, but it might also be on refinement, improvement, or architectural consolidation.

Figure 2.4 displays the iterative enhancement model as described by Basili and Turner with three iterations. The first iteration (checkerboard pattern) develops the core part of the complete system, the second iteration (vertical stripes) and the third iteration (horizontal stripes) both add functionality. A prerequisite for applying the iterative enhancement model is that the problem permits incremental development.

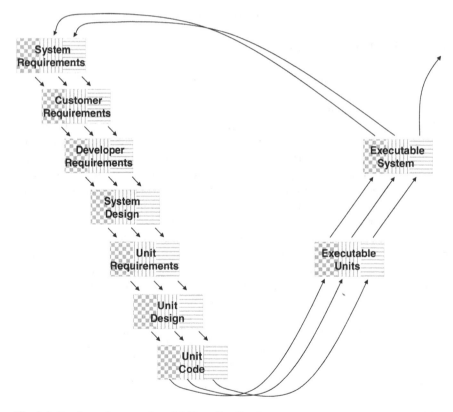

Fig. 2.4 Iterative enhancement model (three iterations)

For example, requirements to be considered in later iterations should not require a complete redesign of the system architecture.

Advantages. Iterative projects support efficient learning. With iterations designed properly, the core of the final product is available very early, thus featuring essential properties of the complete product. This allows for early customer involvement and feedback. Iteratively developing the requirements helps when requirements are not entirely clear or still unstable. Integration testing is supported due to relatively small increments being added at a time. In case of fixed delivery dates, incremental development helps to ensure that the most important functionality can actually be delivered—and the customer can decide what is most important to him.

Challenges. Since the product design is based on the current set of requirements, there is a risk that requirements showing up later may be expensive to fulfill, due to design decisions made earlier. Good and comprehensive version and configuration management is necessary to distinguish increments. Integration may become increasingly difficult with the number of iterations, depending on how well requirements may be partitioned and on the system architecture.

Many modern software process models, such as the Unified Process, Extreme Programming, or Scrum follow an iterative pattern.

2.3.1.3 The Prototyping Model

Another common lifecycle model is the prototyping model. Prototyping concentrates on the development of an executable version of the system that fulfills a limited number of requirements. Specifically, user interfaces are often simplified and/or performance and throughput requirements are reduced or even ignored. In other cases, e.g., for performance-critical components, different designs may be tested for their capabilities. The primary goal of building prototypes is to gain initial experience (e.g., regarding unclear requirements or difficult design aspects). *Getting a first version of the final product should usually not be a goal.* In fact, when all questions have been answered by the prototype, it should be thrown away and a system fulfilling all requirements should be developed based on one of the other lifecycle models.

Figure 2.5 displays the prototyping model. Note that developer requirements or even customer requirements typically directly lead to code, skipping all the other steps encountered, for example, in the waterfall or the iterative enhancement model. As necessary prerequisites to applying a prototyping approach, one must possess a high level of experience with the development techniques used, because all common assistance in the form of designs, modules, etc., is usually missing. In addition to that, the technical infrastructure for creating and evaluating a prototype must be available, e.g., the hardware to run the prototype on.

Advantages. A prototype can be developed when the final properties are not entirely clear. The direct contact between customer and developer reduces misunderstandings. Inconsistent requirements are discovered earlier, either by the developer or by the customer who evaluates the prototype. Comprehensive version

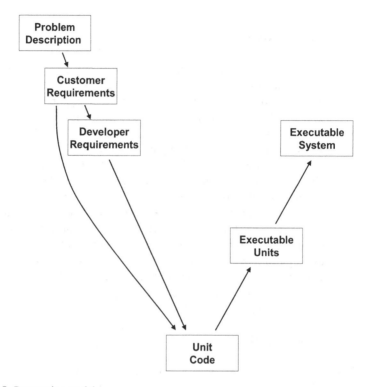

Fig. 2.5 Prototyping model

and configuration management is not necessary because the code produced is not meant to exist for a long time. The risk of project failure (e.g., developing a product that does not satisfy the customer requirements) is reduced due to the early involvement of the customer. In some cases, prototypes may even be used for evaluating business models, before a lot of money is spent on developing the real software.

Challenges. There is an inherent risk that side effects are not sufficiently considered, especially nonfunctional requirements such as reliability or safety. Another risk is that the customer (or the developer) considers the prototype as the first version of the system, and that the system will be evolved from the prototype, potentially leading to poorly documented, badly architected systems. The prototyping phase of a project may also induce higher costs compared to a nonprototyped approach.

A prototype is a great way to clarify ambiguous or unknown requirements; however, don't ever confuse it with the first version of the actual system!

2.3.1.4   The Spiral Model

The spiral model was first published in 1986 by Barry Boehm [4]. It represents a risk-driven approach, i.e., the assessment of risks determines the next project phase. The spiral model combines aspects of the waterfall model, the iterative enhancement model, and prototyping. Figure 2.6 displays the model. The first step of each spiral cycle identifies the objectives of the product part being elaborated (e.g., performance or functionality), the different alternatives for implementing the product part (e.g., different designs or reuse of existing components), and the constraints for each of the identified alternatives (e.g., cost or schedule). The next step evaluates the identified alternatives and identifies and resolves risks that come with the different alternatives. The third step is determined by the risks that remain after the second step. During the third step, the development approach that is suited best for the risks is chosen. This may be the construction of a prototype or the application of a strict waterfall process for implementing a clearly defined feature. Finally, the next phases are planned, and the complete cycle is reviewed by the stakeholders. Obviously, a prerequisite for applying the spiral model is the capability to identify and assess risks, as well as a project context that allows for changing the process model during project run-time.

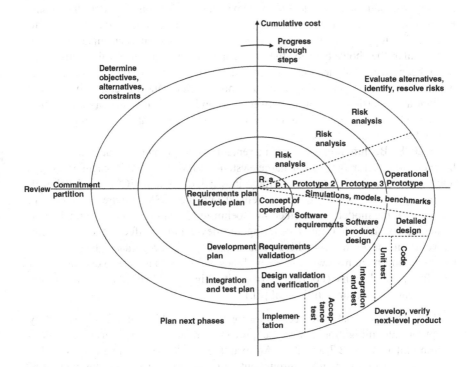

Fig. 2.6 Boehm's spiral model

Advantages. The third step accommodates features of other lifecycle process models as needed. The spiral model is therefore very flexible. The explicit consideration of risks avoids many of the difficulties of other process models. Similarly, unattractive alternatives are identified and eliminated early. The spiral model forms a single approach for software development and maintenance, whereas other models often concentrate on one or the other.

Challenges. For contract software, the spiral model is difficult to apply because individual project phases are not fully determined during project setup. It relies heavily on the organization's expertise with respect to risk assessment—therefore, a bad risk assessment may lead to the selection of bad alternatives or development approaches.

Boehm's spiral model embraces risk as its central aspect, and chooses the best approach for every iteration. This distinguishes it from other lifecycle models, which consider risks, but do not change the basic model accordingly.

2.3.1.5 The Incremental Commitment Spiral Model

The original spiral model demands that for every spiral, a project should identify its objectives, constraints, and alternative solution approaches; evaluate these alternatives; and then decide on the next steps based on the identified risks. By intention, this could be anything from straight waterfall development to completely stopping development. However, this has often been misunderstood; in particular, the choice between the different development process alternatives has often been neglected, leading to "unrolling" of the spiral model into a strict waterfall model or perceiving it as a simple incremental development process without any decision making in between. To address these issues, a new version of the model was developed that makes the decision points and different paths that can be taken explicit: the ICSM.

In 2008, Boehm proposed the incremental commitment model (ICM) as a lifecycle model for developing large systems with high development risks [5]. Such systems are typical for the military, in which context the ICM was developed. In subsequent years, the model was refined into the ICSM. Figure 2.7 shows an overview of the model as described by Boehm in [6]. Similar to the original spiral model, it consists of a spiral covering the development lifecycle of a system. However, it makes the risk-driven decisions explicit, accentuated by the stakeholder commitment reviews 1–6. Each of these reviews constitutes a decision point with four possible exits: (For reasons of clarity, Fig. 2.7 only displays the first three; Fig. 2.8 shows all four in full detail [6].)

- If the identified risks are acceptable for the stakeholders and well covered by appropriate mitigation plans, the project will continue into the next spiral (top exit in Figs. 2.7 and 2.8). An example would be a software system that does not reach its intended throughput, but that scales well with the number of

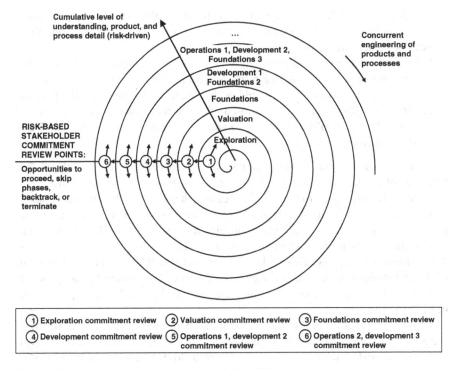

Fig. 2.7 Boehm's incremental commitment spiral model

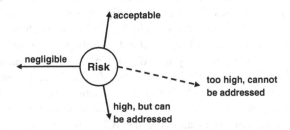

Fig. 2.8 Risk-based decisions

CPUs—the mitigation plan would be to add additional CPUs in order to reach the target throughput.

– If the identified risks are high, but expected to be addressable, the project will remain in the current spiral until the risks are resolved or covered by appropriate mitigation plans (bottom exit in Figs. 2.7 and 2.8). An example would be working out safety cases for a safety-critical system or producing acceptable versions of missing risk mitigation plans.

– If the identified risks are negligible, the project can skip the next spiral(s) (left exit in Figs. 2.7 and 2.8). This means, for example, that if the risks are determined to be negligible during the Exploration spiral, both the Valuation and Foundations spirals can be skipped, and the project can go directly to the

Development spiral. For example, this can happen if the Exploration spiral finds that the solution can be easily produced by tailoring a COTS package rather than developing a custom system.
– If the identified risks are determined to be too high or cannot be addressed, the project should be terminated or rescoped (back exit, indicated by the dashed arrow in Fig. 2.8). An example would be that the market window for the product under development has already closed—hence, the project should either be terminated, or it should be rescoped to address a different market sector whose market window is still open.

Being an incremental model, each spiral concurrently addresses all of the activities of product development: Requirements (objectives and constraints) and solutions (alternatives); products and processes; hardware, software, and human factors aspects; and business case analysis of alternative product configurations or product line investments are all being considered in every spiral. The development team does not only produce (development) artifacts, but also provides evidence of their combined feasibility. This evidence is central to the ICSM; in fact, during each of the stakeholder commitment reviews, all evidence is assessed by independent experts, and significant risks identified are then addressed by appropriate risk mitigation plans.

In [7], Boehm gives an example of total vs. incremental commitment in gambling. A typical *total* commitment game is roulette: you put all your chips (money) on a number and wait to see whether you win or lose. In a software project, you would bet your development budget on the on-time delivery of your product, and then wait and see whether you will make it. Typical *incremental* commitment games are poker or blackjack. You put some chips in, see your cards and some of the others' cards, and then you decide whether and how much more money to commit. If your cards are too bad, you bail out, avoiding losing more money in a situation where it is highly unlikely for you to win. The ICSM enables a similar strategy for software projects: You spend some of your development budget and check the results (for example, whether your application interfaces correctly with another application) in order to find out whether and how to progress.

A necessary precondition to applying the ICSM is the understanding of all involved partners and their willingness to stop a project if the risk analysis suggests that. In other words, the ICSM cannot be applied in projects that must deliver a result, no matter how good (or bad) it is. Applying the ICSM also requires the capability to identify and assess risks.

Advantages. The ICSM prevents premature total commitments, which can lead to a situation where there is no way back. The early identification of project risks and either their mitigation or the adjustment of the project scope facilitates the congruence of expected and actual project results. Additionally, the ICSM opens an exit strategy to stop a project before burning away lots of money, without the need for anyone to lose their face—which can be highly beneficial in projects where politics play an important role.

Challenges. Honestly assessing risks requires great openness within an organization. This may be difficult for certain employee evaluation models. The systems addressed by the ICSM (large, high-risk) are sometimes political projects that normally cannot be stopped, no matter how bad the situation is—in these cases, a cultural change both on the buyer and on the supplier side is required.

The ICSM was developed for very large, very risky projects where one does not know at the beginning whether and to what extent the goal can be reached.

2.3.1.6 Example Lifecycle Models

This section introduces two example lifecycle models that adopt the general concepts described in the previous sections. The Unified Process is a widely used process framework for developing software. The Cleanroom Development Process model is described here as an exemplary model that enforces the use of early defect detection techniques and the use of formal methods. It can be seen as an alternative approach that aims at producing higher quality software than traditional, testing- and debugging-based approaches.

Unified Process

Published by Jacobson, Booch, and Rumbaugh in 1999, the Unified Process is a generic process framework for software development [8]. It consists of a generic description of phases and activities that can—and normally must!—be adapted for different types of organizations, the class of software system to be developed, different application domains, competence levels, and project sizes. The Unified Process distinguishes project phases like the waterfall model does and supports iterative development within the phases like the iterative enhancement model does. It also specifically considers risks during the iterations, borrowing from the spiral model. In addition, it contains traces of the prototyping model, since it recommends building prototypes within iterations under special circumstances.

The Unified Process is *component based*, i.e., the system to be built is compiled from software components that are interconnected via well-defined interfaces. The Unified Modeling Language (UML) is used to model all central artifacts describing the system—e.g., requirements and design. Both UML and the Unified Process were developed in parallel.

Besides focusing on components, the Unified Process is *use-case driven*. Within the Unified Process, use cases replace the traditional functional specification of the system. According to the philosophy of the Unified Process, a functional specification describes what the system is supposed to do, whereas use cases describe what the system is supposed to do *for each user*. Therefore, the Unified Process focuses on the user who will work with the system, as opposed to the system itself. Use cases are central to system development, also driving design, implementation, and test.

The Unified Process is also *architecture-centric*, i.e., it focuses strongly on the system architecture, embodying the most significant static and dynamic aspects of the system. Use cases and system architecture are developed in parallel: Whereas the use cases describe the *function* of the system, the architecture describes its *form*. Therefore, the architecture is influenced by the use cases, because it must satisfy all the stated user needs. It is also influenced by external factors such as the platform. The system architect must find an architecture that satisfies these external factors as well as the requirements stated in the use cases. He typically starts with a part of the architecture that is not specific to the use cases, for example, the aforementioned platform. Still, a general understanding of what the system should do is necessary, in order to go in the right direction. As soon as a set of use cases is available that describes the key functions of the system, the architecture is refined. The more detailed and mature the use cases become, the more details are added to the architecture, which in turn facilitates the maturation of additional use cases. This process continues until the architecture is deemed stable.

Finally, the Unified Process is *iterative and incremental*. This reflects the fact that for large and high-risk systems, a waterfall-like approach is not likely to work very well. Therefore, the Unified Process divides the work into mini projects forming iterations and resulting in increments that are added to the system. An iteration typically groups together use cases that extend the usefulness of the system and deals with the most important risks first. Each iteration contains the core workflows *requirements, analysis, design, implementation,* and *test.* Their intensity varies with the phase the project is currently in: At the beginning of a project, requirements work will be more intensive than towards the end of a project. Not all iterations add functionality; for example, the system architecture may be modified in one increment without adding any new features.

Figure 2.9 displays the core workflows and project phases of the Unified Process together with a rough estimate of the intensity in terms of effort for each workflow as described by Jacobson et al. [8]. A project typically goes through the phases *Inception, Elaboration, Construction,* and *Transition.* The phases are separated by milestones, defined by the availability of a set of artifacts (i.e., certain models or documents are in a prescribed state). The *inception* phase creates a vision of and a business case for the final system. During the *elaboration* phase, most of the system's use cases are specified and its architecture is defined. The *construction* phase builds the system, evolving the architecture to its final state. Finally, the *transition* phase covers the system's beta testing, correcting the defects found by the beta testers.

Each phase contains a number of iterations, adding increments to the system. Each iteration elicits *requirements;* performs an *analysis* that allocates the system behavior to a set of objects of the system; provides a *design* that describes the static structure of the system as subsystems, classes, and interfaces as well as the use cases realized as collaborations among them; creates an *implementation* that includes components (i.e., source code); and finally performs a *test* of the system, using test cases that verify the use cases.

The Unified Process is a popular lifecycle model; however, its application requires some process maturity, e.g., to clearly distinguish the project phases and

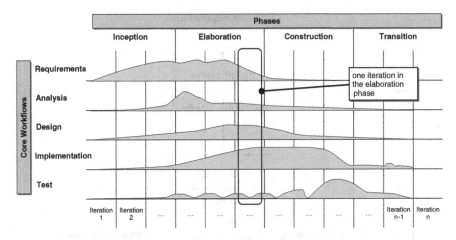

Fig. 2.9   The core workflows and phases of the Unified Process

the development activities. It must be adapted to the respective context—a fact that is often neglected. The iterative nature within the phases may be confusing, because the phases make the Unified Process look like a waterfall process. Another challenge is the fact that the Unified Process "stops" when the system is in beta testing, so actually bringing it into service and operation must be done using other means—a detail that may easily be forgotten.

The Unified Process is a comprehensive development process that must be adapted to the specific organization before it can be applied.

Cleanroom Development Process

Published by Mills, Dyer, and Linger in 1987 [9], the Cleanroom Development Process distinguishes itself from other approaches by focusing on the formal verification of correctness, as opposed to trying to eliminate as many defects as possible by testing a system. This has some obvious advantages: While a formal proof guarantees that something is correct, even successful test cases can never prove the absence of defects—and thus correctness. The Cleanroom Development Process is based on developing and certifying a sequence of software increments that together form the final system. Each increment is developed and certified by a small, independent team. The development teams assure correctness via formal specification, design, and verification. In fact, team correctness verification takes the place of testing and debugging—the development team does not execute the code that it writes! The Cleanroom Development Process is therefore an iterative process, similar to the iterative enhancement model.

Figure 2.10 displays the Cleanroom Development Process as described by Linger [10]. It features two cooperating teams: the development team and the specification team. Initially, both teams together analyze and clarify customer requirements. If requirements are unclear, the teams can develop prototypes to elicit feedback iteratively. During the specification activity, the teams produce a

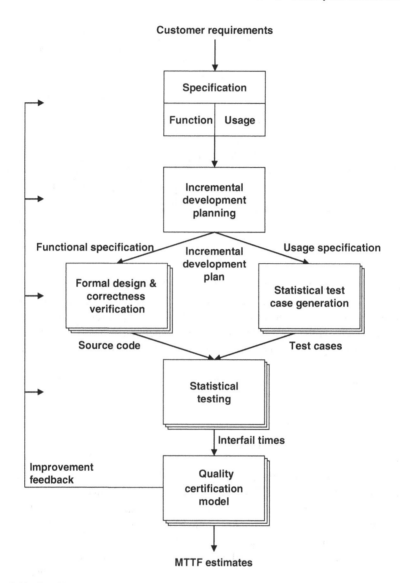

Fig. 2.10 The Cleanroom Development Process

functional specification and a usage specification. The functional specification
defines the required external system behavior in all circumstances of use in a formal
way; the usage specification defines usage scenarios and their probabilities for all
possible system usages, both correct and incorrect ones. While the functional
specification is the basis for the incremental system development, the usage specification is the basis for generating test cases. On the basis of both specifications,
the development and certification teams together define an initial plan for incre-
mentally developing the system.

After that, incremental development starts (indicated by stacked boxes in Fig. 2.10). For each increment, the development team creates a system design and carries out correctness verification for the respective design. The design contains a number of program functions transforming input data into output data. This transformation corresponds to a mathematical function and thus can be formally verified. Since there is only a limited number of program functions (e.g., sequence, alternation, iteration), and since each program function can be verified using a limited number of steps, verification itself is a finite process. The certification team proceeds in parallel, using the usage specification to generate test cases that reflect the expected use of the accumulated increments.

Each completed increment is integrated with the system (i.e., all prior increments) and delivered to the statistical test team. The previously created test cases are run against the system and the results are checked for correctness against the functional specification. The elapsed time between failures (interfail time) is measured and passed to a quality certification model, which computes objective statistical measures of quality, such as mean time to failure (MTTF). All errors found during testing are returned to the development team for correction.

The Cleanroom Development Process has proven to be able to produce high-quality (in terms of number of defects) software [10]. However, it is not widely adopted, which is to be expected. The reasons lie mostly in its prerequisites: In order to correctly develop a software system with Cleanroom, all involved developers must be highly skilled, especially with respect to formal specification and verification. Considering the contexts in which software is being developed today, this prerequisite can only be met under very rare circumstances. Another challenge is the fact that formally specifying software behavior tends to "explode" the requirements and designs. Most success stories are from projects creating up to 100,000 lines of code, with some going up to 400,000. Today's systems, however, often consist of millions of lines of code, making a formal specification extremely laborious and costly. Focusing the Cleanroom Development Process on critical parts of a system and combining it with other process models, however, could be a way to cope with these challenges.

The Cleanroom Development Process is capable of delivering high-quality software; however, it requires extremely skilled process performers, and its scalability for large systems is unknown.

2.3.2 Engineering Process Models

Engineering process models, as opposed to lifecycle process models, typically cover only a relatively small fraction of the complete lifecycle of a software product. This makes the topic they cover smaller; therefore, they typically elaborate more details than lifecycle models. Still, engineering process models do follow the same principles as lifecycle process models, such as waterfall or iterative enhancement.

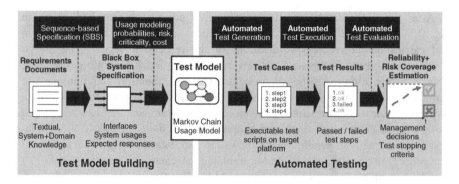

Fig. 2.11 Model-based statistical testing process overview

The following subsections introduce some example engineering process models, covering different areas such as testing, cost estimation, and implementation.

2.3.2.1 Process for Model-Based Statistical Testing

Model-based statistical testing [11] is a system validation technique based on a Markov chain usage model. A usage model represents the actual system usage. (Please note that the term "model" is used ambiguously in this section: "model" within "usage model" is different from "model" within "process model"!) The usage model is used to derive realistic test cases considering the operational profile of the test object. This enables the estimation of system reliability based on the test results. The name of the method comes from the heavy use of statistics, e.g., for constructing and analyzing the usage model, for generating test cases from the model, and for estimating system reliability from the test results. Model-based statistical testing consists of several steps, which are shown in Fig. 2.11 [12].

A functional system specification is derived from the system requirements by applying the sequence-based specification technique (not explained here). Then, the system usage is modeled and a Markov chain usage model is derived. Test case generation, execution, and evaluation are automated using appropriate tools.

Usage modeling. A usage model describes how the system under test is expected to be used. Usage models are finite state machines with transition probabilities. The transitions describe the possible system triggers by external stimuli and the expected system responses. The probabilities express the frequency of system stimuli at certain states and form the probability distribution of the usage model. Several usage profiles might be annotated for one test object, e.g., for different user groups. Usage models have one start state and one exit state, which correspond to the beginning and end of a system use. Any path through the model from the start state to the exit state represents a valid system use.

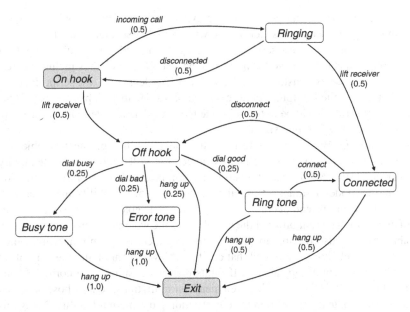

Fig. 2.12 Example system usage model of a telephone

Figure 2.12 shows an example of a usage model of a telephone as described in [13]. Different usage profiles might exist, e.g., to represent a "call-center" environment, which would be different from a "private home" environment.

Test case generation. A test case is a path through the usage model. The transitions of the usage model are annotated with test scripts that drive a test runner. To generate a specific test case, the scripts of the transitions lying on a path through the usage model will be appended one after another and saved as a single test case script. During a test case, the test runner runs each test script sequentially. The statistical testing method includes various ways of automated test case generation, representing various tactics for walking through the usage model:

- Generating the minimum-cost coverage set for a usage model: Simplified, a collection of test cases that visit every arc in a model with the minimum number of test steps is generated.
- Generating tests randomly based on a probability distribution.
- Generating tests in order by weight (most or least probable paths).

In complex usage models with rarely traversed arcs, random test case generation cannot assure the coverage of the whole model, even with a large number of test cases. Therefore, it is advisable to generate the model coverage test cases first in order to pass each transition at least once. Afterwards, a number of random test cases should be generated and executed in order to get statistically relevant test results, which can be used for the reliability analysis.

Test execution. Automated test execution needs a test runner that executes the generated test cases. A test case is a sequence of test scripts (each representing a test step) collected from the usage model transitions during test generation.

The transition from one usage model state to another is performed by invoking the corresponding test script. Test scripts are written in an executable notation.

Test evaluation. The test scripts in the test cases include the required input for the test object and the expected output from the test object, i.e., they include the test oracle. A test case is considered to have failed if at least one test script does not observe the specified output. As an example, consider the telephone again. One possible test script would be to try to lift the receiver. The test step fails if the script does not observe a free line signal.

Test analysis. Based on the test results, the reliability of the test object is estimated by using a particular reliability model, the Miller model [14]. Reliability numbers are estimated for each transition and stimulus. When no prior information is given, the model assumes an initial reliability of 0.5. Reliability increases with successful executions and decreases after failures. The goal is to achieve a reliability of close to 1. The reliability of the test object is the weighted sum of all transition reliabilities. It is also feasible to calculate the so-called optimum reliability, which is the highest reliability estimated that can be achieved by applying the current set of test cases, assuming no failures. If faults that cause failures are corrected, one should therefore first focus on single elements (stimuli, transitions) whose observed reliabilities deviate the most from the corresponding optimum reliability. Using this prioritization, one could achieve higher improvement in single-use reliability due to the same multiplication effect described earlier.

The process for statistical testing introduced here is quite sophisticated and requires in-depth study. Some details have been omitted; the full process can be found in [12].

2.3.2.2 Process for Hybrid Cost Estimation

The CoBRA® method for cost estimation is a method for the systematic utilization of expert and empirical knowledge to estimate the costs for an upcoming project [15, 16]. Based on a combination of measurement data and expert judgment, it predicts the probable costs for projects of the same kind. CoBRA® focuses on a very small fraction of the complete software product development lifecycle (cost estimation at project start) and gives very detailed instructions on what to do and how to do it. The method involves four major steps: *develop causal model, quantify causal model, determine nominal project costs,* and *generate cost overhead model.* Figure 2.13 displays an overview of the CoBRA® method, which will be explained in the following paragraphs.

Develop causal model. The causal model contains factors affecting the costs of projects within a certain context. The causal model is typically obtained through expert knowledge acquisition (e.g., involving experienced project managers). An example is presented in Fig. 2.14 [16]. The arrows indicate direct and indirect relationships. A sign ("+" or "–") indicates the way a cost factor contributes to the overall project costs. The "+" and "−" represent a positive and negative relationship, respectively; that is, if the factor increases, the project costs will also increase

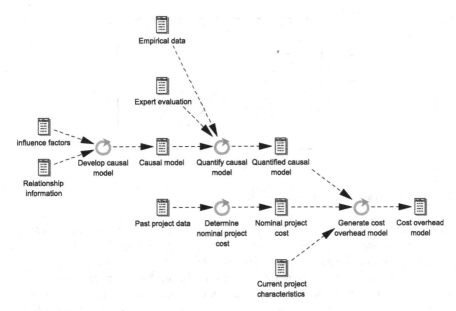

Fig. 2.13   The CoBRA® method for cost estimation

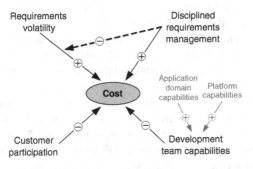

Fig. 2.14   An example CoBRA® causal model

("+") or decrease ("−"). For instance, if *requirements volatility* increases, costs will also increase. One arrow pointing to another one indicates an interaction effect. For example, an interaction exists between *disciplined requirements management* and *requirements volatility*. In this case, increased disciplined requirement management compensates for the negative influence of volatile requirements on software costs.

Quantify causal model. The direct and indirect (through other factors) impact on costs for each factor is quantified using expert evaluation and/or empirical data. The influence is measured as a relative percentage increase of the costs above a nominal project (i.e., a "perfect" project where everything runs optimally). For each factor, experts are asked to give the increase in costs when the considered factor has the worst possible value (extreme case) and all other factors have their nominal values (best case). In order to capture the uncertainty of evaluations, experts are asked to give

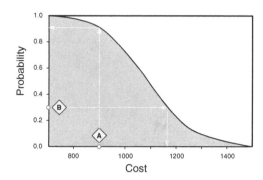

Fig. 2.15 Example cumulative cost distribution

three values: the maximal, minimal, and most likely cost overhead for each factor. These three values are then represented as a triangular probability distribution.

Determine nominal project cost. The nominal project costs, i.e., the costs of a "perfect" project where everything runs optimally, are based on data from past projects that are similar with respect to certain characteristics (e.g., development type, lifecycle type) that are not part of the causal model. These characteristics define the context of the project. Past project data is used to determine the relationship between cost overhead and (nominal) costs. Since it is a simple bivariate dependency, it does not require much measurement data. In principle, merely project size and effort are required. The size measure should reflect the overall project volume including all produced artifacts. Common examples include lines of code or function points. Past project information on identified cost factors is usually elicited from experts.

Generate cost overhead model. Based on the quantified causal model, past project data, and current project characteristics, a cost overhead model is generated for the current project using a simulation algorithm (e.g., Monte Carlo or Latin Hypercube). The probability distribution obtained could be used further to support various project management activities, such as cost estimation, evaluation of cost-related project risks, or benchmarking. Figure 2.15 illustrates two usage scenarios using the inverse cumulative cost distribution: computing the probability of exceeding given project costs (scenario A) and calculating the project costs for a given probability level (scenario B).

Let us assume (scenario A) that the available budget for a project is 900,000 euros and that this project's costs are characterized by the distribution in Fig. 2.15. There is roughly a 90% probability that the project will overrun this budget. If this probability represents an unacceptable risk in a particular context, the project budget might not be approved. On the other hand, let us consider (scenario B) that a project manager wants to minimize the risks of overrunning the budget. In other words, the costs of a software project should be planned so that there is minimal risk of exceeding them. If a project manager sets the maximal tolerable risk of exceeding the budget to 30%, then the planned budget for the project should not be lower than 1,170,000 euros.

Similar to the process for statistical testing, the process for hybrid cost estimation is a sophisticated method. More information, including tool support, can be found in [17].

2.3.2.3   Extreme Programming

Extreme Programming (XP) is an agile approach to software development with a strong focus on producing code, whereas all other activities are only executed if they provide direct benefit for the customer [18]. In practice, this means an enormous reduction in documentation, especially with respect to requirements and design. In XP, traditional requirements are replaced by "user stories" created by the customer that explain a part of the system behavior. A typical user story should not contain more than three sentences and should be realized within 1–3 weeks. User stories not fitting this scheme should be split or merged. User stories are used for schedule planning, not for a detailed problem description. A user story is then broken down into 1- to 3-day programmer tasks. There is no explicit design phase; the programmers write code directly using the tasks as input. If the current system design does not work for the new user stories, it is refactored until the new user stories can be accommodated.

Typically, XP projects feature a weekly cycle. This means that at the beginning of a week, the customer picks a week's worth of user stories to be implemented, and the XP team implements them. Therefore, XP is heavily iterative. A larger iterative cycle plans "themes" quarterly, i.e., larger fractions of the whole product that involve a high number of interrelated user stories. Figure 2.16 displays the two cycles.

Beyond this, XP features more practices that should be obeyed in daily work. These practices are:

- *Sit together*, i.e., the whole team works together in one room.
- *Whole team*, i.e., all required skills are represented by team members (cross-functional teams).

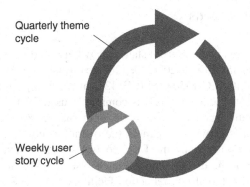

Quarterly theme cycle

Weekly user story cycle

Fig. 2.16 Interaction of XP's weekly and quarterly cycles

- *Informative workspace*, i.e., the workspace the team works in should display all important facts about the project and its status.
- *Energized work*, i.e., people should spend their time working with all their strength—but not more than that, i.e., not spend countless overtime that does not add value to the project.
- *Pair programming*, i.e., when programming, two people sit together at one machine.
- *Slack*, i.e., the prioritization of tasks, so that less important ones can be dropped if necessary.
- *Ten-minute build*, i.e., the whole system can be built and all test cases can be run within 10 min.
- *Continuous integration*, i.e., any changes are integrated into the system and tested after no more than a few hours.
- *Test-first programming*, i.e., writing the test case(s) before the actual program.
- *Incremental design*, i.e., the system design should always reflect what is needed at the very point in time, and nothing more—any additions will change the design as needed.

Extreme Programming has generated much discussion about the "right" way to develop systems. Whereas the reduction of documentation was generally welcomed by most programmers, other quality aspects of an XP-developed system that consists only of user stories and code, such as maintainability, degraded. XP has been successful for the development of smaller systems or of systems without clear requirements; however, for safety-critical systems that mandate certain documentation and verification steps, XP seems less suitable. The discussion about XP is anything but over, however; it seems that XP will find its place among the traditional process models. Beware: In many cases, when organizations claim to do "agile development" or XP, they merely apply one or two practices, but follow a chaotic process otherwise. In these cases, it is necessary to find out what such organizations really do in order to evaluate their performance.

2.4 Process Standards

This section introduces some process standards widely used in industry. ISO/IEC 12207:1995 [19] and ISO/IEC 12207:2008 [20] are the basis for many other, derived standards, such as ISO/IEC 15504 (SPICE) [21] or the European Space Agency's ECSS standards [22]. IEC 61508 [23] is commonly used for the development of safety-critical systems such as automotive or aerospace (embedded) systems. It defines functional safety as "...part of the overall safety relating to the EUC (Equipment Under Control) and the EUC control system which depends on the correct functioning of the E/E/PE safety-related systems, other technology safety-related systems and external risk reduction facilities." ISO/DIS 26262 [24] is an upcoming adaptation of IEC 61508 to comply with needs specific to the application sector of electric and electronic (E/E) systems within road vehicles. Finally, IEC 62304 [25] is a standard describing the software lifecycle for the development of medical devices, with a specific focus on safety aspects after delivery.

2.4.1 ISO/IEC 12207:2008

The international standard ISO/IEC 12207:2008 [20] is a process standard that establishes a common framework for software lifecycle processes, with a well-defined terminology, which can be referenced by the software industry. It addresses the issue that often, the same or similar concepts are referenced using different terms, or that one term is used for different meanings. The standard covers the software lifecycle from collecting the first ideas and concepts via implementing the system to decommissioning obsolete systems. Many other standards, such as CMMI [26] or ISO/IEC 15504 (SPICE) [21], are derived directly or indirectly from ISO/IEC 12207 (either from its first version from 1995 or from the later 2008 version).

The standard groups the activities executed during the software lifecycle into seven process groups. Each of the 44 processes described within the process groups contains a purpose statement and a list of expected outcomes. Furthermore, activities and tasks that are necessary to produce the expected outcomes are described. ISO/IEC 12207:2008 was developed together with ISO/IEC 15288:2008 (System Lifecycle Processes) [27] and in many cases constitutes a software-specific variant thereof. Additionally, ISO/IEC 12207:2008 has been designated explicitly to be used as a process reference model (PRM) within ISO/IEC 15504 (SPICE).

Figure 2.17 shows an overview of the standard. In contrast to its predecessor (ISO/IEC 12207:1995), ISO/IEC 12207:2008 distinguishes processes for stand-alone software products or services (*System Context Processes*, left-hand part of Fig. 2.17) and processes for software products or services that are part of a superior system (*Software Specific Processes*, right-hand part of Fig. 2.17).

Within the *System Context Processes*, the process group *Agreement Processes* contains the processes necessary to reach an agreement between two organizations. *Organizational Project-Enabling Processes* are processes that facilitate and support project execution on a strategic level. *Project Processes* deal with "classic" project management tasks, i.e., planning and controlling, decision management, risk management, configuration and information management, and measurement. Product development, including (system) requirements elicitation, system architecture, implementation, integration, testing, installation, operation, maintenance, and disposal, is described by the *Technical Processes*.

Within the *Software Specific Processes*, the *Software Implementation Processes* describe the activities necessary to create a specific system element that is implemented in software. This includes software requirements analysis, software architecture and design, implementation, integration, and testing. The *Software*

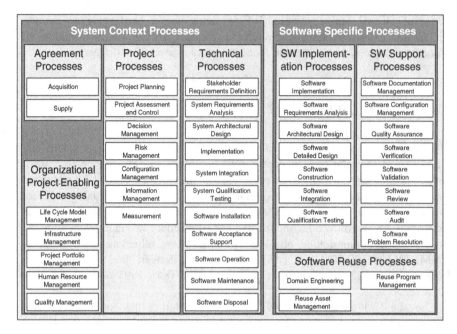

Fig. 2.17 Overview of ISO/IEC 12207:2008

Support Processes contain software-specific processes with respect to documentation, configuration management, quality assurance, verification and validation, reviews and audits, and problem resolution. Finally, *Software Reuse Processes* define processes for systematically reusing system components.

ISO/IEC 12207 is sometimes called "the mother of all standards," because most specialized standards are based directly or indirectly on it. Beware: Many derived standards still reference ISO/IEC 12207:1995, the predecessor of ISO/IEC 12207:2008!

2.4.2   IEC 61508

The international standard IEC 61508 [23] as well as the corresponding German standard DIN EN 61508 [28] set out a generic approach for all safety lifecycle activities for systems comprised of electrical and/or electronic and/or programmable electronic components (E/E/PESs) that are used to perform safety functions in order to ensure risks are kept at an acceptable level.

IEC 61508 is a general standard that shall be refined for different application domains. For the automotive domain, such a refinement is currently in progress: ISO 26262 [24] is an upcoming adaptation of IEC 61508 to comply with needs specific to the application sector of electric and electronic (E/E) systems within road vehicles. However, IEC 61508 will remain the relevant standard for all safety-related automotive systems until it is replaced by ISO 26262.

For that reason, this section gives a brief overview of the specific requirements of IEC 61508 on development processes. The IEC 61508 defines two types of requirements: organizational and technical requirements. This section focuses on the organizational requirements.

With regard to the organizational requirements, a development process for safety-related systems is quite similar to standard high-quality development processes [19, 29, 30]. In general, the organizational requirements of IEC 61508 first influence the organizational processes, including project management and documentation. Second, they influence the supporting processes, including configuration management, quality assurance, and change management.

The following additional tasks, in particular, must be considered in the development of safety-related systems:

– The management of functional safety is added to the project management.
– Additional tasks for ensuring functional safety are required.
– A hazard and risk analysis must be performed.
– Depending on the safety integrity level (SIL), specific methods and measures must be applied, e.g., specific test activities.
– A final assessment of the functional safety is required.

In the following, the organizational requirements of IEC 61508 will be briefly described and related to standard development processes. For this purpose, Sect. 2.4.2.1 gives an overview of the safety-specific requirements on organizational and supporting processes. Section 2.4.2.2 identifies and briefly describes the safety-specific overall lifecycle phases required in addition. The software safety lifecycle is regarded in Sect. 2.4.2.3. Finally, Sect. 2.4.2.4 introduces important aspects regarding the certification of systems.

2.4.2.1   Requirements on Organizational and Supporting Processes

IEC 61508 defines organizational and technical requirements on the development processes for safety-related systems. With regard to the organizational requirements, these are usually fulfilled by mature processes (for example with CMMI-Level 2 [29, 30] or CMMI Level 3 [31]). The most important safety-specific requirements are outlined in the following sections. Regarding the technical requirements, however, it must be clearly stated that reaching a maturity level does not imply compliance to IEC 61508 [32]. The major challenges raised by IEC 61508 are the technical requirements on the engineering process.

Documentation. As a general requirement, IEC 61508 specifies the necessary information to be documented in order for all phases of the overall, E/E/PES, and software safety lifecycles to be performed effectively.

IEC 61508 defines the following general requirements on all documents that are created during the lifecycle:

- The documentation shall contain sufficient information for each phase of the different lifecycles that is necessary for the effective performance of subsequent phases and verification activities. However, it is not explicitly defined what constitutes sufficient information. In fact, this strongly depends on the development context.
- The documentation must contain all information that is required for the management and assessment of functional safety.
- The documentation must be accurate and concise; it must be easy to understand by all stakeholders; it must suit the purpose for which it is intended; and it must be accessible and maintainable.
- Each document shall contain a minimum of organizational information, including titles or names indicating the scope of the contents, some form of index arrangement, and a revision index.
- All relevant documents shall be revised, amended, reviewed, and approved and shall be under the control of an appropriate document control scheme.

Regarding these requirements, there is no significant difference to common process standards and to the requirements of capability/maturity models.

Management of functional safety. An additional, safety-specific task of project management that is required by IEC 61508 is the management of functional safety. As the output of this task, a safety plan is created as an additional work product.

In this step, the management and technical activities during all lifecycle phases that are necessary for achieving the required functional safety of the safety-related systems are defined. Moreover, the responsibilities of each person, department, and organization for the different project phases and activities within the phases are defined.

It makes sense for the project leader to appoint a safety manager who is responsible for performing the management of functional safety and who defines the safety plan [29].

The safety plan must include at least the following information:

- It must be defined which of the lifecycle phases defined in IEC 61508 are actually applied and which of the recommended techniques and measures are used in these phases.
- It must be identified who carries out and who reviews these phases. This means, in particular, that it must be defined who is responsible for taking care of the functional safety of the system. Responsibilities may also be assigned to licensing authorities or safety regulatory bodies.
- The functional safety assessment activities must be defined. Additionally, it is required to define the procedures for how the recommendations of the different review and assessment activities can be resolved.
 - It is required that all persons involved in the overall lifecycle must be adequately trained and periodically retrained.
- Regarding the operation of the system, procedures must be defined that specify that dangerous incidents will be analyzed and appropriate recommendations will be made to improve the system.

- Procedures for analyzing the operation and maintenance performance must be defined.
- Requirements for periodic functional safety audits must be specified.
- Procedures for initiating modifications to the safety-related systems as well as the required approval procedure and authority for modifications must be defined.
- The procedures for maintaining accurate information on potential hazards and safety-related systems must be defined.
- It is further necessary to specify the procedures for configuration management. This includes the definition of the stage at which formal configuration control must be used and the definition of the procedures used for uniquely identifying all constituent parts and for preventing unauthorized items from entering service.

All of these specified activities shall be formally reviewed and implemented and progress is to be monitored. All responsible stakeholders for the management of functional safety activities shall be informed.

Suppliers providing products or services shall have an appropriate quality management system that is compliant with the defined requirements.

Configuration management. The requirements on the configuration management are only defined roughly in IEC 61508. According to [29], in addition to standard configuration management processes, the following aspects must be considered:

- All tools and development environments used must be additional configuration elements.
- All versions of the software must be documented. All released versions of the software and all related documents must be kept throughout the operation lifetime of the system in order to support the maintenance and modification of the software.

Quality assurance. Quality assurance is obviously one of the major aspects regarding the development of safety-related systems. Nonetheless, mature processes already include a sophisticated quality assurance process. In terms of IEC 61508, quality assurance plays an important role in two respects: First, it is necessary to perform a dedicated overall safety validation. Second, the functional safety of the system must be assessed. These issues are addressed by the additional safety-specific development phases that are described in Sect. 2.4.2.2.

Change management. With respect to change management, it is basically necessary to extend the impact analysis in order to identify impacts on the functional safety of the system. As a result of the analysis, it must be decided whether or not a new hazard and risk analysis is required. In the worst case, the latter has to be repeated completely. In turn, the safety requirements and the SILs of the safety functions may change. Further, it must be decided which phases must be repeated. After each modification, it is at least necessary to repeat the verification activities. Depending on the SIL, it might not be sufficient to reverify affected subsystems; rather, the overall system must be verified again.

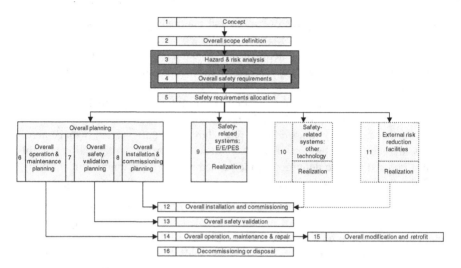

Fig. 2.18 IEC 61508 Safety Lifecycle model

2.4.2.2 Overall Safety Lifecycle

As a major requirement, IEC 61508 defines a lifecycle model for the development of safety-related systems. All development processes for the development of safety-related systems must comply with this lifecycle model or at least the equivalence must be shown. The overall lifecycle model of IEC 61508 is shown in Fig. 2.18. This section will not describe the complete lifecycle model, but will focus on the safety-specific lifecycle phases 3 (hazard and risk analysis) and 4 (overall safety requirements) of IEC 61508.

Hazard and risk analysis. A hazard and risk analysis must be conducted as soon as the overall concept and scope definitions of the future system have been finished. It aims at identifying all hazards and hazardous events, explaining their causes, forecasting their consequences, and finding detection and mitigation possibilities. Often it also contains quantitative aspects, at least the assignment of a SIL or a risk priority number on an ordinal scale, partly also an estimation of occurrence probability or severity of the consequences (e.g., costs). IEC 61508 leaves the choice between qualitative and quantitative techniques open.

A number of techniques are known that help to find all hazards and determine the sequences of events leading to the hazards. Most practically applied techniques are graphical or tabular techniques. Often the same techniques can be applied in later development phases for a more detailed breakdown of hazard influences. Among the recommended techniques in IEC 61508 are:

– Failure modes and effects analysis (FMEA) and its derivatives
– Cause consequence diagrams
– Event tree analysis
– Fault tree analysis

- Hazard and operability studies
- Markov models
- Reliability block diagrams

Annexes B.6 and C.6 of IEC 61508 give a short explanation and further references for these techniques. Other techniques that might be appropriate, according to the literature, are preliminary hazard analysis (PHA) and functional hazard analysis (FHA).

Overall safety requirements. Actually, the definition of the safety requirements is not an additional lifecycle phase. In fact, it is more an extension of already existing requirements analysis phases. In general, those requirements that affect safety functions of the systems must be considered as safety requirements. A safety requirement always consists of two parts:

- *Safety function requirements* define what the safety function does.
- *Safety integrity requirements* define the likelihood of a safety function being performed satisfactorily.

Usually the safety function requirements are derived from the results of the hazard analysis. The hazards identified in this analysis shall be prevented by means of appropriate safety functions. The safety integrity requirements can be derived from the results of the risk analysis.

As an example, consider a machine with a rotating blade that is protected by a hinged solid cover [33]: In order to protect the operator, the motor is de-energized and the brakes are applied whenever the cover is lifted. As a result of the hazard analysis, it is detected that it must not be possible to lift the hinged cover more than 5 mm without the brake activating and stopping the blade within less than a second in order to prevent accidents. During risk assessment, various aspects, such as the likelihood of this hazard occurring and the associated severity, were looked at, and the corresponding safety function was classified to SIL 2. The complete safety requirement could then be defined as follows:

When the hinged cover is lifted by 5 mm or more, the motor shall be de-energized and the brake activated so that the blade is stopped within 1 second. The safety integrity level of this safety function shall be SIL 2.

The higher the SIL of a safety function gets, the more strongly IEC 61508 recommends formal requirements specification techniques such as Z [34] or VDM [35]. During the (ongoing) adaptation of the standard to the automotive industry, this recommendation seems to be weakened and a requirements specification using natural language comparable to the example above will be sufficient.

The safety requirements are initially related to the overall system. Therefore, an additional step is necessary to allocate the safety requirements to different subsystems, including E/E/PES, safety-related systems of other technologies, and external risk reduction facilities. This process is repeated in the context of software development by assigning safety requirements to the software and subsequently to the individual software components. Obviously, allocating safety requirements is no different from allocating functional requirements in a systems engineering process.

Overall safety validation. In order to validate whether or not the overall system meets the specification of the overall safety function and integrity requirements, an overall safety validation phase is required.

Before the actual validation takes place, a safety validation plan must be defined during the safety validation planning phase. This plan specifies the validation of the functional safety and shall include:

– Information about when the safety validation takes place.
– Who is responsible for carrying out the validation.
– Which safety-related systems must be validated in which operation mode.
– The technical strategy for the validation (for example, analytical methods, statistical tests, etc.)
– The measures, techniques, and procedures that shall be used for confirming that the allocation of safety functions has been carried out correctly. This shall include confirmation that each safety function conforms to the specification for the overall safety functions requirements and to the specification for the overall safety integrity requirements.
– The required environment in which the validation activities are to take place (for tests, this would include calibrated tools and equipment).
– The pass and fail criteria.
– The policies and procedures for evaluating the results of the validation, particularly failures.

During the actual overall safety validation phase, the following aspects must be considered:

– All validation activities shall be carried out in accordance with the overall safety validation plan.
– During the validation, the following aspects shall be documented in particular: the validation activities in chronological order with the corresponding results and the discrepancies to the expected results, the version of the safety requirements specification used, the validated safety functions, the tools and equipment used.
– When discrepancies are discovered, it shall be documented whether validation will be continued or whether a change request will be issued.

The overall safety validation phase is certainly not the only validation activity in the lifecycle. In fact, the lifecycles of software and hardware development include specific validation activities. The requirements on these activities, however, are more of technical interest, since they define specific validation and verification techniques that have to be applied.

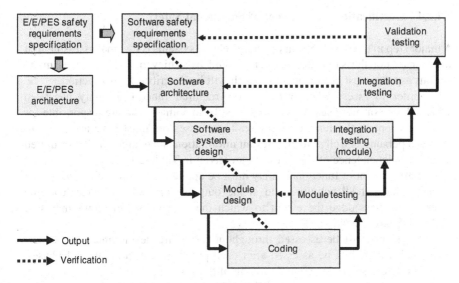

Fig. 2.19 Software safety lifecycle model of IEC 61508

2.4.2.3 Software Safety Lifecycle

The previous section considered the overall safety lifecycle model of IEC 61508. Additionally, the latter defines lifecycle models for the individual realization phases. This section illustrates the safety-specific aspects of the software safety lifecycle as illustrated in Fig. 2.19.

The IEC 61508 software safety lifecycle model is obviously no different from standard lifecycle models. This is particularly true since the individual phases can be (and shall be) adapted to the specific development context. From the point of view of a management process, the development of safety functions can thus simply be integrated into existing software development processes that define comparable development phases.

In general, the safety functions are developed using the standard lifecycle model. However, it is usually necessary to obey additional requirements on the methods and measures applied in order to meet the technical requirements of IEC 61508. For that reason, it is very important to clearly separate safety-related and non-safety-related functions in a system. Otherwise, the whole system development must be compliant to IEC 61508. Further, a clear separation between safety functions of different SILs is very important. Otherwise, all functions must be developed compliant to the highest SIL one of the safety functions is assigned to.

In most cases, the two aspects mentioned earlier are the focus of many industrial activities in the context of IEC 61508. First, appropriate techniques are defined that fit the development processes, techniques, and tools commonly used in the respective domain (e.g., automotive systems). Second, reasonable system and software architectures are defined that enable an economically feasible approach to the development of standard-compliant systems.

2.4.2.4 Certification: Assessment of Functional Safety

A major step in the development of safety-related systems is the final assessment of whether or not the safety requirements could be achieved. For this assessment, various aspects must be considered, which will be described in this section.

In order to assess whether or not the required functional safety has been achieved, one or more safety assessors must be appointed who are responsible for the assessment of the functional safety. These assessors must have access to all involved persons as well as to all relevant information and equipment. The required levels of independence of the assessors are given in Table 2.1.

The assessment of functional safety must be applied to all lifecycle phases. The assessors look at all activities and at the outputs obtained. As a result of the assessment, they judge the extent to which the objectives and requirements of IEC 61508 have been met.

The system must be assessed throughout the entire development cycle. The functional safety shall be assessed after each phase or after a number of phases, but at the latest before the commissioning of the system.

Another important aspect to consider is that any tool that is used during system development is also subject to assessment. This includes, for example, modeling tools, code generators, compilers, and host target systems.

During the assessment, all steps that have been performed since the last assessment, the plans and strategies for implementing further assessments, as well as the recommendations of the previous assessments and the corresponding changes must be looked at.

At the conclusion of the assessment, recommendations shall be produced for acceptance, qualified acceptance, and rejection.

Before the actual assessment takes place, an assessment plan has to be defined and must be approved by the assessors and by the safety manager who is responsible for the assessed safety lifecycle phase. Such a plan shall contain the following information:

– The persons who shall undertake the functional safety assessment
– The outputs from each functional safety assessment
– The scope of the functional safety assessment (in establishing the scope of the functional safety assessment, it will be necessary to specify the documents, and their status, which are to be used as inputs for each assessment activity)
– The safety bodies involved
– The resources required
– The level of independence of the persons undertaking the functional safety assessment
– The competence of those undertaking the functional safety assessment relative to the application

IEC 61508 currently forms the basis for safety-related activities in automotive software engineering. However, it will be replaced by ISO 26262 [24].

Table 2.1 Minimum levels of independence

Minimum level of independence	Safety integrity level			
	1	2	3	4
Independent person	Highly recommended	Highly recommended	Not recommended	Not recommended
Independent department	–		Highly recommended	Highly recommended	Not recommended
Independent organization	–	–	Highly recommended	Highly recommended

2.4.3 ISO 26262

ISO 26262 [24] is an upcoming standard concerned with the functional safety of road vehicles, specifically their electric and electronic (E/E) systems. It currently exists as a Final Draft International Standard (as of June 6, 2011, it was in stage 50.20 "DIS ballot initiated: 2 months") and is expected to be published as an international standard in 2011. ISO 26262 is an adaptation of IEC 61508 [23] for road vehicles. *Please note that all statements with respect to ISO 26262 are based on the current draft and thus should be considered as preliminary.*

The standard provides an automotive safety lifecycle (management, development, production, operation, service, decommissioning) for E/E systems and supports tailoring of the necessary activities during these lifecycle phases. It provides an automotive-specific risk-based approach for determining risk classes called *Automotive Safety Integrity Levels*, or ASILs. The standard uses such ASILs for specifying an item's safety requirements that are necessary for achieving an acceptable residual risk and provides requirements for validation and confirmation measures to ensure that a sufficient and acceptable level of safety is achieved. ISO 26262 consists of ten parts. The general process defined in ISO 26262 is very similar to the one from IEC 61508. Major changes include better consideration of software in general and requirements on software engineering in particular, and the way risks are assessed. Figure 2.20 shows an overview of the nine normative parts (part 10 is informative only).

Part 1: Glossary. This part provides a glossary of the terms used throughout the standard.

Part 2: Management of functional safety. This part specifies the requirements on functional safety management for automotive applications. These requirements cover the project management activities of all phases and consist of project-independent requirements and project-dependent requirements to be followed during development and requirements that apply after product release.

Part 3: Concept phase. This part specifies the requirements on the concept phase for automotive applications. These requirements include the item definition, the initiation of the safety lifecycle, the hazard analysis and risk assessment, and the functional safety concept.

Fig. 2.20 Overview of the normative parts of ISO 26262 (draft)

Part 4: Product development: system level. This part specifies the requirements on
   product development at the system level. These include requirements on the
   initiation of product development at the system level, the specification of the
   technical safety concept, system design, item integration and testing, safety
   validation, functional safety assessment, and product release.

Part 5: Product development: hardware level. This part specifies the requirements
   on product development at the hardware level. These include requirements on
   the initiation of product development at the hardware level, the specification of
   the hardware safety requirements, hardware design, hardware architectural
   constraints, assessment criteria for the probability of violation of safety goals,
   hardware integration and testing, and safety requirements for hardware–software
   interfaces.

Part 6: Product development: software level. This part specifies the requirements on product development at the software level for automotive applications. This includes requirements on the initiation of product development at the software level, specification of software safety requirements, software architectural design, software unit design and implementation, software unit testing, software integration and testing, and software safety acceptance testing.

Part 7: Production and operation. This part specifies the requirements on production as well as operation, service, and decommissioning.

Part 8: Supporting processes. This part specifies the requirements for supporting processes. These include interfaces within distributed development, overall management of safety requirements, configuration management, change management, verification, documentation, qualification of software tools, qualification of software components, qualification of hardware components, and proven-in-use argument.

Part 9: ASIL-oriented and safety-oriented analyses. This part specifies the requirements for ASIL-oriented and safety-oriented analyses. These include ASIL decomposition, criticality analysis, analysis of dependent failures, and safety analyses.

Part 10: Guideline. General guidelines, application examples, and further explanations (informative only).

So far, IEC 61508 is the standard that guides the development of safety-critical systems. For the automotive domain, ISO 26262 will take over this role when it is published.

2.4.4   IEC 62304

IEC 62304 [25] is a standard describing the software lifecycle for the development of medical devices. Similar to the software lifecycle described in IEC 61508, it describes a process for software development, starting with system requirements elicitation and ending with tests. In comparison to the more generic IEC 61508, it explicitly mentions and elaborately describes the handling of the product after commissioning, i.e., during operation. The operation issues, however, are limited to the scope of safety and give information on how to handle safety issues emerging after delivery.

Another difference to IEC 61508 is that IEC 62304 specifically describes the software development process and the implications for risk management. The processes describing the development of the complete (hardware/software) system are elaborated in ISO 60601 [36] (Fig. 2.21).

In addition to the engineering processes described in IEC 62304 and ISO 60601, ISO 13485 [37] describes a comprehensive quality management system for organizations developing medical devices, similar to the DIN EN ISO 9000 [38] and 9001 [39] standards for traditional organizations. ISO 13485 is complemented by ISO 14971 [40], which focuses on risk management for medical devices.

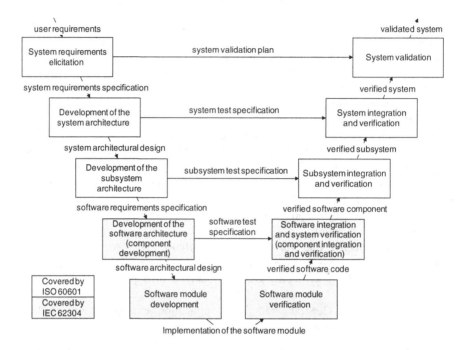

Fig. 2.21 Coverage of IEC 62304 and ISO 60601

IEC 62304 is harmonized, i.e., by proving compliance to this standard, an organization is also presumed to be compliant to the (mandatory) EWG directives 90/385/EWG, 93/42/EWG, and 98/79/EG. IEC 62304 is a process standard for developing medical device software that is complemented by many other standards and should not be viewed as standalone.

2.5 Process Representations in Organizations

This section describes two major alternatives of making process information publicly known in an organization: process handbooks and EPGs. Both can serve various purposes and have their specific strengths, which will be briefly illustrated.

2.5.1 Process Handbooks

This section describes process handbooks as a means of documenting and publishing process information. It describes the typical purpose and content of a process handbook and gives an exemplary outline for structuring a process handbook.

2.5.1.1   Purpose and Content

Process handbooks are generally thought of as information that helps process performers do the *right thing* at the *right time*. As such, they define the work that should be done, expected outcomes, the responsibilities of the various roles, the conditions that control the sequencing of the work, the conditions that can be used to track progress, etc. Process handbooks are usually organized according to a logical decomposition of the work that must be done, with chapters for major subprocesses, sections for major activities within each subprocess, and subsections for specific tasks.

The content and organization of a process handbook should reflect task-related questions posed by *process performers*, i.e., agents who are assigned to a project and responsible for carrying out the process. Some typical questions are:

- What do I have to do to perform an activity?
- What are the prerequisites for performing a task?
- What do I have to produce during the course of my work?
- Why do I have to perform a task in a specific way (rationale)?
- Which tasks am I responsible for?
- How can I determine whether or not I have successfully completed a task?
- Where can I find a particular template?

Across all the roles in a process, there will be many questions of many different kinds. For each kind of question, there should be one or more views that help in answering questions of this kind. For example, an activity decomposition view helps to answer questions about the interdependencies among activities and an artifact lifecycle view helps to answer questions about when to produce which document, and whom to send it to.

One handbook often cannot conveniently meet the needs of all the roles that will have questions about the process and its performance. Actually, many handbooks are needed, each oriented towards some role's domain of questions. This severely complicates the maintenance of an organization's process descriptions because changes and additions have to be accurately and consistently made to a possibly large number of handbooks. Therefore, a mature organization typically maintains only one comprehensive process model, and generates process handbooks for specific audiences out of this, covering the views required by the respective audience.

The content of process handbooks (and their underlying process models) usually comprises at least the following information:

- A description of the *activities* a process performer has to execute,
- A description of the *work products* that are produced by each activity, and thus have to be created by the process performer, and
- A description of the *roles* associated with the activities.

In addition to this, there is a variety of optional information that can be covered by process handbooks, depending on their purpose. This information may include:

- A description of resources or tools to be used during the activities,
- Document templates for the work products,
- Examples of the work products, i.e., an exemplary, "perfect" instance of a particular work product,
- How-tos for specific tasks, e.g., detailed instructions on how to complete the task using a specific tool, and
- Tips and tricks, e.g., workarounds for a bug in a tool.

Process handbooks always address a specific audience and try to convey specific information. Keep this in mind when developing a process handbook!

2.5.1.2 Exemplary Outline and Structure

The structure of process handbooks varies greatly. So far, there exists no common standard for process handbooks, i.e., no specification on where to find which information. Typically, an organization's process handbooks also follow the respective organization's corporate design, which may make the same content look very different across different organizations. This section introduces a generic outline for a process handbook that structures the information in a sensible way.

Introduction

- *Purpose:* What is the purpose of the process handbook—why was it created, e.g., for auditing purposes or for daily usage?
- *Target audience:* Which audience is addressed by the handbook, e.g., programmers or project managers?
- *History:* What is the history of the handbook, which previous version does the current handbook replace, and what was changed?
- *Process specifics:* What is specific about the process that is described in the handbook? Where does it differ from standard/other processes? What makes it special, what should people direct special attention to?
- *Applicability:* In which context(s) is the process applicable, e.g., is it for the development of safety-critical embedded systems or for the development of a Web application?
- *Relationships to other models:* Which other standards (e.g., international standards or other organization standards) or process models is this process handbook derived from? Where does it have similarities, where is it different?

- *Version:* Which version of the process model is described in the handbook? What are the differences to its predecessor/which problems were addressed with this version?
- *Structure:* What is the structure of the handbook? Which information can be found in which section?

Definitions

- *Terminology:* A definition of the terms used in the handbook. This is especially important since different terms are often used synonymously throughout the process community, while other terms have different meanings in different contexts.
- *Abbreviations:* Every organization has its own organizational slang, especially when it comes to abbreviating terms. Therefore, it is important to define the abbreviations used in the handbook.
- *Schemes* for describing products, processes, roles, and their relationships: These descriptions typically follow some kind of (semi-)formal structure. For example, a role can be linked to an activity ("performs") or to a document ("responsible for"). These schemes should be explained in order to enable the reader to understand the relationships described in the handbook.

Process Views

The views displayed in the handbook depend on its purpose and content; therefore, no generally applicable recommendation exists. However, typical views contain:

- *Major entities:* Which are the (sub-)processes/activities/tasks, which are the work products of the processes? Which roles exist, and which resources are used?
- *Control flow:* Which activity is preceded by which other activity, and which activity follows?
- *Product flow:* Which activity produces which work product, and which ones does it consume or modify?
- *Role-specific views:* Which role is participating in which activities? Which role is responsible for which work products?
- *Hierarchical decomposition:* Which activities and tasks belong to which subprocess?

Depending on the purpose of the process handbook, the descriptions will need to be on different levels of abstraction. For example, if the handbook should support assessors in identifying the company processes, detailed task descriptions including methods and techniques are less important. However, in order to assist process performers during their daily work, a precise and concise description of the design method can be most beneficial.

List of Figures and Tables, Index

In order to allow people to quickly find a figure or table they previously discovered somewhere, a list of figures and tables should be added. An index allows for quickly finding relevant information on specific keywords. The index should point to specific entry points and thus complements a full-text search (for electronic handbooks).

List of References

Finally, the list of references should provide additional information to that provided in the handbook. It may contain books on specific methods, tool manuals, or online resources in the organization's intranet or on the Internet. The references should either be referenced from within the process handbook or accompanied by a short explanation of what to expect from the reference.

Appendices

The appendices typically contain additional information that may be relevant for some groups of people, but that is not needed for daily work. For example, traceability information to other standards may become important for assessments or certifications, but is not required for daily project work. Such information is typically stored in appendices to the handbook, where it does not distract from daily work but can be accessed readily when needed. Appendices may also contain document templates, examples, checklists, tips and tricks, information on how to tailor the process for specific contexts, etc.

2.5.1.3 Usability

One of the most important—and difficult to achieve—aspects when it comes to process handbooks is their usability. Process handbooks are created for a purpose, a part of which is usually to support process performers in their daily work. If they do not like the process handbook, for whatever reason, they are less likely to fully apply the described processes, leading to compliance problems and possibly further mayhem. Therefore, the process handbook should make it easy to use it and encourage people to take a look at it.

While every process handbook is different, there are some general directions that should be considered when creating such a handbook:

– *Consistency:* The handbook should be consistent. This means that the same terms should always mean the same thing, and this thing should not be described using different terms. It should also be consistent on a higher level of abstraction.

This means, for example, that when a document is created at some point and a detailed description of the document is referenced, this reference should exist and describe the right document. Of course, the underlying process itself should be consistent, too, i.e., when a document is created, it should also be used somewhere else.

- *Up-to-date-ness:* The handbook should be up to date, i.e., it should describe the currently active process. For example, documents that are not used anymore should not be demanded by the process handbook.
- *Design:* The display of information should be functional, yet look nice. For example, the new 8-point company font may look cool, but it may be very hard to read—and thus should not be used for major content. The same applies to colors: The extensive use of colors may look great on screen—but if most people print the handbook on black-and-white printers and the colors suddenly all look like the same gray, this does not help.
- *Accessibility:* The information in the process handbook should be readily accessible. A single printed version of the handbook on the department's bookshelf is not likely to be used—or applied during daily work. An EPG, prominently linked in the organization's intranet or process portal, with powerful search functionality and direct template download, is much more helpful.

Remember: The best process handbook is worthless if it is difficult to use and is thus ignored!

2.5.2 Electronic Process Guides

This section describes EPGs as another means of documenting and publishing process information that makes the provided information easily accessible. It describes the typical purpose and content of an EPG and offers some examples of EPGs.

2.5.2.1 Purpose and Content

EPGs are typical instruments used to guide process performers in doing the right thing at the right time—much more so than process handbooks. While a process handbook as a linear representation of the process cannot really capture its networked structure, an EPG can. Interlinked Web pages allow following every possible path through the process easily, and are thus much easier to use for process guidance than a handbook that either requires following the given structure, or necessitates a lot of skimming through the pages.

An EPG is typically generated by a process modeling environment, i.e., it uses the process model as input and generates a Web-based representation, i.e., a set of interlinked Web pages. This type of EPG is usually called a "static" Web guide, because it consists of only static elements (Web pages, images). Any changes to the underlying process model result in the regeneration of the EPG.

Another variant generates the EPG on demand, i.e., an active server component reads the necessary information from the process model and generates the appropriate Web pages on demand. This EPG flavor will always represent the underlying process model accurately; however, it typically feels a bit slower when it is used due to the generation process.

Given the purpose of guidance for process performers, the content may be similar to that of process handbooks, yet a lot more useful for performing the process. For example, a template for a specific work product may be provided for download from the intranet—so that the creation of, for example, a requirements specification as prescribed is a lot simpler. A process handbook will typically be less comfortable to use and require, for instance, going to a specific intranet Web site manually (by typing in the URL). While this may sound like a minor issue, it may just be the reason for people not to use the provided template.

An EPG may also provide other helpful material: Besides templates, examples of "good" work products may show the process performers how to create the respective document. Discussion areas provide process performers with the ability to give direct feedback on the process description—what seems perfectly understandable to the process engineer may be rather complicated for a software developer, and vice versa. Similarly, process performers may give helpful tips for performing a certain task themselves—for instance, how to work around bugs in the tools that are used.

Apart from this kind of supportive material, an EPG may also support process performance by providing different views on the process. While a process handbook typically comprises the complete process (and thus features a rather global view), an EPG may provide different views for different roles. For example, a tester might not always need to know how to use the requirements management tool—thus, for his view, such details may be omitted. This helps people to focus on their specific role and does not clutter them with unnecessary (and potentially confusing) details. However, they usually have the option of switching to a different view with all the details. An EPG may even provide specific process views on demand, by generating them from the underlying process model.

The following section gives some examples of EPGs.

2.5.2.2 EPG Examples

Figure 2.22 displays an example of a static EPG that was generated by the process modeling tool SPEARMINT™. Each symbol is clickable, leading to a detailed description of the activity or work product it represents. In addition, the text may contain arbitrary links to other entities of the process model (i.e., to other pages within the EPG) or to any intranet or Internet URL.

Figure 2.23 shows a different variant of a static EPG. It provides basically the same features as the one shown in Fig. 2.22, yet has a completely different look and

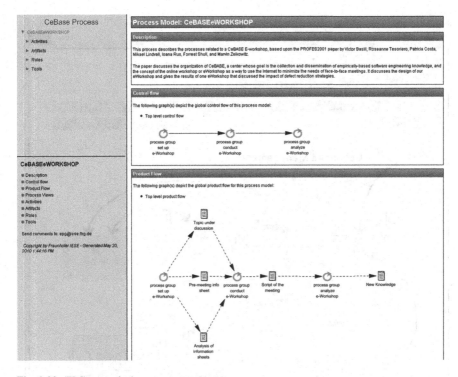

Fig. 2.22 EPG example 1

feel. Most process modeling environments provide a standard look and feel for the generated EPGs, which may then be adopted to follow the organization's corporate design, if necessary.

Figure 2.24 displays a wiki-based EPG. In this case, a MediaWiki installation was used with the Semantic MediaWiki extension, i.e., the process model is contained in the wiki itself [41]. All standard wiki functionality is available, such as commenting and subscribing for changes. In addition to that, the wiki provides a meta model that allows automatic listing of activities, work products, etc.

Figure 2.25, finally, displays another part of the wiki-based EPG. The displayed page is generated completely automatically from the wiki content. It displays a graphical rendition of the process description, which is automatically updated when the process description in the wiki changes [41].

2.6 Deploying Prescriptive Process Models

Process deployment deals with getting a prescriptive process into daily practice, i.e., getting people to follow the new or changed process. As already stated in Sect. 2.2.1, this means changing people's behavior, which is a difficult task to say

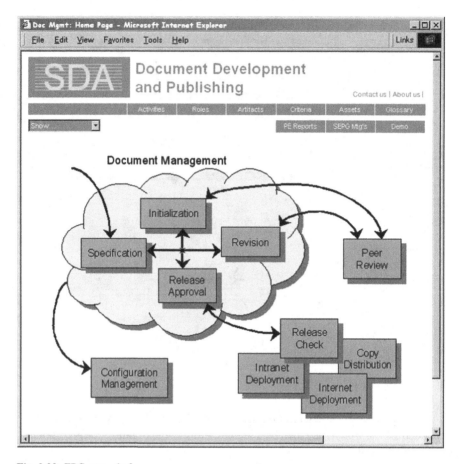

Fig. 2.23 EPG example 2

the least. This section describes possible strategies for deploying processes to an organization. It introduces an approach that has proven to be successful in practice, as well as experience from industrial process deployments, including a number of commonly made mistakes.

2.6.1 Deployment Strategies

Two general strategies for deploying a changed process to an organization are the big-bang and the phased approach:

– *Big-bang:* The complete organization is switched from the old to the new process at the same time. In this case, there will be no confusion resulting

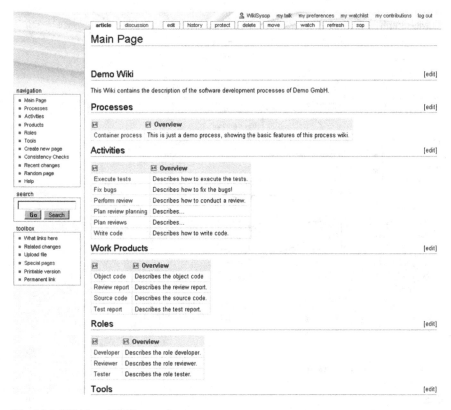

Fig. 2.24 Wiki-based EPG example

from people working in different projects/departments using different processes. However, this strategy requires a large amount of support capability for educating and coaching the employees. An intensified version of the big-bang strategy also switches running projects to the new process. However, this creates a lot of overhead; therefore, this is rarely done.

– *Phased:* The new process is applied only selectively in specific, newly starting projects. This requires only limited training and coaching capabilities and eliminates the switching overhead. However, if this strategy is pursued on a continuing basis, there will be a plethora of process variants active within the organization at the same time.

No matter which strategy is pursued, it is important that the process performers know about the new process. This means they must be educated in its contents and application. It is *not* enough to simply publish the new process handbook on the intranet and expect everyone to follow it! Most people are unwilling to change a behavior they have followed in the past, and they will use all kinds of excuses not to do so. Therefore, their changing behavior must be facilitated and supported. A first

Activity Graph   [edit]

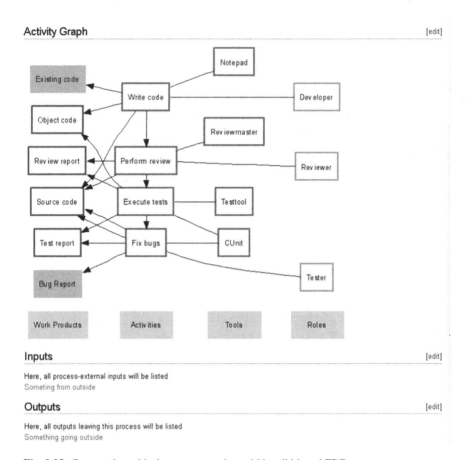

Inputs   [edit]

Here, all process-external inputs will be listed
Someting from outside

Outputs   [edit]

Here, all outputs leaving this process will be listed
Something going outside

Fig. 2.25 Generated graphical process overview within wiki-based EPG

step is to make it easy for them to find out what has changed in the first place. Typically, a process is not changed completely, but only some parts are altered. By pointing out the parts that were kept constant and highlighting those that were actually changed, the process performers will not need to read the whole handbook, but only the parts that apply to them and were actually changed.

This analysis has to be done by the process engineer who is preparing the changed process. This knowledge must then be transferred to the process performers. This can be done through classroom-style education, through coaching, by providing a "diffed" version of the process handbook that highlights changes, or through other means. In addition to a one-time knowledge transfer, process performers should be continuously supported by a helpdesk that assists them with the new process. Many problems and ambiguities will only show up during daily practice, for example, when a new template is to be used. In these cases, it is advisable to help process performers to correctly fill in this template, lest they either do not use it at all or use it incorrectly.

Industry example. A CMMI level 5 organization updates its processes every 3 months, based on feedback collected from all process performers. Every newly started project has to apply the new version from the start. Every already running project has to switch to the new process 3 months after the version was released at the very latest. The new version of the process is taught to all affected process performers in a classroom-style setting. After that, the Software Engineering Process Group (SEPG) provides coaching for the process performers, i.e., they provide a helpdesk that people can contact if they have questions. Every project is audited at least once every 3 months in order to assure that current processes are followed.

The following section describes an exemplary deployment approach for a new or changed software process. For rolling out the process to the organization, it supports both the "big-bang" and "phased" strategies described earlier.

2.6.2 An Exemplary Deployment Approach

With every change to a process, there is a risk that the changed process does not yield its expected benefits, i.e., does not perform better than the old one, or even worse, does not even perform as well as the old process and thus makes the situation worse. Therefore, a changed process should be tested before it is widely applied. A staged strategy permits to do this and has, in fact, proven to be a good choice [42]. Figure 2.26 displays one such approach, which supports both a big-bang and a phased rollout. We will explain this approach in the following subsections.

2.6.2.1 Process Development

During this phase, the changed process is developed, i.e., its model is created and the necessary documentation (handbooks, EPGs, etc.) is prepared. A typical approach is to create a descriptive model of the current process, analyze it for weaknesses, and modify the model to remove these weaknesses. However, this activity is not considered part of process deployment, and therefore is not detailed here.

2.6.2.2 Quality Gate 1: Piloting Maturity

This quality gate checks the changed process to see whether it is mature enough to be piloted. In particular, the following aspects should be checked:

– Goal achievement

  • Are the goals of the changed process documented in a verifiable form?
  • Which problems are addressed?
  • Does a cost/benefit analysis justify changing the process?

– Process handbook (presentation and contents)

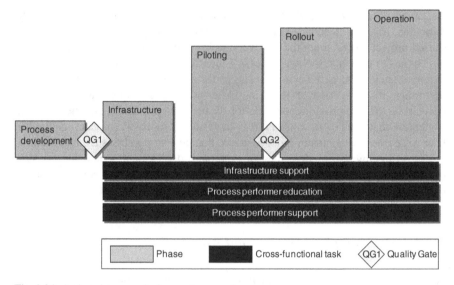

Fig. 2.26 A phased process deployment approach

- Are the essential elements included (cf. Sect. 2.5.1.2)?
- Are the presentation and contents okay for the target audience?
- Is the process handbook complete and correct?

– Quality assurance

- Was the changed process reviewed? By whom? Was the review documented? Was the process reworked according to the review results?
- Were all stakeholders identified and involved?

– Context factors

- What is the environment (technical/social) of the target audience?
- Are document templates available?
- Is there a definition of when the process is "successful"? What are the success criteria?
- Has a deployment strategy been defined?

2.6.2.3   Infrastructure

The infrastructure necessary to adequately support the new process must be supplied before the piloting starts, in order to provide realistic circumstances. This includes providing a sufficient number of tools (e.g., a requirements management tool), workplaces, hardware resources such as engine test beds or test vehicles, as well as education resources such as classrooms, personnel for helpdesk services, and others.

2.6.2.4 Process Performer Education and Support

These tasks are cross-functional, i.e., they are required to run continuously during the deployment of the changed process. At the beginning, education will require more resources, while at the end, this will shift towards supporting the process performers in their daily work. In particular, the following aspects should be considered:

– Process performer empowerment

  • Create trust and acceptance
  • Enable participation of process performers: include their input, let them take responsibility

– Education before project start

  • Common introductory courses
  • Role-specific courses
  • Tool-specific courses

– Process performer support before project start, during project runtime, and after the project finishes

  • Provision of education materials
  • Electronic newsletters
  • Community building: forum, wiki, blog
  • Coaching of process performers during the project
  • Provision of helpdesk service

– Feedback mechanisms before project start, during project runtime, and after the project finishes

  • To decrease the process performers' fear
  • To identify process problems ("you missed a step here")
  • To identify potentially problematic areas ("this is never going to work")
  • To check when the project is over: Was the education adequate? Tool support? Process handbook?
  • To create a "Wishlist" for future changes to the process

2.6.2.5 Piloting

When Quality Gate 1 has been successfully passed, the pilot project(s) using the changed process can commence. During a pilot project, the changed process is tested, i.e., it is applied in a realistic setting and the effects of its application are recorded. The goal of such a pilot project is to evaluate whether the changed process is fit for organization-wide deployment. However, it should not be forgotten that the pilot project itself introduces a bias: By choosing "simple" or "complicated"

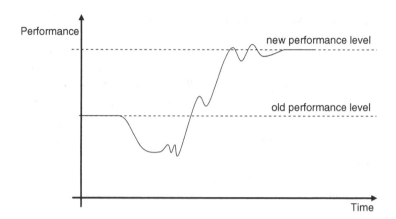

Fig. 2.27 Typical process performance over time

projects, the result can be manipulated. Therefore, a representative project should be chosen. In addition, it is also likely that project performance (e.g., cycle time) will decrease at the beginning. This is because a changed process always introduces a certain amount of confusion, which degrades process performance. It is important not to mistake the confusion-generated performance decrease with a general process failure; however, making this distinction is not easy and requires a certain experience. Figure 2.27 shows the typical performance development over time when deploying a changed process, with a temporary decrease compared to the old performance level, and subsequent increase and stabilization on the new, higher performance level.

For the piloting phase, the following aspects should be considered:

– Pilot project selection

  • Project type (representative for the organization?)
  • What is the influence of the changed process? Parallelization/elimination/ acceleration/...
  • Are fallback scenarios necessary? If yes, are they defined and realistic?
  • Are context factors considered (e.g., higher-level management attention, or an expected new standard, or new technologies)?

– Identification of stakeholder classes within the organization

  • Promoters
  • Supporters
  • Hoppers
  • Opponents

– Success evaluation

  • Along the previously defined success criteria
  • Organization-wide rollout only if successful as defined by the criteria!

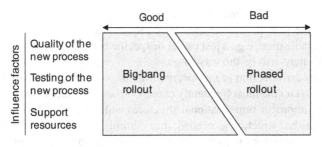

Fig. 2.28 Big-bang vs. phased rollout

2.6.2.6 Quality Gate 2: Rollout Maturity

If piloting of the changed process was successful, it should be evaluated whether the new process has actually been applied—otherwise an untested process could be rolled out organization wide. Such an evaluation typically analyzes those artifacts that should be prepared according to the changed process and/or interviews the process performers who applied the changed process. It should also be evaluated whether it is plausible that the changed process can also reach its goals outside the pilot project.

2.6.2.7 Rollout

The rollout takes the changed process to the entire organization. As mentioned before, there is no common "best practice" rollout strategy (cf. Sect. 2.6.1). Whether to choose a more big-bang-like rollout or a phased rollout depends on various influence factors within the organization, including, but not limited to, factors like the degree to which processes and projects are interwoven, the available support resources, the change climate, and many others.

Typically, it is not a good idea to switch running projects—however, this may be necessary for heavily interrelated projects. This must be decided on a case-by-case basis. Figure 2.28 displays some influencing factors. For example, if support resources are plenty, then a big-bang strategy can work. However, if the quality of the new process is questionable, a phased rollout is more appropriate.

It should also be considered in which order the organizational structure (departments, groups, etc.) and the process organization (workflows) are changed. It is possible to do either one first and then the other, or to change both at the same time.

First change the process organization, then the organizational structure. This is suitable for small process changes, or, in a phased rollout scenario, in the early phases (when only few process performers follow the new process). If the future of the changed process is unknown (i.e., if it is unclear whether it will remain active), it is also a good idea not to change the organizational structure too early.

First change the organizational structure, then the process organization. This is advisable if the new process mandatorily requires certain services or structures within the organization, e.g., a test center or specific hardware. In a big-bang rollout scenario, this may also be the way to go.

Concurrent introduction of new organizational structure and process organization. This is, in fact the most frequently chosen variant. It reduces additional friction losses due to improper organizational structures and allows for the creation of the new organizational structure as needed, thus minimizing overall effort. However, it may increase the effort required for rolling out the process compared to the organizational-structure-first variant.

No matter whether the structure or the process is changed first, there will most likely be some resistance to the intended changes. The deployment approach described earlier is likely to decrease this resistance; however, it will not remove it completely. A proven measure against any remaining resistance is (visible) top-level commitment in combination with maximal openness and transparency. The former makes it clear to everyone that "resistance is futile," i.e., that the changes are actively demanded and supported by the management. The latter will reduce the affected people's fears through information. Since most of the resistance is powered by (founded or unfounded) fears, this helps to reduce resistance as well. Solid trust between management and employees is another important factor: If the employees cannot trust statements made by management, they will resist change automatically, because they typically fear the worst. Rolling out process changes in an organization is thus usually the hardest part of any improvement effort—however, this is often not recognized!

2.6.2.8 Operation

When the changed process has been rolled out to the entire organization, the operational phase starts. During this phase, the process should be closely monitored and evaluated with respect to its effects. However, this activity is not considered part of process deployment, and therefore not detailed here.

2.6.3 Experience from Industrial Practice

In today's software organizations, process deployment is often performed less than optimally. Typical process management failures thus include the following:

- Process handbooks do not fulfill their purpose, e.g., important information is missing or they are too detailed to read.
- Process definitions are vague and incomplete, i.e., the actual problems are not addressed, but hidden underneath soft, meaningless statements.
- Interteam interfaces are poorly defined.

- Nonapplication of the changed process is not sanctioned, i.e., people are not forced to use the changed process and thus do not use it.
- The process engineers are not seen as service providers who assist the developers in their daily work, but rather as enemies of success, i.e., only keeping developers from "doing the real work."

There are more problems, of course. However, these are the most common ones that should be considered in any process organization. Nevertheless, most problems encountered in industrial practice are not technical problems, but social problems. The latter cannot be solved using a specific technology, but only by adequately treating the major influencing factor: humans.

References

1. Rombach HD (2001) Guaranteed Software Quality. In: Keynote address at the third international conference on product focused software process improvement (PROFES), Kaiserslautern, Germany, 10–13 Sept 2001, pp 1–2
2. Royce WW (1970) Managing the development of large software systems. In: Proceedings of IEEE WESCON, Los Angeles, CA, USA, pp 1–9
3. Basili VR, Turner AJ (1975) Iterative enhancement: a practical technique for software development. IEEE T Software Eng 1(4):390–396
4. Boehm BW (1986) A spiral model of software development and enhancement. ACM Sigsoft Software Eng Notes 11(4):22–42
5. Boehm BW, Lane JA (2008) Guide for using the Incremental Commitment Model (ICM) for systems engineering of DoD projects. Center for Systems and Software Engineering, University of Southern California, Los Angeles, CA
6. Boehm BW (2011) Some future software engineering opportunities and challenges. In: Nanz S (ed) The future of software engineering. Springer, Heidelberg. doi:10.1007/978-3-642-15187-3_1
7. Boehm BW (2009) The incremental commitment model (ICM), with ground systems applications. In: Ground systems architectures workshop (GSAW), Torrance, CA, USA, 23–26 Mar 2009
8. Jacobson I, Booch G, Rumbaugh J (1999) The unified software development process. Addison-Wesley, Amsterdam, The Netherlands
9. Mills HD, Dyer M, Linger RC (1987) Cleanroom software engineering. IEEE Software 4(5):19–25
10. Linger RC (1994) Cleanroom process model. IEEE Software 11(2):50–58
11. Prowell SJ, Trammell CJ, Linger RC, Poore JH (1998) Cleanroom software engineering—technology and process. Addison-Wesley, Reading, MA
12. Bauer T, Böhr F, Landmann D, Beletski T, Eschbach R, Poore J (2007) From requirements to statistical testing of embedded systems. In: Proceedings of the 4th international workshop on software engineering for automotive systems (SEAS'07), Minneapolis, MN, 26 May 2007
13. Prowell SJ (2003) JUMBL: a tool for model-based statistical testing. In: Proceedings of the 36th annual hawaii international conference on system sciences (HICSS'03), Hawai'i, HI, 6–9 Jan 2003
14. Miller KW, Morell LJ, Noonan RE, Park SK, Nicol DM, Murrill BW, Voas JM (1992) Estimating the probability of failure when testing reveals no failures. IEEE T Software Eng 18(1):33–43

15. Briand LC, El Emam K, Bomarius F (1997) COBRA: a hybrid method for software cost estimation, benchmarking, and risk assessment. International software engineering research network technical report ISERN-97-24
16. Trendowicz A, Heidrich J, Münch J, Ishigai Y, Yokoyama K, Kikuchi N (2006) Development of a hybrid cost estimation model in an iterative manner. In: Proceedings of the 28th international conference on software engineering (ICSE 2006), Shanghai, China, 20–28 May 2006
17. Fraunhofer Institute for Experimental Software Engineering IESE (2009) CoBRA—master your software projects. http://www.cobrix.org/. Accessed 9 Jun 2011
18. Beck K, Andres C (2005) Extreme programming explained. Addison Wesley, Boston, MA
19. International Organization for Standardization (1995) ISO/IEC 12207:1995. ISO/IEC, Geneva, Switzerland
20. International Organization for Standardization (2008) ISO/IEC 12207:2008, 'Systems and software engineering—software life cycle processes'. ISO, Geneva, Switzerland
21. International Organization for Standardization (2006) ISO/IEC 15504:2004, 'Information technology—process assessment'. ISO/IEC, Geneva, Switzerland
22. European Cooperation for Space Standardization (2009) Collaboration Website of the European cooperation for space standardization. http://www.ecss.nl/. Accessed 9 Jun 2011
23. International Electrotechnical Commission (2005) IEC 61508, 'Functional safety of electrical/electronic/programmable electronic safety-related systems'. IEC, Geneva, Switzerland
24. International Organization for Standardization (2009) ISO/FDIS 26262, 'Road vehicles—functional safety' (draft). ISO, Geneva, Switzerland
25. International Electrotechnical Commission (2006) IEC 62304, 'Medical device software—software life cycle processes'. IEC, Geneva, Switzerland
26. Carnegie Mellon Software Engineering Institute (2002) Capability maturity model integration 1.2. http://www.sei.cmu.edu/cmmi/. Accessed 9 Jun 2011
27. International Organization for Standardization (2008) ISO/IEC 15288, 'Systems and software engineering—system life cycle processes'. ISO, Geneva, Switzerland
28. Deutsches Institut für Normung e.V (2010) DIN EN 61508—Funktionale Sicherheit sicherheitsbezogener elektrischer/elektronischer/programmierbarer elektronischer Systeme. Beuth Verlag, Berlin
29. BMW Group (2005) BMW Group Standard 95014—embedded software development
30. Amsler KJ, Fetzer J, Erben MF (2004) Sicherheitsgerechte Entwicklungsprozesse—alles neu geregelt?. In: Proceedings of Aktive Sicherheit durch Fahrerassistenz, Garching, Germany
31. Benediktsson O, Hunter RB, McGettrick AD (2001) Processes for software in safety critical systems. Software Process Improve Pract 6(1):47–62
32. Jacobs M, Ferré A, Honekamp U, Scheidler C, Chen X, Blecken A, Fitterer E, Josko B (2004) Electronic architecture and system engineering for integrated safety systems—state of the art, EASIS-Report, Deliverable D.0.1.2. EASIS Consortium
33. IEC (2002) Functional safety and IEC 61508—a basic guide. IEC, Geneva, Switzerland
34. Spivey JM (1992) The Z notation: a reference manual. Prentice Hall, Upper Saddle River, NJ
35. Fitzgerald J, Larsen PG (2009) Modelling systems: practical tools and techniques for software development. Cambridge University Press, Cambridge, MA
36. International Electrotechnical Commission (2006) IEC 60601, 'Medical electrical equipment'. IEC, Geneva, Switzerland
37. International Organization for Standardization (2003) ISO 13485:2003, 'Medical devices—quality management systems—requirements for regulatory purposes'. ISO, Geneva, Switzerland
38. International Organization for Standardization (2005) DIN EN ISO 9000, 'Qualitätsmanagementsysteme—Grundlagen und Begriffe'. ISO, Geneva, Switzerland
39. International Organization for Standardization (2008) DIN EN ISO 9001, 'Quality management systems—requirements'. ISO, Geneva, Switzerland
40. International Organization for Standardization (2007) ISO 14971:2007, 'Medical devices—application of risk management to medical devices'. ISO, Geneva, Switzerland

41. Armbrust O, Weber S (2008) Wiki-basierte Dokumentation von Software-Entwicklung-sprozessen—Erfahrungen aus der industriellen Praxis. In: Proceedings of the 3rd Workshop: Vorgehensmodelle in der Praxis—Werkzeuge und Anwendung, 38. Jahrestagung der Gesell-schaft für Informatik (INFORMATIK 2008), Munich, Germany, 8–13 Sept
42. Armbrust O, Ebell J, Hammerschall U, Münch J, Thoma D (2008) Experiences and results from tailoring and deploying a large process standard in a company. Software Process Improve Pract 13:301–309

Chapter 3
Descriptive Process Models

This chapter introduces descriptive process models as a means of capturing the processes being pursued by an organization. It first describes some typical goals of descriptive process modeling efforts and then details a systematic approach for creating a descriptive process model. In addition, alternatives to a part of the approach as well as for the complete approach are presented in order to provide a broader view on the subject. In most process modeling approaches, eliciting process information through interviews is one of the hardest activities; hence the chapter gives some guidelines on conducting efficient and effective interviews. Finally, the chapter introduces some tactics for managing the risks that accompany descriptive process modeling efforts. Figure 3.1 displays an overview of the chapter structure.

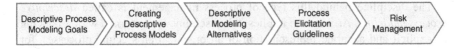

Fig. 3.1 Chapter structure

3.1 Objectives of This Chapter

After reading this chapter, you should be able to

- Define goals for a descriptive process modeling effort
- Plan and conduct a descriptive process modeling effort based on an 8-step approach
- Conduct process elicitation interviews
- Assess and manage the basic risks associated with a descriptive process modeling effort

J. Münch et al., *Software Process Definition and Management*,
The Fraunhofer Series on Software and Systems Engineering,
DOI 10.1007/978-3-642-24291-5_3, © Springer-Verlag Berlin Heidelberg 2012

3.2   Introduction

The last chapter explained that one of the main purposes of prescriptive process models is to provide a reference process framework that an organization can adopt. Since these process descriptions are usually based on well-proven and widely accepted practices, their adoption often constitutes a safe path to process improvement.

The downside of prescriptive models is that, being generic, they cannot exactly fit the particularities of a specific organization. A number of factors can influence the way software development activities are shaped in an organization. Obviously, the strongest of these factors are usually related to the type of product that is being developed, as well as to the technology involved in producing this product. Still, even organizations that produce similar, potentially competing software products often have widely different ways of developing them. These differences can be related to factors such as their organizational culture and history; the social, legal, and political contexts in which the organization operates; and the level of skill and type of education of the people involved, among many others. The result is that, in practice, no organization exactly follows a generic prescribed process, and no two organizations operate according to exactly the same process.

The actual processes present in an organization, those that are used in practice to produce and deliver the organization's products and services, can usually be counted as one of its main assets. Normally, these processes encompass a good deal of the experience and knowledge that make an organization successful. For this reason, managing them appropriately can become a crucial activity for an organization's long-time survival.

The discipline behind this type of process management is called *descriptive process modeling*. As its name implies, this discipline is concerned with producing an explicit and accurate representation of an organization's actual processes, for purposes such as documentation, dissemination, analysis, and improvement.

3.3   Goals of Descriptive Process Modeling

Descriptive process modeling can serve a number of goals in an organization. This section describes some common reasons why organizations decide to describe their processes explicitly.

3.3.1   Stable and Accurate Process Execution

Software processes can be very complex, involving large numbers of interrelated activities. For every software development project, these activities must be carefully orchestrated, so that dependencies are respected and resources are available where and when they are needed. This complexity makes it very hard to guarantee that processes are always executed in the same way. Given the large number of individual activities and their complex interdependencies, there is a high risk that some activities are not planned or are skipped because of external pressure. Also, there is always the risk that people will change the process over time without even noticing it, maybe eliminating beneficial activities.

A documented process helps to mitigate these risks. With a proper process description at hand, both project planners and project performers can make sure that they are performing all important and expected activities, and that they are taking into account all relevant interrelations between those activities. Also, a documented process makes it easier to introduce changes in a controlled fashion, which leads us to our next point: understanding the process.

3.3.2 Process Understanding

Software development processes must change for a number of reasons. Sometimes, external factors—such as changes in laws and regulations, or technological progress—force changes in the development process. Very often, however, the process is changed in order to introduce improvements. In many organizations, this happens in an organic fashion, because people identify situations where work can be done in a better way. There is always the risk, however, that changes that are originally perceived as improvements end up having unintended, detrimental consequences, which may negatively affect the overall process performance. For example, tools are often introduced because they are expected to improve the process by automating parts of it. It may happen, however, that a particular tool is designed with a process in mind that is too different from that of the organization. In this case, the tool is likely to introduce inefficiencies that are not compensated by its potential advantages.

Understanding the process is fundamental for managing this risk. An explicit process representation makes it much easier to assess the overall impact of process changes, thus allowing better management of process changes.

3.3.3 Process Propagation

A common problem, present especially in large organizations, is that different development groups in the organization follow different processes for the same task. Sometimes, these process differences are related to the fact that different groups may have different needs. However, it often happens that they work differently simply because it is difficult for a group to exactly tell what other groups are doing.

By explicitly describing the processes followed by various organizational units, it is easier to achieve a unified process. Differences between groups can still exist, but they are the result of conscious decisions based on analyzing each group's particular needs. A unified process is important because it allows for practices that are widely accepted as being beneficial, to be propagated to all units in a large organization.

3.3.4 Process Measurement

As an organization reaches a higher degree of process maturity, it becomes increasingly important to measure process performance. Aspects that are commonly measured in a process are its productivity (amount of output produced vs. resources invested into producing it), its ability to deliver results on time, and its ability to detect and correct product defects as early as possible, among many others. The reasons for measuring vary widely from one organization to another, but often include the desire to improve planning and increase the quality of software products by reducing the number of defects present in them when they are delivered.

Measuring a process involves acquiring quantitative information about the actual activities, products, and resources involved. This is a hard task requiring high levels of discipline in order to yield satisfactory results, and which therefore must be carefully planned and executed. A proper process description greatly facilitates such planning by making it easier to identify appropriate measurement objects and to specify the procedures necessary to measure them. In addition, it provides the basis for comparing two processes with each other: It is only feasible to compare, for instance, the "duration of code development" if it is known which activities are contained: only coding, or also unit/integration testing?

3.3.5 Process Administration

In the long term, one of the main reasons for explicitly describing an organization's development processes is to be able to define goals for the process and work systematically on achieving them. Doing this involves at least some of the descriptive process modeling goals explained earlier, such as process understanding and process measurement. Long-term goals for a process are often related to improvement (e.g., increase product quality, reduce time dedicated to product rework, etc.), but may be related to other process aspects. For example, many companies are forced by legal regulations, or, simply, by the critical nature of their products, to comply with existing norms and regulations regarding the way their products are produced and validated. For these organizations, one important reason for modeling their processes explicitly is to guarantee that they comply with whatever norms and regulations are considered relevant. Without a proper process description, this can be very difficult or even impossible to achieve.

3.3.6   Process Automation

It happens quite often that once a process has been properly described and stabilized, opportunities for supporting parts of it with automated tools become evident. Analyzing a detailed process description is probably one of the best ways to determine the exact requirements of new process-supporting tools.

One area where processes can be supported in a particularly effective way is information flow. Since process models often contain detailed descriptions of the product and control flows in a process, a tool can effectively support process participants by giving them access to the pieces of information that are relevant for their activities and by providing appropriate mechanisms for storing new work products and informing other process performers about their availability and status. This type of support is especially useful in modern development environments, where developers are frequently distributed geographically, often across several time zones.

3.4   Creating a Descriptive Process Model

This section introduces a systematic approach for creating and validating a descriptive process model.

Process engineers working on describing an organization's processes are confronted with two main challenges. The first of these challenges is the so-called *process elicitation*, namely, collecting information about how the process is actually performed. This can be done by working together with the actual process performers, by observing their work, or by analyzing the results of their work, such as the documents produced during past development projects. Through interviews, direct observation of people's work, and analysis of documents and final products, among other techniques, process engineers gain a detailed understanding of the process.

The second challenge process engineers face is *storing the process knowledge for future use*. The process-related information must be expressed in a clear and unambiguous way that is amenable to the goals of the modeling effort (e.g., process measurement, improvement, analysis, etc.). A number of notations and modeling tools are available to facilitate this task. Notations allow expressing processes using a predefined, standardized set of concepts. They can be formal or graphical in nature, with graphical notations being preferred in recent years because they facilitate communication with process stakeholders. Tools, in turn, help process engineers to deal with the complexity of process models, which, in practice, may easily grow to contain hundreds or even thousands of individual elements.

Normally, descriptive process modeling is performed in an iterative fashion, with the elicitation and modeling phases being interwoven. Process engineers work to gain some initial knowledge of the modeled process, describe this knowledge using an appropriate process notation, and then discuss this initial description with the process stakeholders. This discussion often leads to additional knowledge being collected, which can be incorporated into the description and validated again with the stakeholders. This cycle can be repeated until satisfactory levels of detail and accuracy of the process description have been achieved.

The following sections detail a systematic approach to creating a descriptive process model for an organization. It is based on the 8-step approach presented in [1]. In addition to the approach described in this section, Sect. 3.5.1 describes an alternative to steps 5 and 6, whereas Sect. 3.5.2 introduces a complete alternative to creating a descriptive process model.

3.4.1 Approach Overview

The approach consists of two major phases: a *set-up phase* configuring the modeling approach for the organization, the modeling goals and context; and an *execution phase* performing the actual modeling. The set-up phase consists of these four steps:

1. State objectives and scope
2. Select or develop a process modeling scheme
3. Select (a set of) process modeling formalisms
4. Select or tailor tools

The execution phase consists of these four steps:

5. Elicitation
6. Create the process model
7. Analyze the process model
8. Analyze the process

In theory, these steps should be repeated for every process modeling effort in order to achieve optimal results. In practice, however, the process modeling scheme, formalisms, and tools are likely to be rather stable across different modeling efforts, because in a real-world setting, it is usually not feasible to frequently switch them due to cost reasons. Nevertheless, every modeling effort should clearly state its objectives and scope, because they will likely *not* be stable across different modeling efforts. Steps 5 through 8 will have to be repeated in any case.

The eight steps are explained in detail in the following sections, illustrated by three different case studies highlighting different contexts and goals of a descriptive process modeling effort. Although the case studies are fictitious, they reflect the realities of common process modeling efforts. The general settings in which each of the case studies takes place are as follows.

3.4.1.1   Case Study 1: The Defect Management Process at DocVault

DocVault is a small software development company, with about 50 employees and 6 years in the market. DocVault's main product is an Internet-based document management system that is made available to clients through a subscription-based model (software as a service). The company already has more than 30 corporate customers and good prospects for acquiring several more in the upcoming months.

Since DocVaults's product is already quite large and complex, it is relatively common for clients to be affected by defects in the system that were not detected by the quality assurance procedures used by the company (mainly testing). Until now, the company has relied on email as the main mechanism for clients to report problems they might have found. This simple mechanism has served the company well so far, but with the number of customers quickly increasing, the need for a more elaborate and potentially automated solution is becoming urgent.

For this reason, DocVault wants to start by modeling its defect management process. This process involves not only the actual problem reporting by users, but also the classification of problem reports by company staff, the assignment of potential defect-fixing tasks to developers, and the follow-up of defect fixes until they are released to clients, among other tasks.

3.4.1.2 Case Study 2: Software Development at Selene Aerospace Systems

Selene Aerospace Systems specializes in building complex data transmission and storage systems for satellites and other spacecraft. Selene was founded almost 20 years ago, and currently has about 700 employees, about 250 of whom perform tasks related to software development.

The development process at *Selene* has evolved from the company's long experience in aerospace systems and can be considered quite stable at this time. Since Selene's systems are very often very complex and often subject to strong reliability requirements, the development processes at the company are very elaborate and complex, involving a large number of steps for tasks such as requirements management and quality assurance.

The complexity of Selene's development process can easily become problematic: The only way to make sure that processes are executed as desired is by involving highly experienced project managers and developers in each project. The company keeps growing, however, which makes it impossible to find enough experienced people for all new projects. For this reason, the company is considering modeling its complete set of development processes in order to make them more accessible to less experienced developers and project managers.

3.4.1.3 Case Study 3: Software Customization at Soster

Soster Inc.'s product is an *Enterprise Resource Planning* (ERP) system oriented towards small- and medium-sized companies. Soster is about 10 years old and has about 200 employees. Over the years, Soster has developed a solid, highly customizable core system implementing most of the required ERP functionality. For this reason, its current business centers on customizing this system for specific customers.

Soster's system has already been customized for more than 250 customers, which is a pretty large number given the company's relatively small size. This has been possible because the customization process is very streamlined, consisting mostly of creating a set of UML models for each client, which are used to generate code automatically. The generated code often has to be complemented by hand-written code, but the size of this manually created code can be kept quite small.

Since Soster's revenue comes mostly from customization, the company is especially interested in optimizing this process. In particular, it is important to maximize product quality and project predictability. For this reason, the company has decided to start a modeling effort to describe this particular process.

3.4.2 Step 1: State Objectives and Scope

Section 3.3 described a variety of possible goals a descriptive process modeling effort may have. In order to properly plan and later manage the process modeling effort, it is thus important to state its goals clearly before any modeling has started. The scope of the effort must also be clearly stated. This includes specifying

- Who will use the process model
- What these people expect of the model
- Which processes should be covered
- Which processes are explicitly excluded from the model

With this information as a basis, it is possible to specify the scope more concretely. For example, knowing the general goals of the effort as well as people's concrete expectations makes it possible to determine which processes to model in which detail in order to better fulfill the stated goals and meet the stated expectations.

The following subsection explains how this first step was performed in the exemplary case studies.

3.4.2.1 Case Study 1: DocVault

The modeling effort at DocVault is restricted to the defect management process. This means that the scope is relatively narrow:

- Modeling is limited to the defect management process. It includes taking problem reports from users, classifying them, assigning accepted reports to responsible people in the company, and following them up until fixes are released. Technical processes related to the actual fixing of defects, such as determining the causes of particular failures, designing and implementing code fixes, and testing fixed code, are excluded, however.
- The main users of the description are the developers of the automated defect management system. Notice that these are likely to be not the same people

developing DocVault's product, since DocVault will probably subcontract the defect management system to another company. DocVault's clients, as well as the software developers and quality management team at DocVault, are considered secondary users, as they may use the process description for their own purposes, such as guidance while actually handling problem reports.

– The developers of the defect management system (primary users) expect a detailed description they can use as an initial set of requirements for implementing the process automation. The secondary users, on the other hand, expect a clear description that can be used for guiding internal users at DocVault.

3.4.2.2   Case Study 2: Selene

The modeling effort at Selene has a very wide scope, covering all software development processes in the company:

– The main objective of the modeling effort is to provide guidance for all roles in the organization. This involves describing the processes at a level of detail that allows for processes to be performed reliably even by people who were only recently trained and still lack experience with a particular process.
– All processes related to software development are covered, with no exception. The level of detail is expected to be high.
– The users are all roles participating in development, again with no exception.

3.4.2.3   Case Study 3: Soster

Soster's modeling effort is narrower than that at Selene, since it involves only one process. This process, however, is relatively large and complex and has to be covered in a very detailed way:

– The main objective of the modeling effort is to support improvement. In particular, enough information must be available in the model to make it possible for product quality and project predictability to be optimized. Notice that the goal of the modeling effort is to provide the necessary information for process analysis, but not to perform the actual improvements on the process.
– Processes related to customization are covered, such as requirements elicitation and management, model creation and validation, quality assurance, customization of the generated system through manually written code, and system deployment. The processes related to the development and maintenance of the core system are explicitly excluded.
– The target users of the resulting model are the members of Soster's SEPG, since they are responsible for the improvement effort. Other roles at the company, such as developers and project managers, are explicitly excluded.

3.4.3   Step 2: Select or Develop a Process Modeling Schema

The second step of descriptive process modeling consists of identifying the set of concepts that will be used to describe processes. The following (very simplified) example illustrates how this step may be done in practice.

Example: An organization decides that it will model its processes based on the following informal description:

"We see processes in our company as consisting of a number of individual *activities* (such as Requirements Elicitation, Design Specification, Module Implementation, etc.). Each of these activities has a set of *inputs*, which are *work products* of different kinds (e.g., Functional Requirements Specification, High Level Class Diagram, Module Source File, etc.). The goal of an activity is to produce a set of *outputs* based on the inputs it receives. The outputs, of course, are also *work products*. In this way, activities are interconnected through their associated work products: The outputs of an activity can be inputs to the subsequent activities. Finally, activities are associated to particular people's *roles* (e.g., Requirements Engineer, Software Architect, Programmer, etc.) This means that the people occupying these roles are *responsible* for the corresponding activities."

From this description, it is possible to identify a number of basic concepts that are important for describing processes in the organization:

– Activity
– Work product
– Role
– Product flow between activities and work products, i.e., which products are inputs or outputs to which activities
– Assignment of roles to activities, i.e., which roles are responsible for performing which activities

Usually, a set of concepts such as this used to model processes is called a *process schema*.

Although identifying an appropriate set of modeling concepts may appear to be quite simple from this small example, it is, in practice, a very difficult task, and one that deserves very careful consideration given its importance for the success of the subsequent modeling steps. As a minimum, the following requirements should be taken into account while choosing a process schema:

– The concepts must cover those aspects of a process that are relevant for the current modeling effort. The general concept of a model is related to conveniently representing certain specific aspects of reality, while purposefully ignoring those that are irrelevant for a specific purpose. Process models are no exception in this respect. The chosen set of concepts must cover those aspects of the process that are necessary for achieving the stated modeling goals. For instance, if reducing time to market for new products is a stated modeling goal, modeling the amount of time required by different activities will be fundamental. The chosen process schema must be able to represent this information.

- The concepts must allow for an adequate level of detail and formalism. Achieving an appropriate level of detail and precision while modeling can be very important. Too much detail may be as inadequate as too little detail, depending on the particular situation. For example, a model that is intended for personnel training may be more detailed and informal than one that is intended to provide fine-grained support for process enactment. A set of concepts that does not allow for the level of detail or formalism required by a particular modeling effort, or that requires too much of any of them, will be inadequate and must be adjusted.
- The concepts must facilitate modeling. A process schema that appears adequate at first sight may indeed be very difficult to use in practice. For example, it may happen that common situations are difficult to express and end up requiring too many entities or a convoluted structure of the entities in order to be described appropriately. For this reason, it is important to test modeling concepts in advance before committing to them for a large modeling effort. Trying to model a few, well-known processes or process excerpts may greatly help to assess the relative easiness or difficulty of modeling the complete process.
- Modeling results must be accessible for their intended audience. If process models are intended for people to use, this obviously means that these people must be able to properly read and understand them. If the chosen set of modeling concepts is too complex or unintuitive, chances are that users will be confused when they try to make sense of a model, no matter how careful process engineers were while producing the model.

Designing a set of concepts "from scratch" that fulfills all of these requirements can be a difficult task even for experienced process engineers. The main problem lies in the fact that one cannot determine by simple observation whether a particular schema fulfills any of the criteria. Normally, a schema must be extensively tried in practice before all of its disadvantages become apparent.

For this reason, it is strongly advisable to use an existing schema whenever possible. Fortunately, there are enough schemata available that cover most common modeling needs and that have been extensively tested in practice and are already known to have withstood the proverbial "test of time." If tailoring of a schema is necessary, it should be performed by sufficiently experienced process engineers and the result thoroughly tested before being used in any significant modeling efforts.

3.4.3.1 Case Study 1: DocVault

Given the narrow scope of its modeling effort, DocVault can live with a small set of modeling concepts: *task*, *artifact*, and *role*. Also, modeling more specific dependencies among entities of these types is not necessary, because the involved work flows are relatively simple. For this reason, a *produces* and a *consumes* relationship, together with a relation to associate roles to tasks are enough for this modeling effort.

3.4.3.2 Case Study 2: Selene

Due to the size and level of detail of its modeling effort, Selene requires a large set of concepts. Because of its complexity, only the most important concepts of the Selene schema will be covered:

– Processes with several levels of refinement: *activity, task, step*
– Deliverables, also with several refinement levels: *deliverable, part, chapter*, etc.
– Individual (e.g., Project Manager, Tester) and group roles (Change Management Board)
– A number of secondary concepts associated to the primary ones mentioned earlier, such as

  • Generic methods used to perform an activity or task
  • Templates for deliverables used to facilitate the creation of new documents
  • Level of training and experience required to occupy a role etc.

– A complex set of relationships between concepts, including

  • Grouping and hierarchy
  • Dependencies
  • Associations between main and secondary concepts etc.

Many of the elements in this schema have textual attributes that allow describing them in detail.

3.4.3.3 Case Study 3: Soster

The modeling scope at Soster does not require a schema with the level of complexity required at Selene. Still, a number of concepts are necessary:

– Processes with two levels of refinement: *activity, subactivity.*
– Nonhierarchical deliverables and roles.
– Specialized entity types for modeling project planning and control activities, as well as for modeling quality control activities. These are necessary in order to provide finer-grained modeling for the most relevant concepts, namely, those related to project predictability and product quality.
– Relations to connect the special entities with the basic entities and among themselves:

  • Processes used to plan a given development activity
  • Processes used to monitor the execution of a given development activity
  • Processes used for quality assurance of a particular deliverable etc.

3.4.4   Step 3: Select (a Set of) Process Modeling Formalisms

Process modeling not only requires an appropriate set of concepts but a concrete notation in which these concepts can be expressed. A variety of modeling notations have been used over time, with significant differences in formalism and expressive power. Of course, the notation chosen for a particular modeling effort must be able to express the concepts identified in the previous step. Additionally, process notations can be characterized along a number of dimensions:

– *Graphical vs. textual.* Some notations rely mainly on text, whereas others are mainly graphical. Some combine these aspects to various extents.
– *Formal vs. informal.* Some notations rely on mathematically defined elements, which can only be combined according to strict rules, whereas others rely on natural language text and loosely defined graphical elements. Formal elements are often combined with informal ones to achieve a richer description that is easier to understand.
– *Fine grained vs. coarse grained.* Some notations are intended to describe processes at a macro level, whereas others provide support for producing very detailed descriptions.
– *Predetermined vs. extensible.* Some notations are intended to be used "as-is," with no modifications whatsoever, whereas others allow for extensibility. Extensibility, in turn, may range from very basic, allowing only for simple tailoring that is useful only in certain common cases, to very advanced, allowing for tailoring that can handle almost any practical situation imaginable.

Taking these dimensions into account, it is possible to choose a notation that is appropriate for the needs of a particular modeling effort. For instance, if the main modeling goal is to support automated enactment, a formal and fine-grained notation would be desirable. On the other hand, if the main purpose is to support personnel training, a more informal and coarser-grained notation would likely be enough. Notice that, for both of these examples, the notation could be either graphical or textual, as long as the necessary levels of formality and detail are achieved.

Similar to the identification of modeling concepts discussed in the previous step, selecting an appropriate notation is a demanding task. Indeed, a set of requirements analog to the one presented for the previous step applies here as well:

– The notation must cover the concepts selected in the previous step.
– The notation must allow for an adequate level of detail and formalism.
– The notation must facilitate modeling.
– The modeling results (as represented in the chosen modeling notation) must be accessible to their intended audience.

As in the previous step, these requirements make it very advisable to stick to existing notations whenever possible, and to reduce their tailoring to a minimum.

Given the difficulty of finding appropriate modeling notations, this step is often interwoven in practice with the previous one, that is, the detailed set of modeling concepts and the notation are selected simultaneously. Still, thinking of both steps as conceptually separate remains useful. In particular, by thinking about the necessary modeling concepts in advance, one can guarantee that a notation was chosen because it was appropriate for the modeling effort at hand. Otherwise, there is a high risk that a notation is chosen because it appears convenient (e.g., because it is supported by well-known vendors and/or popular tools) and not because it offers a set of modeling concepts that fulfill the needs of the process stakeholders.

3.4.4.1   Case Study 1: DocVault

Since DocVault's aim is to automate the defect management process, they require a process description that is essentially free of imprecision and ambiguity. For this reason, the process modeling team decides to define a formal, yet simple process notation. This textual notation allows for defining instances of the concepts mentioned in the last section. While defining a process, entities must be given unique identifiers that can later be used for referring to them from other elements, such as relations. Additionally, a formula notation can be used to express pre- and postconditions for tasks. These conditions can later be used by the programmers automating the process.

3.4.4.2   Case Study 2: Selene

In order to provide detailed guidance to a variety of process performers, Selene largely requires using natural language text for describing processes. Maintaining a purely informal description of the large and complex set of processes at Selene would be very difficult, however. As seen in the previous section, Selene's schema involves a significant number of relations between elements. Making these relations explicit in a natural-language description is cumbersome, and verifying them or updating them after changing the model becomes very difficult, because of the need to search for them in a mostly manual way.

For this reason, Selene decided to add a formal structure to the plain-text description. This structure is used to organize the elements in appropriate hierarchies as well as to explicitly represent the many relationships among elements. Individual entities inside this structure are still mainly described using natural-language text, but this text is integrated in the formal structure so that it can be more easily managed. In particular, when the text references model entities other than the one being described, these references use explicit, model-unique identifiers. This way, they can later be traced and corrected when the model is updated.

3.4.4.3 Case Study 3: Soster

For Soster, the ability to identify inefficiencies in their customization processes is an absolute priority, so they wanted a notation that is especially amenable to analysis. For this reason, they decided to express their schema concepts using a graphical representation. This representation makes it convenient for process experts to look at the process, identify potential inefficiencies, and discuss potential improvements.

3.4.5 Step 4: Select or Tailor Tools

Tool support is usually necessary to effectively model complex processes. Among other things, in a descriptive modeling effort, tools are useful for:

- Supporting the use of the chosen modeling notation. The more complex the chosen modeling notation, the higher the need for an editing tool that supports it explicitly. Editing tools not only facilitate creating and changing models, but often help guarantee that the notation is being used properly.
- Storing large models or model collections in a convenient and safe way. Depending on the technology used, modeling efforts may end up producing large numbers of interrelated objects. Tools often help to manage these objects so that they can be conveniently accessed and changed in a safe, controlled way. This type of functionality may be integrated in the modeling tool itself, or it can be provided by separate tools, such as a version management system.
- Producing alternative representations of models. In many cases, different process stakeholders have different needs regarding the way a process model is presented. For instance, project managers may require an overview of the activities involved in a process, whereas the people working on specific activities will need to see the details of how such activities must be performed.

One important aspect about tools is that they do not have to be specialized process modeling tools in order to be adequate for a particular modeling effort. In many cases, standard office tools (word processor, spreadsheet) and/or generic diagramming tools can be effectively used to model processes, as long as the chosen notation is simple enough for them and the models are small and need only little maintenance. Specialized tools, on the other hand, can provide specific support for particular notations and model maintenance, which can be a deciding factor when very large or complex models are involved. Of course, such tools are often accompanied by higher license and user training costs.

3.4.5.1 Case Study 1: DocVault

The relatively small size of DocVault's defect management process as well as the selected, text-based notation make it possible to conduct the modeling without using advanced modeling tools. For this reason, DocVault decided to use standard programming text editors for creating and maintaining the model.

3.4.5.2   Case Study 2: Selene

For its modeling effort, Selene had to edit a significant amount of text. Moreover, this text must be properly formatted, included typical rich text features such as titles, numbering and bullet lists, use of various fonts for highlighting, etc. As explained before, however, Selene's needs are not restricted to editing text, but also involve organizing the edited text into a complex model structure.

In order to support these needs, Selene chose a commercial tool that stores the model structure and text context in a shared, relational database, but uses a standard word processor as its front end. Process engineers can then use the word processor to comfortably create rich text (including, for example, graphics and tables) and then store it in the database for later processing. Formal elements of the model, such as relations between entities, are entered in the word processor using special templates, which are later processed by the tool in order to create the actual relations in the database.

3.4.5.3   Case Study 3: Soster

Soster's emphasis on a graphical process display led them to choose a commercial graphical model editor as their main modeling tool. This editor can be adapted to support a variety of schemata, so they started by customizing it to support their chosen schema.

3.4.6   Step 5: Elicitation

The elicitation step is intended to collect all information necessary for actually describing the target software process. Mainly, the necessary information comprises:

- The process entities. These include activities, roles, work products, tools, and, potentially, many others. Oftentimes, entities form hierarchies. For example, major activities can be decomposed into smaller tasks, and tasks, in turn, can be decomposed into individual steps.
- Relationships between entities. For example, information about which activities produce or consume which products, which tools are necessary for performing a task, or which tasks compose an activity is expressed through relationships.
- Behavioral properties of the process entities, e.g., which conditions must hold in order for an activity to be started *(preconditions)*, or which criteria a work product must fulfill in order to be accepted.

The information items listed earlier can be obtained from a number of sources:

- Individual interviews with process performers
- Group-oriented workshops with process performers
- Direct observation of people at work

- Analysis of preexisting work products
- Analysis of other data left by the execution of a process, e.g., meeting minutes, electronic discussions, issue/bug reports, software version history, etc.

The techniques used to elicit information are a central success factor for a descriptive process modeling effort. Depending on the organization's culture, for example, either individual interviews, group workshops, or a combination of both may be the best option for obtaining direct information from process participants.

One delicate and often very critical aspect of process elicitation is that process engineers should avoid issuing judgments about the process they are eliciting or about the people performing it. The fear of being judged frequently moves people to describe an ideal process that they expect will be accepted better. Of course, this is a very undesirable situation, because the main goal of descriptive process modeling is to produce an accurate representation of the actual process.

3.4.6.1   Case Study 1: DocVault

DocVault used three information sources for elicitation:

- Interviews with members of the quality assurance team
- Interviews with staff members of one large customer, who had reported several problems over the years
- Archived e-mail messages from various problem reports

3.4.6.2   Case Study 2: Selene

In order to cover their large scope, Selene required a comprehensive interview program, covering all roles in the organization. In order to improve the completeness and accuracy of the resulting model, it was decided to conduct separate interviews with several people in the same role whenever possible. Although this additional effort actually helped to collect more complete and detailed information about the process, it also caused difficulties because, oftentimes, several somewhat contradictory or otherwise inconsistent views arose. Solving these inconsistencies required significant effort on the part of the elicitation team, often involving special meetings for discussing the details of a particular activity or set of activities with process participants.

3.4.6.3   Case Study 3: Soster

The elicitation effort at Soster relied on two main information sources:

- Interviews with engineers in charge of the customization process
- Documentation from old and current customization projects

3.4.7 Step 6: Create the Process Model

The information collected during the elicitation step can now be used to create a model using the chosen modeling notation. It is advisable to collect the information in the following general order [2]:

- Start by modeling products, because they are usually the easiest process entities to identify. In contrast to activities, which are often only implicitly defined, a set of products usually explicitly exists in an organization and can be directly modeled.
- Continue with the activities and the product flow.
- When activities are modeled, attach associated roles to the activities or the products.
- Model further entity types, such as resources, as needed.
- As a last step, model behavioral restrictions associated with entities, such as the preconditions that must be met before an activity can start.

Here again, there is a conceptual separation between the elicitation and the actual modeling steps, although, in practice, they are normally interwoven. Once an initial model is available based on elicited information, it must be reviewed by the process participants. Such a review will often result in additional elicitation activities and successive model refinements. In most cases, several elicitation/modeling cycles will be necessary to achieve an adequate level of agreement about the process model.

3.4.7.1 Case Study 1: DocVault

The model creation work at DocVault was conducted by two process engineers, who prepared detailed step sequences in a regular programming text editor using the defined formal notation. In order to review the resulting model, a workshop was conducted where selected members of DocVault's Quality Assurance team worked together with the process engineers. The process engineers presented the model, while the QA members were encouraged to criticize it and make suggestions. Issues were written down during the workshop and corrected afterwards.

3.4.7.2 Case Study 2: Selene

After the interview phase was completed at Selene, the process engineers moved on to creating the model. They proceeded in two main steps:

1. Create a high-level model. This model contained the basic structure and relations, but no detailed text descriptions. Meetings with small groups of process performers were conducted in order to validate this high level model.
2. Add textual descriptions. When the high-level structure was considered sufficiently stable, detailed textual descriptions were added. The process engineering team used the help of technical writers to conduct this step.

When the model was completed, an Electronic Process Guide was generated from the model and validated with selected performers in small focused meetings.

3.4.7.3   Case Study 3: Soster

The use of a graphical notation and editor had a particular advantage for Soster: Initial versions of the process models for particular activities could be created "live" during interviews with process participants. This made it easier to determine whether the interviewer's view of the process matched that of the interviewee. After the interviews, the process engineers proceeded to merge these views into a single, unified, graphical model.

3.4.8   Step 7: Analyze the Process Model

As process models become complex, there is an increasing risk of defects being inadvertently introduced into the model by the process engineers. The purpose of the process model analysis step is to detect such defects and correct them.

Depending on the notation used, there are many possible types of defects that may arise in practice. The following list contains a few examples of possible process model defects:

– Dangling reference: An entity references another, undefined entity, e.g., an activity description mentions an input work product that has no definition of its own in the model.
– Inconsistent precondition: The start conditions stated for an activity are contradictory and cannot be fulfilled in practice.
– Inconsistent references: The same entity is mentioned in the model using different, inconsistent names.
– Orphan entity: An entity is defined in the model, but is not referenced by any other entity in a meaningful way.
– Dependency cycle: An activity depends on a particular input product in order to start, but, according to the model, this input product cannot be produced unless the activity has already been finished.
– Incomplete descriptions: Important entity attributes, such as activity or product descriptions, are missing or empty in some or all of the process entities.

The analyses that can be performed to detect defects such as those listed earlier roughly fall into three categories:

– *Completeness analyses.* Even if a model correctly describes a process, the level of detail or the amount of information in the description could be insufficient. Completeness analyses are concerned with making sure that all relevant information is available and at a sufficient level of detail. Checking for empty fields in entity description forms, and making sure that all activities in a process are refined to the level of individual tasks, are two examples of possible completeness analyses.

- *Consistency analyses.* This type of analysis is related to making sure that elements of the model do not contradict each other. An example of a consistency analysis is to make sure that all products mentioned by the natural language description of an activity are modeled explicitly as inputs or outputs of the activity, and that they are mentioned using the same name used in the corresponding product description.
- *Dynamic analyses.* These analyses are concerned with problems that may arise when the process described by the model is executed. A typical dynamic analysis is to search for potential deadlocks that may occur while executing the process.

Depending on the levels of formality and detail of the chosen process model notation, process analysis can be automated. Indeed, this is one of the main benefits of using a formal modeling notation. Automated model checks can be described in a declarative fashion as rules (e.g., for all entities of the type "Activity," the attribute "description" must not be empty) or as arbitrary programs that navigate the model elements checking for particular conditions.

In many cases, however, automation is not possible, either because the information is not formal enough (e.g., it is available only as natural language text) or because checking for a particular property may be beyond the ability of a computer algorithm (in certain cases, making sure that a model does not contain deadlocks is equivalent to solving the halting problem for a nontrivial computer program). For these cases, manual model reviews must be conducted, possibly using disciplined inspection techniques similar to those intended for inspecting software programs.

3.4.8.1 Case Study 1: DocVault

Since DocVault's model ended up being relatively small, most checks were conducted by manually inspecting the model. However, the process engineering team also created a simple syntax checker to make sure that a set of minimal syntactic requirements was fulfilled by the text-based specifications.

3.4.8.2 Case Study 2: Selene

At the end of the initial modeling effort, Selene's model contained almost 1,000 separate entities and several thousand relations. It was absolutely necessary to check this model for potential errors. Most checks were achieved automatically by writing simple programs that checked the structural properties of the model by consulting the model database and looking for potentially problematic elements or constructs.

3.4.8.3 Case Study 3: Soster

For checking, Soster relied mainly on the built-in capabilities of the graphical model editor they were using. The editor allowed for defining a set of basic correctness and consistency rules, and Soster used those to detect basic problems in the model.

3.4.9 Step 8: Analyze the Process

The final step of descriptive process modeling is perform a process analysis, i.e., to use the process model to track or analyze process performance, depending on the process modeling objectives stated in step 1. One possibility is to track the process by asking process performers to log, for example, the start and finish times for their activities. Another option is to make "snapshots" by asking people about their current activities at regular intervals. The resulting data can be used for qualitative or for quantitative analyses.

Qualitative analyses aim at identifying weaknesses of the processes, e.g., when too many responsibilities are pinned to a single role, or when too many roles are assigned to a single person, or when feedback loops become so excessive that they consume more time than productive project work.

Quantitative analyses aim at identifying correlations between process attributes, e.g., when the number of requirements is more than 30% higher than average, the number of defects rises by 70%.

Both kinds of analysis results can then be used to modify the process (in order to remove the weaknesses), or the process model (in case it does not fit the process after all), or to influence project planning (e.g., allocate more resources to requirements reviews when the number of requirements is more than 30% higher than average).

3.4.9.1 Case Study 1: DocVault

Although the defect management process at DocVault had been handled manually for the most part, it actually left traces in a number of data repositories. First, a good portion of the communication and software defects happening between customers, QA people, and developers were reported via email, and those messages were archived. And, second, changes made to the software because of defects found were always registered in the version management system, together with a log entry explaining the reason for the change.

The process group then proceeded to isolate a number of defect-fixing cases and to identify email messages and entries in the version management system that were relevant to each case. By looking at this data, the process engineers were able to create detailed profiles for these cases, identifying the people involved, the activities that were conducted, and the time for each event.

With these profiles at hand, the process group then proceeded to check their models. The basic question was to determine whether the process model could be instantiated for each one of the particular cases, and how difficult this would be. Together with the primary users (developers of the defect management system) and the secondary users of the model (developers of the defect management system and DocVault's clients, as well as the software developers and quality management team at DocVault), they decided that the model adequately describes the process and proceeded with the implementation of the automated defect management system.

3.4.9.2 Case Study 2: Selene

Since Selene's primary objective was to provide guidance for all roles in the organization with respect to its processes, the process itself was of secondary interest. However, Selene instructed all performers to watch for potential problems or inconsistencies and to report them actively. An issue report system was set up to collect these reports, and the SEPG conducted regular meetings to evaluate the reports and follow up as necessary.

3.4.9.3 Case Study 3: Soster

Since Soster's goal was to gather information for improvement, a detailed process analysis was conducted. A number of influence factors for product quality and project predictability was identified, including the frequency of requirements changes and the time available for reviews (quantitative data); as well as role assignments, people overloading, and tool availability (qualitative data). From the data gathered, Soster's SEPG developed a strategic improvement plan, covering 3-month Quick Wins and long-term goals to be realized within 3 years.

3.5 Descriptive Process Modeling Alternatives

This section presents two alternatives to the approach described in Sect. 3.4. The *Multi-View Modeling* method [3] replaces steps 5 and 6 with an approach that collects and integrates multiple views on the same process, and the *Elicit* method [4] completely replaces the eight-step approach with a perspective-based tactic.

3.5.1 Multi-view Process Modeling

Multi-view process modeling [3] provides a specific way to conduct the elicitation step and build a model based on it (steps 5 and 6 described in Sects. 3.4.6 and 3.4.7). The main assumption behind multi-view process modeling is that, given the complexity of actual software processes, no single process participant has a complete, unified, and sufficiently detailed view of the process. Quite on the contrary, participants are normally experts in rather narrow areas of the process. For this reason, multi-view modeling starts by modeling the process as understood by individual participants. This results in separate, *role-specific* process views that contain potentially detailed but partial process information. In a later step, the individual views are systematically integrated to form a single, complete process model. This procedure is illustrated in Fig. 3.2.

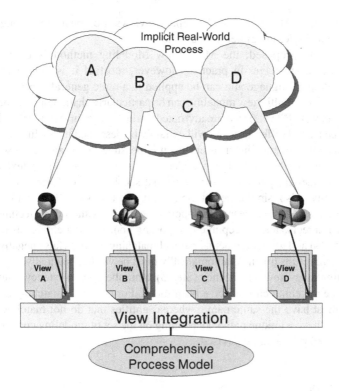

Fig. 3.2 Multi-view process modeling overview

The integration of role-specific views is an iterative process comprising four steps:

1. Modeling. In the modeling step, role-specific views are created by independently interviewing participants. The resulting views are partial process models that contain all activities performed by a role, together with related process entities such as work products or other roles with which the analyzed role interacts. Role-specific views are expected to be internally consistent, but they are not guaranteed to be consistent with each other.

2. Similarity analysis. In this step, the various role-specific views are analyzed to identify common objects, such as shared activities or work products. Notice that, due to the fact that each view comes from a different person or group of persons, there may be inconsistencies in naming and other modeling aspects. For this reason, a combination of manual and automated techniques is used to find matching entities.

3. Inter-view consistency checking. Once matching elements have been identified, a number of consistency checks are performed between interrelated views in order to detect potential inconsistencies between them. Whenever inconsistencies are found, they are resolved by changing the views as necessary.

4. Integration. At this point, the separate views are consistent enough to be merged into a single, integrated process model.

As originally proposed, the Multi-View Modeling method is based on the MVP-L process language. In practice, however, most of it is independent of a specific modeling language and can be applied in a quite general way.

Steps 2 and 3 of multi-view modeling can be particularly challenging. In the case of similarity analysis (Step 2), as already noted earlier, matching entities in different views can be named differently and will certainly be described using different words. In order to deal with such inconsistencies, it is possible, for example, to search for names that are similar (although not identical) or to use advanced text analysis techniques to identify pairs of descriptions that speak (with different words) about the same entity. Also, similarities in the structure of a product flow can be used to suggest possible matching areas. It is important to note that all of these techniques are potentially imprecise and susceptible to reporting nonmatching entities as matching (false positives) and to missing actual pairs of matching entities (false negatives). For this reason, all results obtained automatically must be verified manually.

Regarding inter-view consistency (Step 3), a number of consistency rules can be applied once matching entities have been found. For example, matching entities in all views must have the same name, whereas entities that do not match any other entity should have a unique name. Depending on the set of modeling concepts used, more advanced rules can be devised.

3.5.2   Elicit

Elicit [4] is a general framework for process elicitation. Its main difference to the general, eight-step approach presented in this chapter is that it does not expect the organization to select a schema, a modeling language, or a set of modeling tools. Elicit provides all of these elements, together with a set of methodological steps for using them, thus making its application somewhat simpler.

Elicit works by looking at the process from a variety of viewpoints, which are later consolidated into a unified view. The Elicit schema is structured as a set of five so-called *perspectives*, together with three types of properties that must be described for each perspective. The Elicit perspectives are *artifacts, process steps, roles, resources,* and *constraints,* and the property types are *descriptive, static,* and *dynamic.* The combination of a perspective and a property is called a *view* in Elicit. This means that there are 15 possible views (5 perspectives times 3 property types). For each of these views, Elicit provides a set of so-called *attributes.* For example, the descriptive view of the *artifacts* perspective contains the following attributes:

- Identifier
- Has purposes
- Stored in formats
- Is of artifact type
- Characterized by artifact description

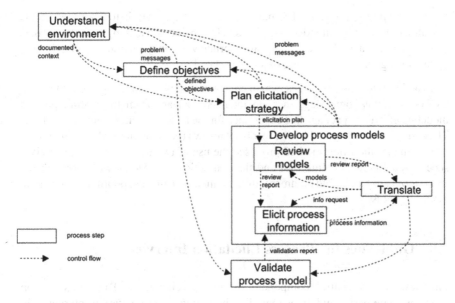

Fig. 3.3 The steps of the Elicit method

Models are created by providing values for these and similar attributes in all views.

As already mentioned earlier, Elicit provides a set of steps for producing descriptive models. These steps are illustrated in Fig. 3.3 (adapted from [4]) and can be summarized as follows:

1. *Understand organizational environment.* This step consists of understanding key aspects of the organization, such as its size, management structure, number and size of the running projects, common roles played by people in projects, etc. Understanding these issues is considered fundamental for process engineers to be able to do their job in later steps.
2. *Define objectives.* This includes defining the exact scope of the model—e.g., its granularity and the degree of consistency, completeness, accuracy, and clarity that must be achieved—and setting goals for the modeling effort itself, such as its targeted costs and time frame.
3. *Plan the elicitation strategy.* Given the set of goals produced in the previous step, it must be defined how to achieve these goals. A key aspect of this step is to allocate appropriate resources for the modeling effort. For example, it must be decided which people will be interviewed, when reviews are going to be conducted, etc.
4. *Develop process models.* This step involves collecting information according to the Elicit process schema, as explained earlier. The collected information is then used to create models using process modeling tools and submitted for review. If reviews find deficiencies in the model, further information collection and modeling must be performed.

5. *Validate process models.* The main objective of this step is to have the models validated by their intended recipients. This includes checking that the models represent the actual process in an appropriate way, and, generally, validating the models against the modeling objectives stated originally.

In addition to these five steps, which are concerned with modeling itself, the Elicit method contains some steps that are intended to learn from the overall process modeling effort and package this experience for the benefit of future modeling efforts. These steps are represented by the feedback arrows (pointing upward) in Fig. 3.3.

Originally, the Elicit method proposed the use of two modeling tools, namely a specialized Elicit modeling tool and the simulation tool *Statemate*. Although the Elicit tool is not available commercially, the method can be supported with generic modeling tools.

3.6   Guidelines for Process Elicitation Interviews

Interviews are a central component of process elicitation. Thus, this section provides some basic guidelines regarding how to conduct elicitation interviews in a software organization.

3.6.1   Interview Preparation

Before conducting a set of elicitation interviews in an organization, a number of preparation steps should be taken:

- Get to know the organization. As a minimum, interviewers should have basic knowledge about the organizational structure, the roles played by their interviewees in that structure, and the software domain in which the organization works. It is also advisable to begin the interviews with quality assurance people or with project managers, since they will be able to provide a better overall view of the organization.
- Find out if the organization is being restructured or was restructured recently. Large changes in the organization's structure normally have an impact on the software process and on people's roles. If restructuring is recent or is in progress, the interviewer must find out in advance which version of the process he is being told about.
- Take a look at existing documents and other work products. This not only helps the interviewer to acquire a general idea of how the process is executed, but it makes it easier to speak with interviewees about their usual tasks.

Before conducting interviews, it is important to make sure that the interviewees were selected according to the requirements of the elicitation effort. It is to be expected that the people who are most knowledgeable about a process are also most likely to be busy. For this reason, there is always the risk that interviewers will be "diverted" to less critical, but also less knowledgeable people. It is important to make sure that your interviewees are knowledgeable and experienced enough to provide you with the necessary information. Otherwise, insist on interviewing the right person.

3.6.2 Beginning the Interview

The first minutes of an interview are crucial, because during this time, a proper relationship with the interviewee must be established. In particular, it is important to create an environment of confidence and teamwork. The interviewee must understand that s/he is not being evaluated and that the purpose of the interview is to achieve a better understanding of the actual process. In order to create this positive environment, it is advisable to:

- Make sure that the interviewee has proper knowledge regarding the overall elicitation process, i.e., how it is being conducted, who is taking part, and what its general objectives are.
- Explain the goals and purposes of the interview. Let the interviewee know why s/he is being interviewed and why her/his knowledge is important for the overall elicitation effort.
- If necessary, make a confidentiality agreement with the interviewee. Explain clearly how the information acquired during the interview is going to be handled in terms of privacy and security (if relevant). In some cases, it may be appropriate to present interview results anonymously. If this is your intention, make sure that you mention it.
- Formulate some general questions about the interviewee and her/his role in the process. In particular, try to confirm any knowledge you may have previously acquired about the interviewee and his/her job.

3.6.3 The Main Interview

After the introduction, you can concentrate on its actual purpose: eliciting process information. Some general guidelines are:

- Behave neutrally. It is fundamental that the interviewer avoids being judgmental about the process. Any remark in this direction may destroy the confidence created with the interviewee and cause the interview to fail. Remember that you are there for understanding the process, not for criticizing it. Also, take into account that aspects of the process that, at first sight, may appear outlandish or even nonsensical may be supported by very good justifications that you do not yet understand.

– Ask first about products. As already explained, products are sometimes easier to identify for software engineers, so it may be wise to start by asking people which work products they usually work on and in which exact ways they are involved with their creation. When asking about products, take into account that different organizations may use widely different words to refer to process work products. Document, system, program, module, and report, to mention but a few, are terms that may be used to refer to work products in practice.

– Ask about processes. After a clear view of the documents has been created, you can move to ask about the processes related to producing these products. Some of the relevant questions are: Which inputs are necessary? Which other roles participate in the processes? Which conditions must be met in order to start creating the product? When is the product considered finished? Who reviews the product and how?

– Look for typical deviations. If the interviewee has not spoken of deviations already, make sure to ask about them. What are typical problems that happen during this process? How are they normally handled?

– Try to identify variants. Processes are often subject to variation depending on factors such as the availability of certain resources (e.g., "if the project budget allows for a separate test team, we do X, otherwise we do Y"), the presence of specific product requirements (e.g., "if the product is intended for the international market, we conduct an additional internationalization review. . ."), or particular customer characteristics ("when the customer is a government institution, we have to produce an additional accounting report as required by current law. . .").

When conducting the interview, always try to make sure that you are getting a consistent picture of the process. In particular, make sure that you ask questions even in those cases when you only see small ambiguities: It often happens that major deficiencies in understanding are hidden behind an apparently minor issue.

3.6.4 Interview Closure

The final part of the interview should help to involve the interviewee in the whole elicitation effort. Before you finish the interview:

– Speak about future steps. Explain to the interviewee which steps will follow. In particular, make clear how the information obtained in the interview will be used during the remainder of the elicitation process. If the interviewee is expected to actively participate in further steps of the elicitation effort such as a review, this may be a good time to clarify the schedule.

– Thank your interview partner. Make sure that you stress the importance of the interviewee's contribution to the overall elicitation process, and thank her/him for that.

When further steps of the elicitation process are completed, it is advisable to inform all participants of the progress and to let them know how their individual contributions are shaping up into a detailed picture of the software process. In particular, interview results can be written down, summarized, and presented to the interviewees for revision.

3.7 Managing Risk in Descriptive Process Modeling Efforts

Modeling a process is a potentially highly complex task, which involves dedicating a significant amount of work and time to it. It is hence not surprising that many risks are involved in a process modeling effort. In order for such an effort to be successful, these risks must be taken into account and mitigated whenever possible. This section explains the most common risks and possible countermeasures.

Although it is impossible to predict every possible problem that may arise during a process modeling effort, experience collected over the years allows us to enumerate some issues that are likely to be present. The remainder of this section discusses these issues as well as potential countermeasures.

3.7.1 Resistance of Participants

A disciplined, detailed process modeling effort can easily awaken resistance in an organization. Considering how the modeling effort may be seen by process participants, the reasons for this become obvious:

- Participants may see the process experts as the people who are placing their daily work "under the microscope." They fear that, as soon as their work practices are made explicit, they will be judged for any deficiencies or limitations of the process that may become visible through process analysis. In a similar vein, participants may see the renewed interest in their daily work activities solely as a way to control them.
- Participants may perceive a defined process as a way to constrain them. They may fear that, once a defined process is in place, they will have no freedom to change and adjust the way they work according to their needs.
- Participants may generally perceive processes as bureaucratic. They may expect explicitly defined processes to introduce significant additional administrative overhead that will divert them from the technical and managerial tasks they are pursuing.
- Finally, participants may simply not see any added value in the process modeling effort and may thus be reluctant to put time or work into it.

In order to mitigate the risk of a process modeling effort failing because of resistance—or even active sabotaging—from process participants, it is important that the processes and their definition are "owned" by the participants themselves. Acquiring deeper knowledge about the process should never be seen as a means of control, but rather as a way to improve project execution and product quality, with obvious benefits for everyone involved.

Some ways to put the process modeling effort "into the hands" of the process participants are:

- Promote the benefits of proper process management. Better process management can significantly contribute to improving a participant's work life. For example, better project planning can reduce or eliminate the need for working long hours, and better product quality can reduce the stress associated with unexpected product failures. Before a process modeling effort starts, process participants should know the potential benefits and properly understand how process modeling can contribute to achieving them.
- Whenever possible, involve process participants in the definition of the goals for the modeling effort. A process modeling effort (and, in general, a process improvement effort) that is only intended to benefit an organization's management is much more likely to meet resistance from the people at lower organizational levels, since they do not see any direct, personal benefits. When participants are involved from the bottom up in the definition of goals for the effort, they can pursue their own goals while contributing to the effort, making it much more likely to succeed.
- Actively involve process participants in all process modeling activities. Apart from goal definition, interested participants can be engaged in various activities, ranging from detailed elicitation to high-level process description and review. This is not only likely to turn these engaged participants into "process proponents," but will help guarantee that the resulting process represents the views and goals of all stakeholders.
- Make the modeling effort as open as possible. Make sure that the results of the modeling effort are visible and that participants have a voice if they disagree. For example, it is advisable to provide an official mechanism for reporting problems with the process definition and to make sure that such reports are promptly reviewed and answered, too, either by correcting the process definition or by providing an explanation of why changes will not be made.

By taking these and similar measures, it is possible to achieve much higher commitment by the process participants, consequently increasing the chances that the process modeling effort will be successful.

3.7.2   Inaccurate Reporting

When participants are interviewed about the way they work, there is a significant risk that their description of their own activities will not fit reality to a certain extent. Reasons for why this may happen include self-protection, forgetting process details, and idealization of the process.

As explained in the previous subsection, people may fear that a process modeling effort will immediately expose them to judgment and criticism. For this reason, and in order to protect themselves, they may try to "embellish" the process in ways that they expect to be more satisfactory to external observers than "the naked truth" about how things are done. As also explained in the previous section, active involvement of the process participants in the modeling effort is probably the best way to minimize this problem.

A related problem may arise when process participants are discontent with their organization or management. In this case, they may tend to present the process worse than it really is, in order to stress the problems they are currently going through. Although such an attitude is a clear signal of potential process-related problems and should not be dismissed, there may still be strengths to the actual process that are being unnecessarily downplayed by disgruntled process participants.

Even when participants have a positive attitude towards their organization and the modeling effort, they may end up reporting incomplete or outright false information about a process. This may be caused by people forgetting details, which should not be surprising given the high complexity and variability of many software-related processes. Also, people who are fond of a particular procedure may tend to idealize it, and to present it as being simpler and more straightforward than it really is.

The usual way to deal with problems of this type is to gather information redundantly from various sources whenever possible in order to spot possible inconsistencies caused by missing or (either deliberately or inadvertently) false information. Redundancy can be achieved, for instance, by interviewing many participants who play the same role or by comparing the process described by people with the actual work products that resulted from past instances of the process.

3.7.3   Underestimating Necessary Investments

Descriptive process models involve potentially large investments. First of all, it should be clear from the modeling steps discussed in Sect. 3.5 that modeling the whole set of software development processes in an organization represents a significant amount of work. In particular, the elicitation step requires the involvement of a possibly large number of people in the organization. In order for the process modeling effort to be successful, these people must dedicate considerable time to interviews, reviews, and other process-related activities.

Additionally, it often happens that the improved understanding of the process brought on by process modeling triggers changes to a process, sometimes in an immediate fashion. Although these changes are likely to eventually bring improvements, in the short term they may involve increased operation costs, for example due to a temporary reduction in productivity.

Underestimating these costs is, of course, a serious risk for a process modeling effort. An effort can easily fail if the organization's management is not conscious of its potential costs. Proper planning is, thus, necessary to properly estimate these costs from the ground up and guarantee appropriate commitment of the organization's management.

3.7.4 Underestimating Process Model Complexity

When planning a process modeling effort, it is easy to underestimate the complexity of the final model. Process model complexity is mainly related to the number of entities and entity relations in it, and less so to the number of concepts in the selected process schema. Since estimating the number of entities in a model before creating it is difficult, the risk of underestimation during planning can be high.

For this reason, descriptive process models should not overemphasize accuracy, but rather concentrate on achieving a level of detail that is adequate for the stated modeling goals. Also, organizations that lack process modeling experience should start with pilot modeling efforts that are restricted to relatively small and well delimited processes. The experience obtained from such pilot efforts should help to estimate the potential model size (and involved modeling effort) for larger and more complex processes.

References

1. Becker U, Hamann D, Verlage M (1997) Descriptive modeling of software processes, ISERN Report 97-10. Fraunhofer Institute for Experimental Software Engineering IESE, Kaiserslautern, Germany
2. Bröckers A, Differding C, Threin G (1996) The role of software process modeling in planning industrial measurement programs. In: Proceedings of the 3ird international software metrics symposium, Berlin, March 1996
3. Verlage M (1994) Multi-view modeling of software processes. Lect Notes Comput Sci 772:123–126
4. Madhavji NH, Holtje D, Hong W, Bruckhaus T (1994) Elicit: a method for eliciting process models. In: Proceedings of the 3rd international conference on the software process (ICSP 3), Reston, VA, USA

Chapter 4
Process Modeling Notations and Tools

This chapter introduces notations for process modeling and gives an overview of tool support for process modeling and management. The chapter is structured into three main parts. First, it introduces a set of criteria for process modeling notations in order to enable the reader to distinguish different process modeling notations and to understand that different purposes might be addressed by different notations. Second, it discusses two different process modeling notations, namely, MVP-L and SPEM 2.0, and characterizes them according to the previously defined criteria. Finally, it introduces process management tools by discussing the ECMA/NIST framework and the Eclipse Process Framework (EPF) Composer. Figure 4.1 displays an overview of the chapter structure.

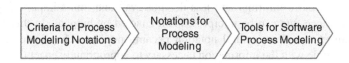

Fig. 4.1 Chapter structure

4.1 Objectives of This Chapter

After reading this chapter, you should be able to

- Distinguish different process modeling notations and assess their suitability with respect to different purposes
- Explain and use the basic concepts of MVP-L
- Explain and use the basic concepts of SPEM 2.0
- Understand and explain the components of process management tools

J. Münch et al., *Software Process Definition and Management*,
The Fraunhofer Series on Software and Systems Engineering,
DOI 10.1007/978-3-642-24291-5_4, © Springer-Verlag Berlin Heidelberg 2012

4.2   Introduction

When we think of process modeling notations, we can identify a plethora of different approaches. This is due to the fact that during the historical development of process modeling notations, different communities have influenced the discipline of process modeling. In terms of software engineering processes, two major groups that influenced the development of process modeling notations can be identified [1].

The first group was significantly influenced by tool developers and programmers. Within this group, notations for the representation of processes were developed or adopted aimed at creating representations that could be interpreted by machines. Thus, this group focused on process automation and the notations used were typically not designed to be interpreted by humans. The underlying vision was to create software development environments where the execution of software development tools would be controlled by a process-driven engine. The main focus was on small, low-level processes such as the code–compile–test–fix cycle. As a result, this approach focused on processes with a high potential of automation.

The second group has its origins in the community that was concerned with software process improvement. In this discipline, the aim was to make software development more mature by means of introducing best practices and establishing learning cycles. For this reason, the need arose to represent software processes in order to understand and improve the processes of software development performed by humans. The notation constructs developed in this context aimed at describing real-world concepts and creating models that humans can interpret. This approach, and in particular the representation of software engineering processes, focused on higher level processes and a minor degree of automation. Therefore, processes are described in a more informal and less detailed way and, most importantly, they provide guidance that can be interpreted and enacted by humans. In this context, process guides based on natural notation became popular. They concentrate on providing people with the information necessary to appropriately enact the process.

Currently, an abundance of different process modeling notations exists and, therefore, a strong need for standardization has developed. As a result of this development, the Software Process Engineering Metamodel (SPEM) was created. Its goal is to enable the representation of different software engineering concepts.

4.3   Criteria for Assessing Process Modeling Notations

The multitude of existing process modeling notations has been developed due to different motivations and needs. As needs usually differ greatly for different stakeholders, purposes, and contexts, there is no best representation for processes, and thus different representations cannot be assessed from a general point of view. But it can be useful to compare different concepts in order to understand the specific aspects that are addressed by a specific representation.

This section will introduce concepts for characterizing process modeling notations and furthermore define requirements for process modeling notations from different perspectives. These concepts are useful for comparing different notations for the representation of processes.

4.3.1 Characteristics of Process Modeling Notations

In order to understand the context and motivation of a certain representation, Rombach and Verlage [1] use the following aspects for characterizing process modeling notations.

4.3.1.1 Process Programming vs. Process Improvement

A major distinction can be made between process modeling notations for the implementation of processes (i.e., process programming) and notations for the conceptual modeling of processes (i.e., process improvement). Process programming notations focus on a representation for interpretation and execution by machines. Process improvement notations focus on representation of real-world concepts and provision of a representation that can be interpreted by humans.

4.3.1.2 Hidden vs. Guiding

When the process model is used, the representation of the process models can be hidden or presented to the process user. When hidden, the process instantiation is completely encoded in the process models or tools that support process enactment. Thus, only filtered information is provided concerning the current project state. If used for guiding, the process models themselves are used to inform the user and to provide guidance during process instantiation.

4.3.1.3 Prescriptive vs. Proscriptive

In the early days of software process research, the main focus was placed on automating process execution with the help of software development tools. Therefore, the user of such tools would be guided by an execution mechanism in a prescriptive manner. This approach of prescribing the process and thus also the human activities has been subject to criticism and is difficult to implement. The proscriptive approach represents a nonrestrictive way of formulating processes. The process models provide guidance in order to enable performance of the required process steps, but process users have a certain freedom in deciding which actions to take at a particular stage of the project.

4.3.1.4 Single Person vs. Multiperson

Software development projects are not performed by a single person and, in consequence, collaboration and cooperation between persons, teams, and organizations is highly relevant. Process models should support all these different levels in order to make collaboration and cooperation possible. Historically, process representations have evolved from a single-person focus in order to ensure proper application of specific techniques by individuals. For the purpose of cooperation, a multiperson focus is needed in order to coordinate the processes of different persons. Therefore, a process representation should contain constructs for modeling concepts of collaboration.

4.3.2 Requirements for Process Modeling Notations

In the following, a set of requirements for process modeling notations will be described in accordance with [1]. The fulfillment of these requirements can be seen as an indicator for the suitability of the notation to support process management for software engineering organizations. Based on the viewpoint, the purpose, and the context, different requirements might be relevant. A process engineer who wants to automate a build process of a business unit might select different requirements than an education department that aims at introducing a company-wide training program. The stated requirements help to find suitable process modeling notations by first selecting the relevant requirements and afterwards selecting such notations that fulfill the requirements. The following requirements can be applied [1].

– *R1—Natural Representation:* A process modeling notation should not only be able to capture all relevant aspects of software development, but it should also be able to represent these aspects in a natural, intuitive, and easy-to-identify manner. A mapping between real-world phenomena and process model elements that is as complete as possible facilitates the modeling and maintenance of these models.
– *R2—Support of Measurement:* A process modeling notation should take into account the measurability of the process model. In order to enable software process improvement, the impact of different technologies on products and processes has to be observed. Furthermore, the scientific evaluation of the efficiency and effectiveness of these technologies should be based on measurement. For this reason, the notation has to take into account the definition of attributes and measurement within process models.
– *R3—Tailorability of Models:* On the one hand, a process modeling notation should enable a generic representation of information in order to allow for process models that can describe commonalities of processes from several different projects. On the other hand, no development project is completely similar to another one and therefore, the process environment is most likely to

change for each project. Thus, in planning a project, the differences must be considered and the process model has to be instantiated and tailored accordingly. The use of tailorable models limits the number of process models and thus reduces maintenance efforts. Therefore, concepts for defining and supporting process variability and tailoring are needed.

- *R4—Formality:* A process modeling notation should allow for the creation of process models with a certain degree of formality. Formality is needed to support communication among different process participants and to foster a common understanding of the process model by different people. Fulfillment of this requirement means that process model constructs are defined formally within the process model.

- *R5—Understandability:* Understandability is a key aspect of a process modeling notation, as process models are used as a reference during projects. Most activities related to process engineering rely on human interpretation rather than interpretation by a machine and understandability is therefore a crucial factor for the success of any process representation. Understandability refers to the style of presentation and to how difficult it is for its users to retrieve needed information.

- *R6—Executability:* A process modeling notation should support the interpretation and execution of the process representation by a machine. This need arises due to the fact that standard procedures of software development are often supported by tools that aim at providing automated support for the process user.

- *R7—Flexibility:* A notation for process representation should account for handling decisions made by humans during process performance. These decisions are characterized by creativity and nondeterminism. A process modeling notation thus should contain constructs that are capable of capturing these aspects.

- *R8—Traceability:* Traceability should be ensured within and across layers of abstraction (i.e., horizontal and vertical traceability). This means that, for each piece of information, it should be possible to determine its context, the processes that rely on it, and how it was transformed. A process modeling notation should thus support process representations that provide constructs for the explicit description of different relationships between various process elements.

These characteristics and requirements can be used to define a framework that helps to distinguish different process modeling notations and their purpose. All elements of this framework are summarized in Table 4.1 (adapted from [1]). For the evaluation of requirements satisfaction, (+) represents full, (O) partial, and (−) no fulfillment of the respective requirement.

In the following sections, two software process modeling notations, MVP-L and SPEM 2.0, will be introduced. MVP-L represents a notation that offers a comprehensive set of modeling constructs. SPEM 2.0 will be introduced because it has the potential to become a future process model notation standard. The framework of characteristics and requirements that was introduced earlier will be used to give an overview and characterization of these notations.

Table 4.1 Characterization framework

Characterization	
Process programming vs. improvement	Prescriptive vs. proscriptive
Hidden vs. guidance	Single person vs. multiperson
Requirements satisfaction	
R1—Natural representation	(+/O/−)
R2—Support of measurement	(+/O/−)
R3—Tailorability of models	(+/O/−)
R4—Formality	(+/O/−)
R5—Understandability	(+/O/−)
R6—Executability	(+/O/−)
R7—Flexibility	(+/O/−)
R8—Traceability	(+/O/−)

4.4   Multi-view Process Modeling Language

4.4.1   Overview

Multi-view process modeling language (MVP-L) was developed in the 1980s at the University of Maryland. Subsequent development was conducted at the University of Kaiserslautern, Germany. MVP-L has its origins in the Multi-view process modeling (MVP) project, which focused on process models, their representation, and their modularization according to views, as well as their use in the context of software process improvement, namely, the quality improvement paradigm. MVP-L was developed to support the creation of descriptive process models, packaging of these models for reuse, integration of the models into prescriptive project plans, analysis of project plans, and use of these project plans to guide future projects [2].

The main focus of MVP-L is on modeling "in-the-large." It is assumed that the ability to understand, guide, and support the interaction between processes is more beneficial than the complete automation of low-level process steps [2].

4.4.2   Concepts

The main elements that are used in MVP-L for the description of process models are processes, products, resources, and quality attributes, as well as their instantiation in project plans [2]. A process model is actually a type description that captures the properties common to a class of processes. For easy adaptation of process models to different project contexts, the process models are structured using the concepts of a process model-interface and a process model-body. An interface describes a generalization of the formal parameters that are relevant to all models of a particular kind. As an example, a process model "Design" (Fig. 4.2, based on [2])

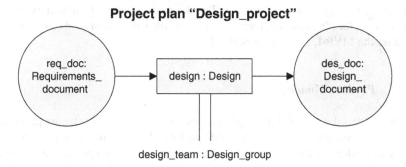

Fig. 4.2   Example of process model "Design"

could describe a class of processes that require an input of the product type "Requirements_document," which must produce an output of the product type "Design_document," and which must be executed by a resource of the type "Design_group." These product and resource model declarations are part of the interface of the process model "Design." The actual implementation of the process model is "hidden" in the body of the process model. Thus, MVP-L models implement the important concept of information hiding [3]. The model-body contains information that is only visible internally, whereas the model-interface contains information that is visible to other models. By implementing the concept of information hiding, changes to models or parts of models can be performed and handled locally without affecting other models.

4.4.3   Notation Constructs

Processes, products, and resources can be used for modeling the basic elements of a software project. Attributes can be used for defining specific properties of these three basic elements. MVP-L calls the constructs for describing these elements "models." However, they can be understood as types [2].

- *Product_model:* Software products are the results of processes for development or maintenance. In addition to the final software product, by-products, artifacts, and parts of a product's documentation are called products as well.
- *Resource_model:* Resources are the entities that are necessary for performing the processes (e.g., people or tools).
- *Process_model:* Processes are the activities that are performed during a project. They produce, consume, or modify products.
- *Attribute_model:* Attributes define properties of products, resources, and processes. The attributes that are used are process_attribute_model, product_attribute_model, and resource_attribute_model. Attributes correspond to measures and their values correspond to specific measurement data.

In the following, these constructs will be discussed in more detail and examples will be given for illustration purposes. The following descriptions and examples are based on the MVP-L language report [2].

4.4.3.1   Product Models

Product models describe the structure and properties of a class of software products. Product models do not only describe code artifacts, but all artifacts that are part of software development activities and supporting activities. Each product representation consists of an interface and a body. Information in the <product_interface> is visible to other objects. The product attributes are declared in the <exports> clause, and their type must first be imported in the product interface's <import> clause.

```
Example- Product Model: Requirements document

product_model Requirements_document (status_0 : Product_status) is
        product_interface
                imports
                        product_attribute_model Product_status;
                exports
                        status : Product_status := status_0;
        end product_interface

        product_body
                implementation
                {textual description}
        end product_body
end product_model Requirements_document.
```

The product model "Requirements_document" imports a product attribute model "Product_status" in order to declare a product attribute "status." The formal instantiation parameter "status_0" is used to provide the initial value for the attribute.

4.4.3.2   Resource Models

Resource models describe resources involved in performing a process. Resources can be differentiated into organizational entities (e.g., groups or teams) and human individuals (active resources) or tools (passive resources). Active resources perform processes and passive resources support the performance of processes. Note that traditional software tools can be represented in MVP-L as resources as well as processes. A compiler, for example, could be represented as an MVP-L process integrated into an MVP project plan dealing with program development. In contrast, an editor may be used as a passive resource within a project plan to support the design process. Like product models, resource models consist of a <resource_interface> and a <resource_body>. For instantiation, parameters can be defined. Parameters are special kinds of attributes for passing values to objects when the objects are instantiated. In the example below, the parameter "eff_0" of the type "Resource_effort" is used. It contains the effort that is available to a designer for the execution of the process in the context of a specific project plan.

```
Example – Resource Model: Designer

resource_model Designer(eff_0: Resource_effort) is
        resource_interface
                imports
                                resource_attribute_model Resource_effort;
                exports
                                effort: Resource_effort := eff_0;
        end resource_interface


        resource_body
                implementation
                { - An instance of this model represents a single member
                of the design team.
                - Persons assuming the role of a designer must be qualified.}
        end resource_body
end resource_model Designer
```

4.4.3.3   Process Models

Process models contain the information that is relevant for performing a specific task. In particular, process models combine the basic elements of products and resources in a manner that allows producing the resulting product. Similar to product and resource models, process models are structured into a model-interface and a model-body.

The process interface is described through <imports>, <exports>, <consume_produce>, <context>, and <criteria> clauses, as shown in the following example, which describes an exemplary design process. The process body is defined in terms of an <implementation> clause. The <imports> clause lists all externally defined models used to declare formal parameters within the <product_flow> clause or attributes within the <exports> clause. The <exports> clause lists all externally visible attributes that can be used by other models. These constructs provide a clear interface to other models. In the example described later, the attribute "effort" of the type "Process_effort" is made available to all models importing the process model "Design." A *product flow* is implemented in the process model through the <product_flow> clause, which lists all products that are consumed, produced, or modified. Products that are modified are declared in the <consume_produce> clause. For the exemplary process model "Design," a product "req_doc" of the type "Requirements_document" is consumed and a product "des_doc" of the type "Design_document" is produced.

Furthermore, *constraint-oriented control flows* can be defined by using *explicit entry and exit criteria* as well as *invariants* within the MVP-L process models. The <criteria> clause within the process model interface describes the pre- and postconditions that have to be fulfilled in order to enter or exit the respective process. In addition, invariants are used to describe states that need to be valid throughout the enactment of the process. Criteria are specified as Boolean expressions. The expression following the keyword <local_entry_criteria> defines the criteria necessary to execute the process in terms of locally defined attributes and local interface parameters. In this example, the local invariant specifies that the actual effort spent for any instance of the process model "Design" should never exceed a value specified by "max_effort." Invariants can be used to implement elements that need to be tracked permanently during process performance and are not allowed to exceed a certain limit. In particular, this accounts for monotonously rising or falling elements. Project effort, for example, should not exceed its maximum value. In the example, the local entry criteria state that any process of the type "Design" can only be executed if the attribute "status" of the product "req_doc" has the value "complete" and the attribute "status" of the product "des_doc" has either the value "non_existing" or "incomplete." The expression following the keyword <local_exit_criteria> defines the criteria expected upon completion of process execution in terms of local attributes and the local interface. In the example, the locally expected result upon completion is that the attribute "status" of the product "des_doc" has the value "complete." Thus, the concept of entry and exit criteria can be used to describe an implicit constraint-oriented control flow. MVP-L also provides constructs for defining global criteria and invariants that address global attributes, such as calendar time.

The <implementation> clause describes how an elementary process is to be performed. This can either be a call of a supporting tool, or simply an informal comment characterizing the task at hand for performance by a human. Processes are related to products via explicit <product_flow> relationships, to attributes via <criteria> clauses, and to resources via a separate <process_resources> clause. In the example of the process model "Design," a resource "des1" of the type "Designer" is designated to execute any process of the type "Design."

Example – Process Model: Design

Process_model Design(eff_0: Process_effort, max_effort_0: Process_effort) **is**

process_interface

    imports

        process_attribute_model Process_effort;

        product_model Requirements_document, Design_document;

    exports

        effort: Process_effort := eff_0;

        max_effort: Process_effort := max_effort_0;

    product_flow

        consume

            req_doc: Requirements_document;

        produce

            des_doc: Design_document;

        consume_produce

    entry_exit_criteria

        local_entry_criteria

            (req_doc.status = "complete") **and** (des_doc.status = "non_existent" **or** des_doc.status = "incomplete");

        local_invariant

            effort <= max_effort;

        local_exit_criteria

            des_doc.status = "complete";

end process_interface

process_body

    implementation

    {textual description}

end process_body

process_resources

    personnel_assignment

        imports

            resource_model Designer;

        objects

            des1: Designer;

    tool_assignment

and process_resources \

end process_model Design

4.4.3.4   Attribute Models

Each attribute model refers to a certain model type and consists mainly of a definition of the <attribute_model_type> (and <attribute_manipulation>, which is not discussed here). The <attribute_model_type> characterizes the type of values the attribute stores. This type could be an integer, a real, string, Boolean, or enumerated type (see example).

Example - Attribute Model: Product status

product_attribute_model Product_status () **is**

       attribute_type

               ("non_existing", "incomplete", "complete");

       ...

end product_attribute_model Product_status

4.4.4   Instantiation and Enactment

The basic MVP-L models described so far can be refined and combined to create complex process models, which can be used to describe typical software and systems engineering processes. The instantiation of a process model allows operationalizing the process model and creating a concrete project plan, which can then be used for project analysis or execution. This section introduces the MVP-L representation of project plans, with an emphasis on the instantiation of processes and process enactment as described in [2]. The creation of project plans in MVP-L allows for creating executable <project_plan> objects.

4.4.4.1   Instantiation

Software process models in MVP-L are instantiated through <project plan> objects. A <project_plan> is described through <imports>, <objects>, and <plan_object_relations> clauses. The imports clause lists all models that are used to specify the process, product, and resource objects that make up the project plan. These objects are declared in the <objects> clause. The objects are interconnected according to their formal interface definition in the <plan_object_relations> clause. A project plan needs to be interpreted by a process engine (a human or a computer) in order to enact the contained processes.

Example – Project Plan: Design Project 2

project_plan Design_project_2 **is**
    imports
            product_model Requirements_document, Design_document;
            process_model Design;
            resource_model Design_group;
    objects
            requiremements_doc: Requirements_document(„complete");
            design_doc: Design_document(„non_existent");
            design: Design(0, 2000);
            design_team: Design_group(0);
    object_relations
            design(req_doc => requirements_doc, des_doc => design_doc,
            designers => design_team);
end project_plan Design_project_2

The project plan example consists of four objects: one process "design," two products "requirements_doc" and "design_doc," and one resource "design_team." The interconnection of these products and the resource with the process "design" is performed according to the formal interface specification of the process model "Design." In this example, a complete requirements document ("requirements_doc") is provided, the design document "design_doc" does not yet exist, and the time that is available for the performance of the process "design" is restricted to 2000 time units. Finally, only members of the "Design_group" are allowed to perform the process "design."

4.4.4.2   Enactment

The notion of a *project state* is the basis for the enactment model in MVP-L [2]. A project state is defined as the set of all attribute values (i.e., all attributes of all objects instantiated within a project plan). Thus, the project state provides valuable information about the status of the projects at any given time. This is an important foundation for effective project control. The initial project state is defined in terms of the initial values of all user-defined attributes and the derived values of built-in attributes.

The values of attributes of the built-in type "Process_status" depend on the entry and exit criteria. The only triggers that change the current project state are user invocations of the kind "start(<object_id>)" and "complete(<object_id>)" to start and complete processes, or the invocation "set(...)" to address external changes of attributes. In each case, the new values of all user-defined and built-in attributes

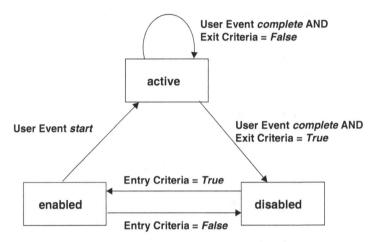

Fig. 4.3 State transition model for processes

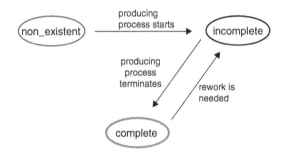

Fig. 4.4 State transition model for products

are computed to determine the new project state. A new project state provides information about the processes that are in execution (i.e., the value of the process status is "active"), ready for execution (i.e., the value of the process status is "enabled"), or not ready for execution (i.e., the value of the process status is "disabled"). The different states of a process can be represented in a state transition model (Fig. 4.3). Starting in the disabled state, processes may only get enabled when the entry criteria are true. An enabled process may get active when it is triggered by a user with the "start" invocation. As long as the exit criteria are not fulfilled and the user does not trigger the user invocation "complete," the process will remain in the active state. When the exit criteria are fulfilled and the user invocation "complete" is triggered, then the process gets disabled. Additionally, for each project state, the state of the associated work products is represented as "non_existent," "incomplete," or "complete" with the built-in type "Product_status."

Consequently, a state transition model can also be defined for products (Fig. 4.4). At the beginning, the product does not exist. When the producing process starts, the product state changes to incomplete. Finally, when the producing process

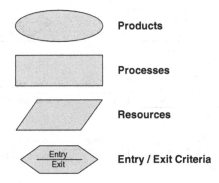

Fig. 4.5 Elements of graphical MVP-L representation

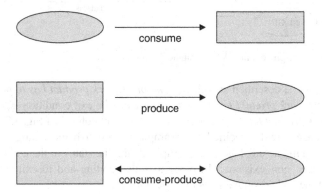

Fig. 4.6 Elements of MVP-L product–process relations

terminates, the product state turns to complete. When rework is needed, several iterations between the product states complete and incomplete are possible.

In addition to the textual representation of MVP-L, a graphical representation is defined for MVP-L in order to facilitate understanding and support process model reviews by process users [4]. Figure 4.5 introduces a graphical representation for MVP-L's products, processes, resources, and entry as well as exit criteria. Figure 4.6 displays the product–process relationships.

For illustration purposes, a simple example of an actual project is provided (Fig. 4.7). This example illustrates the notion of the project state as well as the capabilities of MVP-L in implementing a constraint-oriented control flow using entry and exit criteria. The exemplary process consists of three process instances, namely, requirements specification, design, and coding. In this example, the process is strictly sequential. There are four work products that constitute the product flow within this process. According to Fig. 4.6, an arrow from a product to a process indicates that a product is consumed by this process. An arrow pointing from a process to a product indicates that a product is produced by this process. Control of the process flow is realized implicitly via pre- and postconditions of the process. Since the process is sequential in our case and every subprocess creates one work product, the entry

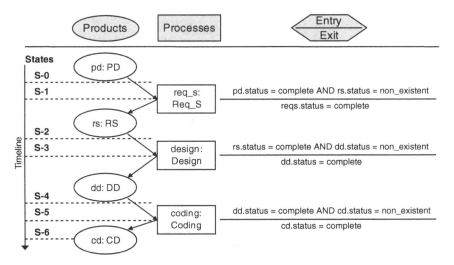

Fig. 4.7 Exemplary process in MVP-L graphical representation

condition could be described as follows: *The prior work product has to be complete AND the next work product has to be nonexistent.* The exit condition is defined as: *The next work product has been completed.* In the right column of Fig. 4.7, entry and exit criteria are explicitly specified. For example, in order to begin coding, the status of the design document "dd" has to be "complete" and the status of the code document "cd" has to be "non_existent." In order to finish coding and to exit the process, the status of the code document has to be "complete."

Finally, on the left of Fig. 4.7, project states are represented that correspond to the enactment scenario provided in the state table in Fig. 4.8 (adapted from [5]). The state table provides a sequence of project plan execution states. Starting in project state S-0, let us assume that the product description "pd" is already "complete" and other products are "nonexistent." As the product description is "complete," the process instance requirements specification can be enabled. The process instance is initiated with the invocation "start(req_s)" and state S-1 is reached. In S-1, the requirements specification process instance is "active" and the requirements specification document "rs" is being produced and is therefore in the state "incomplete." Upon completion of the requirements specification, "complete(req_s)" triggers another project state change. In state S-2, the requirements specification document is "complete," and thus the exit criterion for requirements specification is fulfilled. The requirements specification process instance gets "disabled." Now the entry conditions for the design process are fulfilled, state S-3 can be achieved ("start(design)"), and the design process instance becomes "active." The active design process instance creates the design document and therefore the design document is "incomplete." All other process instances are "disabled." State S-4 is triggered upon completion of the design document (i.e., its exit criterion is fulfilled and "complete(design)" is triggered). Now the entry criteria for the coding process are fulfilled and state S-5 can be entered.

State table		S-0	S-1	S-2	S-3	S-4	S-5	S-6
Product	pd	complete	complete	complete	complete	complete	complete	complete
	rs	n-existent	incomplete	complete	complete	complete	complete	complete
	dd	n-existent	n-existent	n-existent	incomplete	complete	complete	complete
	cd	n-existent	n-existent	n-existent	n-existent	n-existent	incomplete	complete
Process	req_s	enabled	active	disabled	disabled	disabled	disabled	disabled
	design	disabled	disabled	enabled	active	disabled	disabled	disabled
	coding	disabled	disabled	disabled	disabled	enabled	active	disabled

start(req_s) complete(req_s) start(design) complete(design) start(coding) complete(coding)

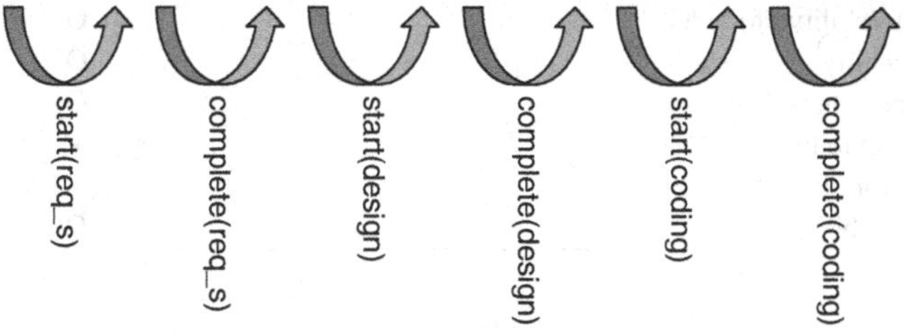

Fig. 4.8 Example of a state table

In S-5, the code document is under creation (code document: "incomplete") and the coding process instance is "active." When the code document reaches the state "complete," the exit criterion for coding is fulfilled and state S-6 is reached through user invocation "complete(coding)." In S-6, all work products are "complete" and all process instances are "disabled" (Fig. 4.8, adapted from [5]).

In this section, the basic concepts of MVP-L were introduced. For more information, the interested reader may refer to [2] and [4].

4.4.5 Assessment with Respect to the Defined Criteria

Table 4.2 describes the four characteristics of MVP-L as well as the satisfaction of the eight requirements R1–R8, based on a subjective assessment. In this context, (+) represents full, (O) partial, and (−) no fulfillment of the respective requirement.

4.5 Software Process Engineering Metamodel

4.5.1 Overview

The first version of the SPEM standard was introduced by the Object Management Group (OMG) in 2002 and was built upon UML 1.4. It was revised in 2005 and again in 2007, when major changes led to version SPEM 2.0, which is compliant with UML 2. Due to UML compliance, standard UML diagrams such as activity diagrams or state chart diagrams can be used for visualizing processes models.

Table 4.2 MVP-L characteristics and requirements

Characterization: MVP-L	
Improvement	Proscriptive
Guidance	Multiperson
Requirements satisfaction: MVP-L	
R1—Natural representation	+
R2—Support of measurement	+
R3—Tailorability of models	O
R4—Formality	O
R5—Understandability	O
R6—Executability	+
R7—Flexibility	+
R8—Traceability	O

The development of SPEM was motivated by the abundance of different concepts for process modeling and software process improvement. These different concepts are usually described in different formats using different notations. Since achieving consistency between different approaches became increasingly difficult, the need for standardization arose. The SPEM standard for modeling software development processes has the following characteristics:

"The Software and Systems Process Engineering Meta-Model (SPEM) is a process engineering metamodel as well as conceptual framework, which can provide the necessary concepts for modeling, documenting, presenting, managing, interchanging, and enacting development methods and processes." [6]

4.5.2   Concepts

In the following sections, the basic SPEM concepts will be introduced. The conceptual framework of SPEM will be discussed, as will the basic notation constructs and the structure of the SPEM standard.

4.5.2.1   Conceptual SPEM Framework

The conceptual framework of SPEM mainly summarizes the aims of the standard. These are, on the one hand, to provide an approach for creating libraries of reusable method content and, on the other hand, to provide concepts for the development and management of processes. The combination of these two basic goals is seen as a solution that enables the configuration of more elaborate process frameworks and finally their enactment in real development projects (Fig. 4.9, based on [6]).

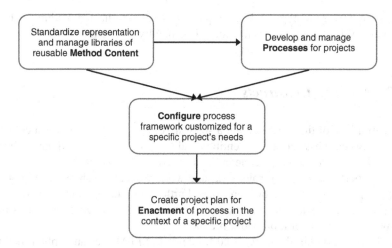

Fig. 4.9 SPEM 2.0 conceptual framework

As depicted in Fig. 4.9, the conceptual SPEM framework consists of four main elements: method content, processes, configuration, and enactment.

Libraries of method content address the need to create a knowledge base containing methods and key practices of software development. Method content captures key practices and methodologies in a standardized format and stores them in adequate libraries. This allows creating and managing reusable practices and methodologies. Such standardized content enables inclusion and integration of external and internal method content according to the current development requirements of an organization, and thus provides methodological support throughout different lifecycle development stages. Furthermore, the standardized method content elements can be used as a basis for the creation of custom processes.

The creation of processes can be supported based on the reusable method content. Processes can be defined as workflows and/or breakdown structures and, within this definition, the selected method content is supposed to be adapted to the specific project context. SPEM intends to provide support for the systematic development and management of development processes as well as for the adaptation of processes to specific project context.

As no two development projects are exactly alike, there is a need for tailoring specific processes from the organization's set of standard processes. With the element of configuration, SPEM aims at addressing concepts for the reuse of processes, for modeling variability, and for tailoring, thus allowing users to define their own extensions, omissions, and variability points on reused processes.

In order to support the enactment of processes within development projects, processes need to be instantiated in a format that is ready for enactment with a "process enactment system" (e.g., project and resource planning systems, workflow systems). Although SPEM 2.0 provides process definition structures, which allow process engineers to express how a process shall be enacted within such an enactment system, support for enactment is generally regarded as weak [7].

4.5.3 Notation Constructs

The central idea of the SPEM is that a software development process is a collaboration between abstract active entities called process *roles*, which perform operations called *tasks* on concrete entities called *work products* [8].

The associations between role, task, and work product are shown in Fig. 4.10. Tasks are performed by one or more roles. Furthermore, tasks require one or more work products as input. They produce one or more work products as output. A role is responsible for one or more work products.

As described within the conceptual framework, SPEM uses an explicit distinction between method content and process, and the basic three entities must therefore be defined for both approaches.

> The SPEM *method content* represents a library of descriptions of software engineering methods and best practices. It defines the "who, what, and how" of work increments that have to be done.
>
> A SPEM *process* represents descriptions of coherent process steps, which enable performance of a certain task. It defines the "when" of work increments that have to be done.

Method content elements can be defined by using work product definitions, role definitions, and task definitions. Furthermore, Category and Guidance can be used. Guidance represents supporting resources, such as guidelines, whitepapers, checklists, examples, or roadmaps, and is defined at the intersection of method content and process because Guidance can provide support for method content as well as for specific processes. Table 4.3 gives an overview and description of basic notation construct elements belonging to Method Content.

Figure 4.11 shows an example representing a tester and all the tasks he performs (create test case, implement test, perform test) as well as the work products he is responsible for (test case, test log) within the software development process.

For the description of a Process, activities are mainly used as the major structuring element. Activities can be nested in order to define work breakdown structures or related to each other in order to define a flow of work. Furthermore, activities may have references to method content elements. These references refer to explicit method content by "using" the concepts *Task Use, Role Use,* and *Work Product Use.* Table 4.4 gives an overview and a description of basic notation construct elements belonging to Process.

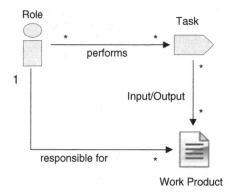

Fig. 4.10 Core method content concepts of role, task, and work product

Table 4.3 Key elements used for method content

Element	Description
Work product definition	Defines any artifact produced, consumed, or modified by a task. Work products can be composed of other work products. Examples: document, model, source code
Role definition	Defines a role and thus related skills, competencies, and responsibilities of one person or many persons. Is responsible for one or many work product(s) and performs one or many task(s). Examples: software architect, project manager, developer
Task definition	Defines work being performed by one or many role(s). A task has input and output work products. Inputs are differentiated into mandatory and optional inputs. Tasks can be divided into steps that describe subunits of work needed to perform the task
Category	Category is used for structuring other elements
Guidance	Can be associated with any SPEM model element to provide more detailed information about the element. Examples: checklist, template, example, guideline

4.5.4   Assessment with Respect to the Defined Criteria

Table 4.5 describes the four characteristics of SPEM 2.0 as well as the fulfillment of the eight requirements R1–R8, based on a subjective assessment. In this context, (+) represents full, (O) partial, and (−) no fulfillment of the respective requirement.

4.6   Tools for Software Process Modeling

Practitioners and process engineers are in need of software support for process modeling in order to be able to deal efficiently with process model creation and the administration of changes and modifications. For example, typical process guidelines

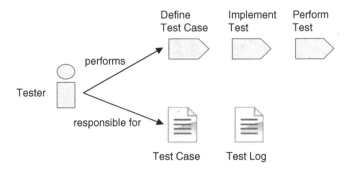

Fig. 4.11 Example for the role "Tester" with related elements

Table 4.4 Key elements used for process

Element	Description
Work product use	Instance of a work product defined within Method Content. Can be used multiple times within process context
Role use	Instance of a role defined within Method Content. Can be used multiple times within process context
Task use	Instance of a task defined within Method Content. Can be used multiple times within process context. Additionally, definition of task-specific steps can be performed
Activity	Activities can be used to define work breakdown structures or workflows and thus group tasks within a software development process, which can then be used multiple times. Activities are used to model software development processes
Process	Can be used for structuring subprocesses by associating activities or tasks to it
Guidance	Can be associated with any SPEM model element to provide more detailed information about the element. Examples: checklist, template, example, guideline

are not only extensive but also cross-referenced, and, consequently, changes in certain areas lead to changes in other parts. Support is therefore useful for maintaining consistency. Such supporting software can have different functionalities. In order to be able to compare different solutions, the introduction of a reference model is useful. Therefore, in the first part of this section, the ECMA/NIST Reference Model for Software Engineering Environments will be introduced, which provides a framework for the discussion of different Software Engineering Environments (SEE). The second part will give an overview of the Eclipse Process Framework (EPF) and especially of the EPF Composer, as a specific tool for process modeling.

4.6.1 The ECMA/NIST Reference Model

The ECMA/NIST Reference Model for Frameworks of Software Engineering Environments was developed jointly by ECMA (European Computer Manufacturers

Table 4.5 SPEM 2.0 characteristics and requirements

Characterization: SPEM 2.0	
Improvement	Proscriptive
Guidance	Multiperson
Requirements Satisfaction: SPEM 2.0	
R1—Natural representation	+
R2—Support of measurement	O
R3—Tailorability of models	+
R4—Formality	O
R5—Understandability	+
R6—Executability	−
R7—Flexibility	O
R8—Traceability	O

Association) and NIST (National Institute of Standards and Technology, USA). The reference model provides a framework for describing and comparing different Software Engineering Environments (SEE) or Computer Aided Software Engineering (CASE) Tools [9]. As such, it is not a standard, but should help to identify emerging standards. In order to promote comparability, different services are grouped in this framework. These services are Object Management Services, Process Management Services, Communication Services, User Interface Services, Operating System Services, Policy Enforcement Services, and Framework Administration Services.

Furthermore, tools (respectively tool slots) are provided, which represent software that is not part of the SEE platform but uses services of the platform and can add further services to the platform. Based on [9], Fig. 4.12 displays an overview of the ECMA/NIST reference model.

In the following, the services that provide the core functionalities that a SEE should implement in some way are described in more detail (based on [9]):

- Object Management Services: The objective of these services is the definition, storage, maintenance, management, and access of object entities and of the relationships they have with other objects.
- Process Management Services: The objective of these services is the definition and computer-assisted performance of software development activities throughout the whole software lifecycle. As this service group addresses processes, the specific services will be described below in more detail. They are:

  - Process Development Service (process modeling)
  - Process Enactment Service
  - Process Visibility Service
  - Process Monitoring Service
  - Process Transaction Service
  - Process Resource Service

- Communication Services: The objective of these services is to provide information exchange among the services of an SEE.
- User Interface Services: These services are designed to allow interaction between the user and the SEE.

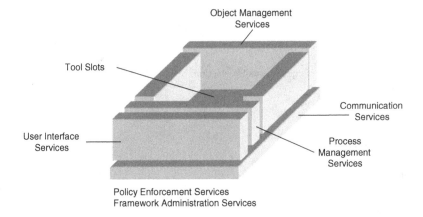

Fig. 4.12 ECMA/NIST reference model

- Operating System Services: These services provide descriptions for and integration with operation systems on which the SEE can be realized.
- Policy Enforcement Services: The purpose of these services is to provide security in an SEE.
- Framework Administration Services: These services provide support for constant adaptation of changes for the SEE.

All these service groups are further refined into specific services within the reference model, but a detailed discussion of all services is beyond the scope of this section. After this brief overview of the reference model, a closer examination of the six services from the Process Management Services group will be provided below (based on [9]):

The *Process Development Service* as described by ECMA/NIST shall enable the modeling of processes within the SEE. Therefore, a form for documenting the process models should be defined, and operations for the creation, modification, and deletion of process models should be included. The formalism of the process description is not restricted, thus allowing informal process description in natural language as well as the use of formal process modeling notations.

The *Process Enactment Service* should facilitate control and support for the enactment of processes defined in the SEE. The operations that are regarded as appropriate in this context are:

- Instantiation of process definitions
- Linking together of process elements
- Enactment of instantiated process definitions
- Suspension and restart of an enacting process
- Abortion of an enacting process
- Tracing of an enacting process
- Checkpoint and rollback
- (Dynamic) Change of enacting instances of a process definition

The *Process Visibility Service* aims at the definition and maintenance of visibility information, by defining which information should be visible to other entities and when and where it should be visible. Operations that are regarded as appropriate for visibility are:

– Establishing access to specified information for an entity
– Hiding information from other entities
– Defining and managing visible areas and communication structures
– Visualizing defined areas and communication structures
– Controlling access rights

The *Process Monitoring Service* observes the evolving process states, detects the occurrence of specified process events, and enacts necessary actions based on observation and detection. In this context, the definition of specific process events and derived actions should be supported. Relevant operations are:

– Definition, modification, deletion, and querying of event definitions
– Manipulation of the control process definitions
– Attaching/detaching actions to/from events
– Querying of the state of a process

The *Process Transaction Service* provides support for the definition and enactment of process transactions, which can be understood as process elements composed of a sequence of atomic process steps. Such a transaction should be either completed entirely or rolled back to the preenactment state. Appropriate operations, which are described in this context, consist of:

– Creation, initiation, abortion, deletion, modification of transactions
– Commit of transactions
– Checkpoints and rollback of process states
– "Login" and "logout" of long-lived transactions

The *Process Resource Service* accounts for allocation and management of resources during enactment of a defined process. The operations defined for the Process Resource Service are:

– Definition, creation, modification, and deletion of process resource types and resource entities
– Mapping of project resources to resource model instances
– Mapping of resource model instances to process instances
– Adaptation of mapping

In this section, an overview of the ECMA/NIST Reference Model for Software Engineering Environments was given, which is useful for describing and comparing tools for process management and its functionalities. In the following section, one example of a tool that supports process modeling will be given by introducing the Eclipse Process Framework and the EPF Composer as well as its main functionalities.

4.6.2   The Eclipse Process Framework (EPF) Composer

The Eclipse Process Framework (EPF) is an open-source project within the Eclipse Foundation and was initiated in January 2006. The EPF project has two main objectives. The first objective is to provide an extensible framework and exemplary tools for software process engineering. This includes support for method and process authoring, library management, configuration, and publishing of processes. The second objective is to provide exemplary and extensible process content for a range of software development and management processes, and thereby support a broad variety of project types and development styles [10].

The EPF Composer has been developed in order to fulfill the first objective. Its conceptual framework is based on SPEM 2.0, and for this reason, the aforementioned concepts in the section about SPEM are useful for understanding the functionality of this tool. The EPF Composer is equipped with predefined process content, which addresses the second objective. The process framework provided with the EPF Composer is called Open Unified Process, and is strongly influenced by IBM's Rational Unified Process [10]. As it was not the aim of the project to provide a process framework, this process content can be understood as a suggestion. In the meantime, further process content has been provided (e.g., agile practices).

4.6.2.1   Basic Concepts

According to SPEM 2.0, the EPF Composer[1] [10] implements the distinction between Method Content and Process, providing capabilities for creating method libraries.

Using the authoring capabilities of EPF Composer, method content can be defined. This definition of method content resembles the creation of method content libraries according to SPEM 2.0.

Tasks are a main element of method content. For tasks, a description can be provided that contains general information. It is also possible to provide detailed information and versioning. Tasks can be refined into the steps that should be performed during task performance. These steps can be defined, ordered, and their content can be described in detail. Moreover, the associated roles, work products, and guidance can be added. Those are defined and described as separate entities within the method content library and then related to a task during task definition. This approach represents an implementation of the task concept provided by SPEM 2.0.

The EPF Composer addresses mainly two audiences. By providing authoring capabilities, it addresses process authors/engineers and provides them with a tool for creating and publishing method content and processes. Simultaneously, it provides functionalities that address process consumers/users by integrating the

---

[1] The content presented here is based on the EPF Composer Version 1.5.0.3.

possibility to publish content in the form of websites that can be browsed. There, the user can find necessary information concerning processes, methods, and guidance (checklists, concepts, guidelines, etc.).

In addition to Method Content, EPF Composer provides capabilities for process definition and adaption. Similar to method content, processes can be authored and published. Within the authoring view, new processes can be composed by creating a sequence of tasks that were already defined in method content. In this way, tasks are integrated that contain associated roles and work products. During process composition, the predefined tasks can be modified, and it is therefore possible to tailor specific processes from predefined method content. Furthermore, it is also possible to tailor previously defined process compositions. The concepts of method content and process variability will be discussed in more detail in the next section.

4.6.2.2   Method Variability

Method variability provides the capability of tailoring existing method content without directly modifying the original content. This is an important ability, as future updates might lead to inconsistencies in the dataset. Variability can be used, for example, to change the description of a role, to add/change steps to an existing task, or to add/change guidance.

The concept used is similar to inheritance in object-oriented programming. Thus, it allows reuse of content with further specialization/modification. For realizing this concept, the EPF Composer uses "plug-ins." After such a plug-in has been created, it can be defined which existing content should be "inherited."

There are four types of method variability [10]:

– Contribute: The contributing element adds content to the base element. The resulting published element contains the content of the base element and the contributing element.
– Replace: The replacing element replaces the base element. The resulting published element is the replacing element.
– Extend: The extending element inherits the content of the base element, which can then be specialized. Both the base element and the extending element are published.
– Extend and Replace: Similar to extend, but the base element is not published.

4.6.2.3   Process Variability

Concepts for process variability are based on activities, which are the elements used to compose processes. Activity variability is based on the same four types of variability as method content (see above: contribute, replace, extend, and extend and replace).

Additionally, activities may be used to create capability patterns. Capability patterns can be defined as a special type of process that describes a reusable cluster of activities for a certain area of application/interest. Processes can be created by using capability patterns in the following ways [10]:

- Extend: The process inherits the properties of the capability pattern. Updates to the capability pattern or respective activities are also realized in the respective process.
- Copy: A process is created based on a copy of the capability pattern. In contrast to extend, the respective process is not synchronized with the capability pattern when changes occur.
- Deep Copy: Similar to copy, but is applied recursively to activities of the respective capability pattern.

References

1. Rombach HD, Verlage M (1995) Directions in software process research. In: Zelkowitz MV (ed) Advances in computers, vol 41. Academic Press, Boston, MA
2. Bröckers A, Lott CM, Rombach HD, Verlage M (1995) MVP-L language report version 2, Technical Report Nr. 265/95, University of Kaiserslautern, Department of Computer Science, Software Engineering Chair
3. Parnas D (1972) On the criteria to be used in decomposing systems into modules. Commun ACM 15(12):1053–1058
4. Bröckers A, Differding C, Hoisl B, Kollnischko F, Lott CM, Münch J, Verlage M, Vorwieger S (1995) A Graphical Representation Schema for the Software Process Modeling Language MVP-L, University of Kaiserslautern, Department of Computer Science, Software Engineering Chair
5. Rombach HD (1991) MVP-L: a language for process modeling in-the-large. University of Maryland, College Park, MD
6. Object Management Group (2008) Software & systems process engineering meta-model specification version 2.0. OMG, Needham, USA
7. Bendraou R, Combemale B, Crogut X, Gervais M (2001) Definition of an Executable SPEM 2.0. In: Proceedings of the 14th Asia-Pacific Software Engineering Conference (APSEC'07), Nagoya, Japan, 5–7 Dec 2007. doi: 10.1109/ASPEC.2007.60
8. Object Management Group (2005) Software process engineering meta-model specification version 1.1. OMG, Needham, USA
9. ECMA/NIST (1993) Reference model for frameworks of software engineering environments, Technical Report ECMA TR/55
10. Eclipse Foundation (2009) EPF composer: open UP library. http://www.eclipse.org/epf/downloads/tool/tool_downloads.php. Accessed 27 Jun 2011

Chapter 5
Process Improvement

This chapter introduces concepts for improving software processes. The chapter is structured into four main parts. First, it describes model-based improvement approaches in general and furthermore introduces two specific model-based improvement frameworks, CMMI and SPICE. Second, it introduces continuous improvement approaches, beginning with a short overview of commonly used continuous improvement approaches and furthermore introducing specific software engineering concepts, especially the Quality Improvement Paradigm (QIP) and the Experience Factory (EF). Third, it focuses on the role of measurement in the context of process improvement. Operationalizing process improvement creates a need for measurement and therefore, the goal/question/metric (GQM) method is presented, which is a de-facto-standard for goal-oriented software measurement. Finally, the organizational and business context of process improvement is discussed by introducing the Balanced Scorecard (BSC) and the GQM+Strategies approaches, which can be used as means to align specific improvement activities with business goals and strategies. Figure 5.1 displays an overview of the chapter.

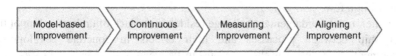

Fig. 5.1 Chapter structure

5.1 Objectives of This Chapter

After reading this chapter, you should be able to

- Differentiate between continuous and model-based improvement approaches
- Understand the principles of model-based process improvement
- Know important model-based improvement approaches such as CMMI and ISO 15504 and their relevance for software and system development

J. Münch et al., *Software Process Definition and Management*,
The Fraunhofer Series on Software and Systems Engineering,
DOI 10.1007/978-3-642-24291-5_5, © Springer-Verlag Berlin Heidelberg 2012

- Know how a process is evaluated by using an assessment model
- Understand the principles of continuous process improvement
- Know the basics of important continuous improvement approaches (e.g., QIP)
- Know how GQM measurement can be used for process improvement
- Understand the importance of aligning improvement goals and strategies with business

5.2   Introduction

A lot of organizations still face a multitude of problems when it comes to creating high-quality software products. On a regular basis, the Standish Group publishes the so-called "Chaos Report," which documents these problems in terms of IT project success and failure [1]. The Chaos Report regularly surveys a large set of IT projects and distinguishes three categories of projects (Fig. 5.2):

- Successful: Projects that have achieved the given target on time and within budget.
- Challenged: Projects that have been completed, but with extensive additional effort and/or budget.
- Failed: Projects that were cancelled without having achieved the given target.

The results of these surveys have been quite stable over many years: many projects failed or needed more effort and budget than planned. There are many reasons for these problems and a lot of them can be related to processes. Some are related to a lack of indispensable processes such as sound project management, configuration and change management, and validation and verification processes. These problems impose significant risks and consequently potential damage on the organization. The resulting risks include financial risks, liability risks, the risk of losing important customers, or the risk of losing the organization's good reputation, to name but a few.

Another, more fundamental challenge resides in the lack of understanding of the relationship between processes and their effects in concrete development environments (e.g., what is the relationship between a specific test process and the resulting reliability of a tested electronic control unit in the automotive domain?). Nowadays, this is not sufficiently understood yet. Based on the widely accepted assumption that there is a relationship between process quality and the quality of the resulting software product [2], the following four cases can be distinguished (Fig. 5.3).

As shown in Fig. 5.3, investing in process improvement and thus high process quality is promising. Low process quality often leads to bad product quality, as chaotic ad-hoc realization of software projects is very defect-prone (quadrant 1 in Fig. 5.3), although achieving good product quality with bad processes can sometimes be seen in practice (quadrant 2 in Fig. 5.3). However, this is usually due to the work of excellent

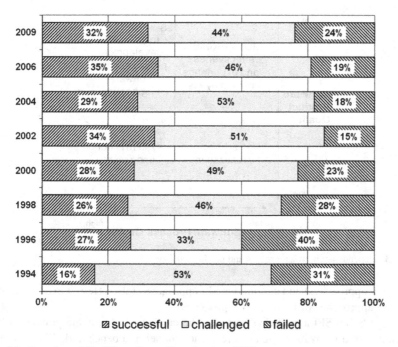

Fig. 5.2 Overview of the "Chaos Report" results since 1994

developers in combination with enormous effort and overtime work. Such software development conditions are not beneficial for an organization, as it is difficult to repeat and institutionalize success when developing high-quality software. Additionally, organizations with such bad development conditions often are subject to high person- nel fluctuations. Therefore, the experts who contributed to the last success might not be available anymore for the next software development project. The institutionaliza- tion of processes can help to build up and preserve organizational knowledge with respect to software development (quadrant 3 in Fig. 5.3). Thus, mature software development processes can be seen as a prerequisite for high-quality software products [2]. In consequence, without good process quality and an understanding of the effects that processes have in a specific development environment, success is not easily repeatable. This is true in particular for processes that rely solely on some sort of "high-quality process documentation" without adapting and improving the processes in the context of the development environment (quadrant 4 in Fig. 5.3). If processes do not evolve with the development context and do not support developers in an adequate way, the resulting product quality often remains low. Past experience with insufficient process quality has motivated the development of software process improvement (SPI) approaches that address these issues. These approaches will be discussed in the following.

Currently, mainly two types of SPI approaches are being used in practice: model-based SPI approaches (also referred to as problem-oriented approaches or

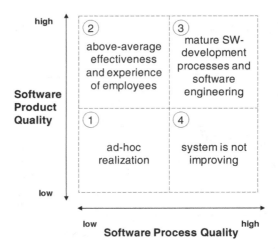

Fig. 5.3 Dependency between process and product quality

top-down approaches) and continuous SPI approaches (also referred to as solution-oriented approaches or bottom-up approaches).

Model-based SPI approaches compare the current processes and practices of a development organization against a reference model or a benchmark. They can be used to identify problematic process areas with respect to the used reference model. Using the identified problematic process areas helps to derive potential improvement options. Usually, model-based SPI approaches provide different so-called capability or maturity levels with different sets of processes and practices. These levels often define an improvement roadmap.

Continuous SPI approaches focus on solutions for the most important challenges of a software development organization and usually involve improvement cycles based on an initial baseline. Continuous approaches focus on solving a specific problem by analyzing the problem, implementing and observing problem-focused improvement actions, and measuring the effects of the actions. The interpretation of the measurement data is used as input for further optimization of the solution.

Model-based and continuous SPI approaches can be seen as being complementary: Model-based approaches can be used to identify problem areas and potential improvement options, and continuous approaches can be used to solve respective company-specific problems. Continuous approaches can be successfully applied, independent of the maturity of an organization, whereas model-based approaches usually require continuous improvement from a certain point on.

The need for SPI is being widely recognized nowadays. In the following sections, model-based and continuous SPI approaches will be introduced. Due to the fact that software development processes are usually human-based and depend on the development context (including domain characteristics, workforce capabilities, and organizational maturity), changes to these processes typically cause significant costs and should be considered carefully. Alternative improvement options need to be evaluated with respect to their implementation cost and their potential impact on business goals. To address these organizational aspects, concepts of business alignment will be discussed in the last section of this chapter.

Model-based SPI approaches compare organizational processes with a reference model and can be used to identify coarse-grained problem areas and potential improvement options.
Continuous SPI approaches can be used to develop company-specific solutions for important problems and assess the effects of improvement actions.

5.3   Model-Based Improvement Approaches

Model-based SPI approaches such as ISO/IEC 15504 (SPICE) [3] or CMMI [4] compare an organization's processes or methods with a reference model containing proven processes or methods. To be precise, such a reference model often contains only requirements for such processes or methods that result from experience collected in successful organizations. Typically, the elements of such a reference model are associated with different levels that are supposed to reflect an organization's different capability or maturity levels. Therefore, this type of model is often called *capability* or *maturity model*. One key element in model-based improvement approaches are assessments. An assessment (sometimes also called appraisal) determines to which degree an organization complies with the demands of the respective model and is typically performed by comparing the processes actually used against the requirements for these processes as stated in the reference model. Such assessments may serve to evaluate an organization with respect to its process maturity, or to identify improvement options for an organization's processes. From this, a coarse-grained overview of potential improvement areas and alternative improvement options and, in consequence, an improvement roadmap can be derived.

Model-based improvement approaches are widely used and provide a number of benefits:

– Creating quality awareness: Model-based approaches can be easily used to create and enforce awareness for quality issues in large organizations because many different stakeholders (e.g., managers, project managers, developers) are involved in the improvement actions.
– Measurable goals: Improvement goals like "reach maturity level 3" can be easily understood, independent of technical details, and are thus, easier to communicate to and by managers. Additionally, from the management point of view, reaching a specific capability level can be defined as a clear, measurable, and assessable goal.

- Process areas and important base practices: The reference models contain relevant process areas and the maturity levels prescribe a way to process improvement, which is perceived as being reasonable. Furthermore, the models feature the early introduction of important base practices such as project management practices.
- Focused improvement actions: Model-based approaches support the prioritization and selection of the most important improvement measures. Thus, improvement actions with high impact can be performed first and the resulting benefits can be realized within a short timeframe.
- Independent assessment: Assessments are usually performed by external experts and thus, an independent assessment and evaluation of the respective organization is facilitated.

The basic assumption behind model-based improvement approaches is that the selected reference model is suitable for an organization. However, since software development highly depends on the context, this is a questionable assumption. Many software development activities are human-centered and thus, nondeterministic. Therefore, individual processes or practices may have very different effects in varying contexts and might not be suitable at all under certain circumstances. Because of this, model-based improvement approaches seem applicable especially for establishing and improving base practices, such as project and product management, which are mostly context-independent. Context-dependent activities, such as software design, are much more difficult to improve, which is why the application of fixed reference models is rather questionable in this context. These models typically only prescribe some generic policies, but detailed elaboration is left to the user – as is the selection of the right practices to achieve the improvement goals.

Model-based improvement approaches may be criticized in a number of points:

- Generic nature of model-based SPI approaches: Model-based approaches typically do not assess the impact of processes on product characteristics and therefore, cannot be used to analytically identify process problems that cause concrete product deficiencies. Moreover, the process reference models (PRMs) are generic and typically lack guidance for tailoring. The practices described in reference models are usually based on the hypothesis that they can be successfully applied in the domain the approach is intended for.
- Unclear business goal alignment: Typically, model-based improvement approaches are independent of an organization's goals. Assessments can be characterized as syntactic activities; during an assessment, it is checked whether a process or practice is in place, but its impact on a business goal or its value for the organization is not evaluated. In particular, this means that reaching a certain maturity level does not automatically lead to the achievement of the organization's business goals. Therefore, having a high maturity level does not mean that the organization is successful in fulfilling its business goals (such as an appropriate trade-off between time to market and product quality). As a consequence, most maturity models explicitly demand a reference to the organization's goals on the higher maturity levels; however, they often elaborate only little on how to do this.

- Unclear value of improvement activities: As the improvement actions are not linked explicitly to the organizational business goals, the added value of the improvement measures suggested by the models and implemented in the organization often remains unclear.
- Conflict of objectives: Performing assessments and appraisals has become a successful business model for consulting companies. These companies are therefore, actively involved in the creation and maintenance of model-based improvement approaches. This creates the danger that the primary goal of achieving high process quality is undermined by business interests, i.e., the generation of consulting business.
- Low acceptance in small enterprises: Model-based approaches do not enjoy high acceptance in small enterprises, as certain costs are involved, for example for the assessments. The International Organization for Standardization, for instance, addresses this problem by offering an approach for small companies with up to 25 employees [5]; however, with limited success so far.

The following sections will present the model-based SPI approaches CMMI and ISO/IEC 15504 (SPICE) in more detail.

5.3.1   Capability Maturity Model Integration

In 1991, the Software Engineering Institute (SEI) at Carnegie Mellon University (CMU) published an approach that supported the evaluation and improvement of an organization's processes by using a best-practice model. The model has been continuously refined. Version 1.2 of the Capability Maturity Model Integration was published in 2006 [6] and updated to Version 1.3 in November 2010 [4]. Since most organizations are still using CMMI 1.2, yet are moving toward 1.3, we will describe the major concepts of CMMI 1.2 and the changes performed in CMMI 1.3.

In general, CMMI describes processes for development (CMMI-DEV), for acquisition (CMMI-ACQ), and for services (CMMI-SVC). CMMI can be used for the evaluation of processes using *appraisals* as well as for process improvement, using the reference model as a template. The following paragraphs introduce the core concepts of CMMI for software development projects (CMMI-DEV 1.2). CMMI-ACQ and CMMI-SVC are constructed similarly.

CMMI-DEV 1.2 distinguishes 22 *process areas* in four groups:

- Project Management
- Engineering
- Process Management
- Support

The processes of the *Project Management* group are provided to manage and control development projects, including risks and purchased components or entire software systems. *Engineering* describes constructive processes for software development as well as verification and validation processes. The *Process Management* group describes processes for the definition, establishment, and control of organizational processes, including training of employees and organizational innovation management. The *Support* group describes cross-functional processes like configuration management, measurement, process and product quality assurance, and others.

In its purpose statement, each process area explains the goals that should be fulfilled by means of the described process. The main elements of the process areas are the *specific goals* and the *generic goals*. The *specific goals* are individual for each process area and should be reached by performing the processes of the particular process area. For example, the process area *Technical Solution (TS)* has the following specific goals:

- (SG 1) Select Product Component Solutions
- (SG 2) Develop the Design
- (SG 3) Implement the Product Design

If these goals are achieved, product alternatives are identified and evaluated, and one is selected, designed, and implemented. Thus, the *specific goals* help to reach the goals of the specific *process area*.

In contrast to the *specific goals*, the *generic goals* are defined globally and need to be instantiated for every process area. Generic goal 1 (GG 1), for example, essentially demands that the specific goals must be reached for the particular process area. This means that for the *Technical Solution (TS)* process area, GG 1 demands that the specific goals SG 1, SG 2, and SG 3 as noted above are achieved. For a different process area, GG 1 demands achieving its specific goals accordingly.

Higher-level generic goals pose requirements that exceed pure activities. While GG 1 essentially demands that certain things be done (no matter how, and consuming whichever effort), GG 2 demands *managing* the respective activities. This means that within a project, performing the respective activity has to be planned and controlled, resources and responsibilities must be considered, stakeholders must be identified and involved, etc. This applies to every process area.

GG 2 demands certain things to be done in a managed fashion. However, every project may decide independently *how* to implement the required activities. GG 3 takes care of this by demanding that the processes and activities performed in projects must be derived from an organization-wide standard process, and that improvement information is collected systematically. Beyond that, GG 4 demands quantitative process management and GG 5 finally establishes continuous, active improvement of those processes that are especially important for the organization to reach its business goals.

During an *appraisal,* an organization's finished projects are evaluated with respect to which generic goals were achieved. CMMI supports two representations [7]. *Continuous representation* allows for appraising any selection of process areas. For each process area, a *capability level* (CL) is assigned, leading to a comb-shaped capability profile (Fig. 5.4). *Staged representation* appraises a very specific selection of process areas, looking for specific generic goals, and assigns an

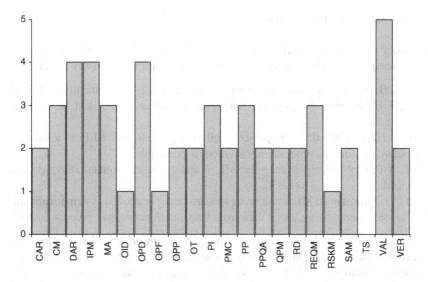

Fig. 5.4 Comb-shaped profile of a CMMI appraisal in continuous representation

organization a single *maturity level* (ML). Both representations will be explained in the following sections.

5.3.1.1 Continuous Representation

Continuous representation allows for appraising any selection of process areas. For every process area, a capability level (CL) is determined that symbolizes the organization's process capabilities with respect to this process area. CMMI defines six capability levels:

- CL 0 (Incomplete): No requirements (every organization automatically achieves CL 0).
- CL 1 (Performed): The process achieves its specific goals (GG 1).
- CL 2 (Managed): CL 1 and the process is managed (GG 2).
- CL 3 (Defined): CL 2 and the process is derived from a standard process (GG 3).
- CL 4 (Quantitatively Managed): CL 3 and the process is under statistical/ quantitative control (GG 4).
- CL 5 (Optimizing): CL 4 and the process is continuously improved, using data from the statistical/quantitative process control (GG 5).

Evaluating an organization using *continuous representation* typically results in a comb-shaped process capability profile (Fig. 5.4) that includes all CMMI process areas (for more details on the process areas, refer to the next section). This representation is similar to that produced by SPICE assessments (see Sect. 5.3.2).

5.3.1.2 Staged Representation

Originally taken from CMMI's predecessor CMM, *staged representation* assigns a single *maturity level* (ML) to an organization. There are five *maturity levels:*

- ML 1 (Initial): No requirements (every organization is automatically on ML 1).
- ML 2 (Managed): Projects are managed, a similar project can be repeated successfully.
- ML 3 (Defined): ML 2 and projects follow a process derived from a standard process; continuous process improvement is performed.
- ML 4 (Quantitatively Managed): ML 3 and statistical (quantitative) process control.
- ML 5 (Optimizing): ML 4 and processes are being improved systematically and in a goal-oriented way, using data from statistical/quantitative process control.

Since *maturity levels* are supposed to make different organizations comparable, for every maturity level (ML), CMMI precisely defines the process areas and their required capability levels (CL). For ML 2, the following process areas must at least reach CL 2:

- Requirements Management (REQM)
- Project Planning (PP)
- Project Monitoring and Control (PMC)
- Supplier Agreement Management (SAM)
- Measurement and Analysis (MA)
- Process and Product Quality Assurance (PPQA)
- Configuration Management (CM)

To reach ML 3, the aforementioned process areas plus the following process areas must reach CL 3:

- Technical Solution (TS)
- Product Integration (PI)
- Validation (VAL)
- Verification (VER)
- Organizational Process Focus (OPF)
- Organizational Process Definition (OPD)
- Organizational Training (OT)
- Requirements Development (RD)
- Decision Analysis and Resolution (DAR)
- Integrated Project Management (IPM)
- Risk Management (RSKM)

For ML 4 (ML 5), process areas that are especially relevant for reaching the appraised organization's business goals must reach CL 4 (CL 5). For example, an organization featuring a process profile such as the one displayed in Fig. 5.4 would achieve ML 2, but not ML 3, because TS only achieves CL 0. Deriving a maturity level from the determined capability levels is called *equivalent staging*.

The maturity level representation determined with CMMI's staged representation makes organizations (partially) comparable; however, it also carries some risk. If an organization achieves ML 2, this only means that the process areas REQM, PP, PMC, SAM, MA, PPQA, and CM achieve CL 2. ML 2 makes no statement whatsoever about the other process areas, such as TS, which covers actual software construction!

5.3.1.3   CMMI 1.3

In November 2010, CMMI 1.3 was published by the SEI [4]. Apart from refinements in many descriptions and much of the informative material, two changes from version 1.2 should be noted in particular:

– *Changes in process areas.* The CMMI 1.2 ML 5 process area of *Organizational Innovation and Deployment* (OID) has been reshaped so that it addresses the overall performance management. Remaining a ML 5 process area, it has been renamed to *Organizational Performance Management* (OPM). Furthermore, the IPPD extensions of CMMI 1.2[1] were integrated into the respective process areas.
– *No more capability levels 4 and 5.* CMMI 1.3 contains only 4 CLs where CMMI 1.2 had 6. The top two CLs (4, "Quantitatively Managed" and 5, "Optimizing") were removed together with their generic practices. This means that the highest CL an organization can reach in CMMI 1.3 is CL3 ("Defined"). The maturity levels remain the same, though. Up to ML 3, the rules for equivalent staging are the same for CMMI 1.2 and CMMI 1.3. For ML 4, CMMI 1.3 demands that all process areas assigned for this ML reach CL 3, which includes the process areas OPP and QPM. This means that for process areas that are especially relevant for the business success of the organization, process performance measures are defined, collected, and statistically analyzed. This aims at making the selected processes predictable in a quantitative way. For ML 5, the two process areas of OPM and CAR must fulfill the same requirement, leading the organization to continuous improvement based on quantitative data.

These changes constitute a gentle refinement of CMMI 1.2, but not a major revision. The process areas, though revised, remain well-known. The changes regarding ML 4 and ML 5 clarify the high-maturity section of CMMI, which has always been somewhat blurry in CMMI 1.2.

---

[1] Integrated Product and Process Development, an addition to CMMI-DEV that aims at specifically supporting organizations with respect to the collaboration of all product stakeholders throughout the entire product lifecycle, in particular nonsoftware-specific stakeholders.

5.3.2 *ISO/IEC 15504 (SPICE)*

ISO/IEC 15504 [3], often simply called SPICE, is an international standard for evaluating and improving an organization's software processes. The international standard consists of five parts. Part 1 (ISO/IEC 15504-1:2004) defines concepts and vocabulary, part 2 (ISO/IEC 15504-2:2003) the requirements for performing process assessments, as a basis for process improvement and capability level determination. Part 3 (ISO/IEC 15504-3:2004) supports the users of the standard in fulfilling the requirements for an assessment as stated in part 2. Part 4 (ISO/IEC 15504-4:2004) assists with utilizing SPICE-compliant assessments for process improvement and capability level determination.

Usually, the most important part of SPICE is part 5 (ISO/IEC 15504-5:2006). Part 5 provides an exemplar *Process Assessment Model* (PAM), which fulfills the requirements stated in part 2. This PAM uses ISO/IEC 12207:1995 [8] as its *Process Reference Model* (PRM). Most SPICE assessments are based on this PAM. More PAMs exist for specific domains, e.g., Automotive SPICE [9] for the automotive domain. For the remainder of this section, SPICE will refer to ISO/IEC 15504-5:2006.

In addition to the five parts of the international standard, two additional parts were released as technical report (TR): part 6 (ISO/IEC TR 15504-6:2008) and part 7 (ISO/IEC TR 15504-7:2008). Part 6 describes an exemplar PAM for system life cycle processes, conformant with the ISO/IEC 15504-2 requirements for such a PAM. It is derived from the PRM defined in ISO/IEC 15288 [10]. Part 7 defines the conditions for an assessment of organizational maturity (similar to CMMI's staged representation). It defines a framework for determining organizational maturity, based upon profiles of process capability derived from process assessment, and defines the conditions under which such assessments are valid.

Similar to ISO/IEC 12207:1995, SPICE defines three process categories that cover 49 processes for developing and acquiring software products and services in nine process groups. Figure 5.5 displays an overview of process categories and process groups.

Within the *Primary Life Cycle Processes*, the *Acquisition* group ACQ contains the processes for the party acquiring software components, whereas the *Supply* group SUP contains those for the party delivering such components. *Engineering* (ENG) describes the engineering processes necessary to develop the software, and *Operation* (OPE) those for later operation of the finished software product.

The *Organizational Life Cycle Processes* affect the whole organization. *Management* (MAN) describes the management of projects and individual activities. *Process improvement* (PIM) takes care of improving all processes, while *Resource and Infrastructure* (RIN) provide the necessary infrastructure for all other processes. Finally, *Reuse* (REU) facilitates systematic reuse of previously developed software components.

The *Supporting Life Cycle Processes* contain only a single process group. *Support* (SUP) contains cross-functional processes that support the other two process categories. These include, in particular, processes for quality assurance,

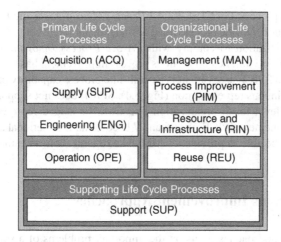

Fig. 5.5 ISO/IEC 15504 overview

verification, validation, reviews, and audits. Furthermore, documentation, configuration management, problem resolution management, and change request management are described.

A SPICE assessment evaluates a defined subset of the 49 SPICE processes, assigning each evaluated process a *Capability Level* (CL), similar to CMMI's continuous representation (see Sect. 5.3.1.1). Evaluation is performed using predefined *Process Attributes* (PA). CL 1 requires only one PA; all higher levels require two. A SPICE process description states the *Process Purpose,* expected *Outcomes* that should be produced by the process, and *Base Practices* and *Work Products,* indicating the extent of achievement of the process purpose and outcomes. In addition to that, typical inputs and outputs are defined.

Like CMMI, SPICE defines six capability levels:

- CL 0 (Incomplete): No requirements (every organization automatically achieves CL 0).
- CL 1 (Performed): The process exists and achieves its specific goals.
- CL 2 (Managed): CL 1 and the process is managed (planned, monitored, and adjusted), and its work products are established, controlled, and maintained.
- CL 3 (Established): CL 2 and the process is implemented using a defined process that is capable of achieving its process outcomes.
- CL 4 (Predictable): CL 3 and the process operates within defined limits to achieve its outcomes.
- CL 5 (Optimizing): CL 4 and the process is continuously improved to meet relevant current and projected business goals.

In order to reach CL 1, a process must achieve its outcomes *(PA 1.1 Process Performance).* For CL 2, the two attributes *PA 2.1 Performance Management* and *PA 2.2 Work Product Management* must be achieved, i.e., the process and its work products, in particular, must be managed. CL 3 demands *PA 3.1 Process Definition* and *PA 3.2 Process Deployment,* i.e., it is required that the organization follows a defined standard process. For CL 4, *PA 4.1 Process Measurement* and *PA 4.2 Process Control* are required, i.e., the process must be under quantitative control. CL 5, finally, requires an organization to comply with *PA 5.1 Process Innovation* and *PA 5.2 Continuous Optimization*, i.e., continuous process improvement has to be performed.

The result of a SPICE assessment is a comb-like process capability profile, similar to CMMI's continuous representation (Fig. 5.4). SPICE does not support assigning a single maturity level to an organization like CMMI's staged representation does. However, when the new SPICE parts 6 and 7 become an International Standard (IS), SPICE will also be able to provide a CMMI-like organization-wide maturity level.

5.4 Continuous Improvement Approaches

Continuous SPI approaches focus on the important problems of a software development organization and usually involve improvement cycles (like Plan-Do-Check-Act (PDCA) or QIP) based on an initial baseline that defines the respective starting point of each improvement action. Continuous improvement approaches focus on solving a specific problem by analyzing the problem, implementing and observing problem-focused improvement actions, and measuring the effects of the actions. The interpretation of the measurement data is used as input for further optimization of the solution. In addition, solving one problem typically reveals further improvement potential in related areas. Thus, further improvement actions can be defined and an improvement roadmap can be created "bottom up."

Continuous improvement approaches provide a series of benefits:

– Focused: Continuous approaches can often be focused on specific problems or improvement opportunities within an organization or its processes; as a consequence, the improvement actions are often highly effective and efficient.
– Specific: Continuous approaches are organization-specific and are therefore suitable for achieving the desired process characteristics. Additionally, the inclusion of measurement can illustrate the immediate impact of an improvement action on process and product quality aspects.

Continuous improvement approaches can be criticized for:

– Need of experience: Setting up a continuous improvement approach usually requires a lot of experience in the area of process improvement; additionally, domain knowledge is beneficial.
– Missing external view: Often, continuous improvement approaches are conducted and driven by internal process experts and, as a result, an external view on the software process environment might be missing that would help to identify critical improvement options.
– Danger of isolation: Due to the fact that continuous improvement approaches are focused, they are often not well suited for creating an overall awareness for quality issues in large software organizations. Thus, it is beneficial if they are embedded into an organizational improvement framework.

In the following, different continuous improvement approaches will be introduced, starting with an overview of the PDCA cycle and the associated organizational framework of Total Quality Management (TQM). After presenting this outline of continuous improvement approaches, software-specific approaches will be introduced with the presentation of the QIP and its associated organizational framework, the Experience Factory (EF).

5.4.1 PDCA Cycle (Deming Cycle)

Continuous improvement approaches concentrate on problems in an organization's development process. Generally speaking, these approaches consist of iterative improvement cycles based on the PDCA cycle, which was made popular by W. Edwards Deming and is based on the work of Walter A. Shewhart [11]. PDCA is not explicitly focused on software development, but has traditionally been used for industrial production and business processes. It consists of a four-step problem-solving process (Fig. 5.6):

Plan: Perform a problem or potential analysis. Based on the results, define measurable improvement goals and plan appropriate improvement actions that will allow achieving the defined improvement goals. Additionally, determine the results expected from a successful implementation of the planned improvement actions.

Do: Implement and perform improvement actions.

Check: Analyze the success of the improvement actions. In particular, compare the results of the improvement actions against the expected results and record any observed differences.

Act: Analyze the differences between the actual and the expected results, determine their causes, and define appropriate means to achieve the expected results. A new cycle may be initiated, e.g., for follow-up improvement activities or with modified improvement activities in the event of failure. In case of successful improvement actions, determine where else the performed improvement actions can be applied within the organization and deploy them.

The PDCA cycle represents a very basic approach for the performance and institutionalization of continuous improvement, and is the basis for the organizational framework of TQM.

5.4.2 Total Quality Management

TQM is a holistic management approach toward quality management and, in particular, continuous improvement within an organization. The TQM approach was mainly developed in the context of industrial production processes. Although classic production processes and software development processes differ, it was possible to transfer basic TQM concepts to the domain of software development [12].

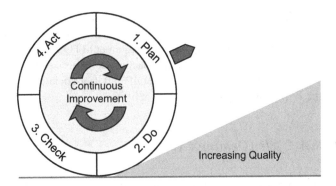

Fig. 5.6 The PDCA cycle

TQM has its origins in the United States, but it became popular due to its application in Japan after World War II. In the aftermath of the war, American specialists in statistical control methods, such as Dr. W. Edwards Deming, came to Japan to support the Training Within Industry (TWI) program designed to restore the country. Deming, Feigenbaum, and others made approaches like the PDCA cycle popular and focused on statistical control of production processes as well as continuous improvement. Since many different individuals were involved, multiple ideas and developments regarding continuous improvement led to the concept of TQM. Throughout the 1970s and 1980s, the popularity of TQM grew in the United States and in Europe. As the subject of quality became more and more important, the U.S. government supported the TQM approach with the Baldrige award for quality, while in Europe, TQM was promoted by the European Foundation for Quality Management with the EFQM framework for organizational management systems [13].

Figure 5.7 (adapted from [11]) shows the evolutionary development of TQM from inspection to quality control, to quality assurance, and finally to TQM. In brief, the main focus of an inspection was to identify and sort out products with defects. Quality control introduced a broader view of quality and provided the first methods (e.g., product testing, basic quality planning) for improving quality. Quality assurance then started to focus on the prevention of defects and on statistical process control. Finally, TQM took a holistic approach to the subject of quality. "Total" means that customers, employees across all departments and the overall organizational environment need to be considered. "Quality" refers to quality of the products, processes, and the organization. Management relates to leadership and goals with respect to the other two aspects [14].

The objective of TQM is to have an organization achieve long-term success by focusing on customer satisfaction. A definition highlighting these characteristics of TQM is provided in Ref. [15]:

> "All work is seen as a process and total quality management is a continuous process of improvement for individuals, groups of people, and whole organizations. What makes total quality management different from other management processes is the concentrated focus on continuous improvement. Total quality management is not a quick management fix; it is about changing the way things are done within the organization's lifetime."

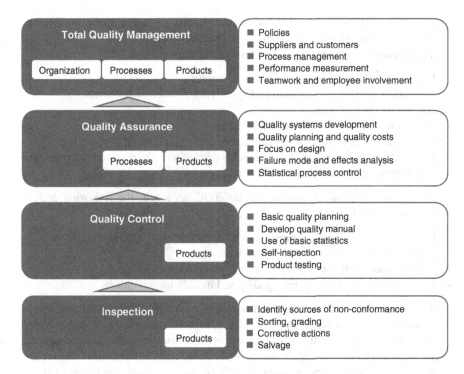

Fig. 5.7 Evolution of the TQM approach

As indicated, TQM has a long history and many different influences have formed what we understand today as TQM. The following sections will introduce the important approaches of Total Quality Control (TQC), Company-Wide Quality Control (CWQC), Kaizen, Zero Defect Program, and finally Six Sigma.

5.4.3   Total Quality Control

The term TQC was coined by Armand Feigenbaum and introduced in 1951 in his book "Quality Control" [16]. TQC was a major step in the development toward TQM and describes a system that integrates quality development, maintenance, and improvement within an organization in order to enable the economical creation of products that achieve full customer satisfaction. In his book, Feigenbaum emphasizes the importance of quality to customers:

> "Quality is the basic customer decision factor for an explosively growing number of products and services today—whether the buyer is a housewife, an industrial corporation, a government agency, a department store chain or a military defense program." [16]

TQC is based on the assumption that as quality improves, productivity improves and costs are reduced. Feigenbaum used the term TQC to describe the importance of all employees within an organization with respect to responsibility for the quality of the products. Thus, not only those employees who are directly involved in manufacturing are responsible for product quality, but employees on different levels of hierarchy share responsibility for product quality [12].

The implementation of TQC includes several steps [16]:

- Finding out what the company needs to improve
- Analyzing the present situation and specifying a problem statement
- Analyzing the problem
- Developing actions to address the problem
- Controlling results through measurement
- Establishing and standardizing processes that effectively resolved the problem
- Establishing continuous improvement

In order to successfully implement the TQC approach, the following factors have to be accounted for:

- Continuous quality improvement guides organizational actions.
- Statistical data are the basis for decisions.
- Organization members must be focused on customer needs.
- Customer requirements define quality and quality improvement.

The positive impact of the TQC approach is based on all organizational levels being involved in quality matters. The TQC approach is assumed to have a positive effect on the required production effort, as improvements in quality reduce rework, waste, and associated customer complaints. Thus, costs related to a product are expected to be reduced and the overall profit of an organization increases [17].

5.4.4 Company-Wide Quality Control

Karou Ishikawa introduced the concept of CWQC in his book "What is Total Quality Control? The Japanese Way" [18]. He was strongly influenced by the works of Deming and particularly Feigenbaum and his concept can be seen as an extension of TQC. In contrast to Feigenbaum, who mainly focused on the participation of all organizational levels of hierarchy in quality improvement, Ishikawa introduced an approach that emphasized the participation of all employees. Consequently, all employees, from top managers to workers, should contribute to product quality in their area of work and responsibility.

Furthermore, Ishikawa advocated cooperation and communication across functions/departments. He came up with the idea that "the next process is your customer." He had this idea because of his experience of work reality at the time, where workers referred to the people in the next process as "enemies." From this experience, he concluded that the strict separation of functions needs to be abolished in order to enable CWQC [19].

In the context of CWQC, Ishikawa developed methods for quality control in order to implement continuous improvement. One of the most popular methods is the Quality Control Circle. Quality Control Circles aim at involving workers in the continuous improvement of quality and at using this institution for educational purposes at the same time [20].

5.4.5   Kaizen

The Japanese word "Kaizen" stands for "improvement" and was adopted in business to describe the philosophy of continuous improvement [21]. The evolution of this term took place in the context of the development of continuous quality improvement concepts such as TCQ or CWQC. The Kaizen philosophy includes continuous improvement in manufacturing activities, business activities, or even all aspects of life depending on the specific context of usage.

Kaizen is based on the following five elements [22]:

- Quality planning
- Teamwork
- Personal discipline and responsibility
- Involvement and suggestions for improvement
- Quality circles.

Kaizen can be characterized as an omnipresent continuous process of evolutionary improvement that aims at eliminating waste and inefficiency and furthermore strives toward standardization [22].

5.4.6   Zero Defect Program

The Zero Defect Program was pioneered by Philip Crosby and is a business practice aimed at minimizing the number of defects and errors in a process and at doing things right the first time. As emphasized by the name of the program, the ultimate objective of this method is to reduce the level of defects to zero, which most probably is not completely possible in practice, but should still be the aim:

> "The quality manager must be clear, right from the start, that zero defects is not a motivation program. Its purpose is to communicate to all employees the literal meaning of the words "zero defects" and the thought that everyone should do things right the first time." [23]

The core of this methodology is based on four principles [24]:

1. *Quality is defined as conformance to requirements.* Requirements represent a description of customer needs and expectations. When a product meets customer requirements, it thereby achieves a level of quality that is high enough to satisfy the customer.
2. *Defect prevention is preferable to correction.* It is better to spend some effort on defect prevention than to spend a lot of effort on inspections and rework. Defects are understood as nonfulfillment of customer requirements and therefore, failure to satisfy the customer.

3. *Zero Defects is the quality standard.* This is the objective of the approach.
4. *Quality is measured as price of nonconformance.* Every defect represents costs, which sometimes may not be obvious. Defect costs include inspection time, rework, wasted material and labor, loss of revenue, and costs associated with customer dissatisfaction. The aim should be to quantify the price that has to be paid for nonconformance, as this yields several benefits. Quantification or measurement provides justification for costs created through quality improvement. Additionally, measurement allows tracking progress and thus, maintaining management commitment for improvement activities.

The concept of zero defects is of great importance in the context of continuous improvement and was an important step from quality control, which stands mainly for identification of defects, to quality assurance, which aims at prevention of defects. In consequence, this was also an important step toward TQM. Additionally, the concept of zero defects led to the development of the widely known Six Sigma methodology.

5.4.7 Six Sigma

Six Sigma (6σ) is widely associated with highly efficient, customer-focused companies that are able to reduce their costs while increasing customer satisfaction [25]. Six Sigma has its origins in statistics, as the term itself comes from statistics and Sigma describes variance. The main objective of Six Sigma is to reduce variance in processes and prevent defects that interfere with customer satisfaction. By achieving these goals, it becomes possible to reduce the costs of production processes and, furthermore, to continuously improve quality and achieve high customer satisfaction. Processes are analyzed by means of statistical methods, and a process operating at the Six Sigma level produces only 3.4 defects per million opportunities. Table 1.1 gives an overview of different Sigma levels. Note that every defect leads to certain costs and that there is a factor of approximately 2,000 when comparing the number of defects of level-4 and level-6 processes (see Table 5.1).

Although Six Sigma comes from statistical analysis and was introduced in manufacturing, by now it has developed into a broader framework that is also applied to software development. The term encompasses different concepts and tools supporting the achievement of nearly perfect processes and can also be applied beyond manufacturing. This is possible due to the understanding of the term defect, which can be nearly everything that leads to customer dissatisfaction. The Six Sigma framework is based on the following aspects [26]:

1. Prevention of defects
2. Reduction of variation
3. Focus on the customer
4. Decision making based on facts
5. Teamwork

Table 5.1 Number of defects on different Sigma levels

Sigma level	Percentage correct	Number of defects per million opportunities
3	93.3193	66,807
4	99.3790	6,210
5	99.9767	233
6	99.9997	3.4

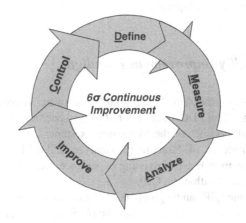

Fig. 5.8 The Six Sigma scheme

The Six Sigma framework contains methodologies for continuous improvement of processes as well as for the design of processes to satisfy Six Sigma requirements. The Define Measure Analyze Improve Control (DMAIC) method is used for process improvement and the Define Measure Analyze Design Verify (DMADV) method, also known as Design for Six Sigma (DFSS), is used for process design. Since this section focuses on process improvement, the DMAIC method will be introduced.

The DMAIC method can be used to find problems in existing processes and to improve the processes in order to solve the problems. It can also be used to expand the current capabilities of an existing process by identifying opportunities for improving the processes. The continuous DMAIC approach is represented in Fig. 5.8 and its phases are explained below [26]:

- Define: Identify the problem and the customers. Define and prioritize the customers' expectations and describe the current process on a high level. Initiate the improvement project.
- Measure: Confirm and quantify the problem by measurement. Measure the steps of the process to collect data about current processes. Revise and clarify the problem statement if necessary. Define the desired outcome of improvement.
- Analyze: Determine the cause of the problem and identify solutions to decrease the gap between the current performance level and the desired performance level.
- Improve: Prioritize the different available solutions. Then implement those solutions with the highest benefit for reaching the desired improvement.

- Control: Measure the improvements which were achieved and perform the maintenance of the improved process in order to ensure sustainability of the improvement.

After this presentation of the historical outline and evolution of TQM and further important continuous improvement approaches, the following sections will focus on other concepts of continuous improvement that were developed exclusively for the domain of software development.

5.4.8   The Quality Improvement Paradigm

The QIP is a six-step procedure for structuring software improvement activities [27]. The QIP is based on PDCA and tailored to the specifics of software development. Thus, the QIP consists of the following six steps: (1) Characterize, (2) Set Goals, (3) Choose Process, (4) Execute, (5) Analyze, and (6) Package (Fig. 5.9). In order to explicitly support reuse of existing experience, steps 1 and 6, in particular, are of great importance within the QIP.

The six steps of the QIP can be grouped into three phases: planning, performing, and evaluating the improvement activities. The planning phase at the start of a new improvement cycle is based on the explicit characterization of the initial situation and organizational context (step 1—characterize); the identification of desirable learning or improvement goals and associated hypotheses (step 2—set goals); and the development of a suitable plan, identification of (pilot) projects for investigating the hypotheses and selection of adequate processes for achieving the planned goals (step 3—choose process).

The performing phase consists of one step. The created plans guide the execution of the improvement or project as well as the collection of measurement (step 4—execute). The subsequent evaluation phase involves analyzing the performed actions with respect to the goals and hypotheses (step 5—analyze), and packaging the experience into reusable artifacts for future use (step 6—package). The analysis and packaging should allow for effective reuse in similar projects in the future and may even set future learning goals. Thus, the gained experience can be used to support the planning phase of further iterations of the QIP [28].

Due to the fact that software development is very context-specific, reuse of experience artifacts is usually achieved through the creation of models, which should fulfill the following requirements [27]:

- The experience models should be annotated with respect to their scope of validity (e.g., a defect profile is stored in step 6 together with a description of the project context it was gained from).
- The model can be tailored to a specific context (e.g., a defect profile originating from a project with highly experienced quality assurance engineers needs to be adapted if the actual project is performed with quality engineers having a low experience level).

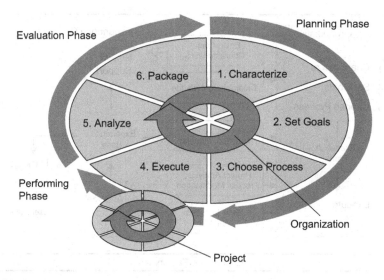

Fig. 5.9 Quality improvement paradigm (QIP)

- The selection of models should be based on a characterization of the actual situation (i.e., the context of a reused defect model needs to be applicable in the project where it will be used).
- The models should be systematically maintained over time. One reason for this may be, for instance, that relevant impact factors were not considered until now or project contexts have been changed. In consequence, existing models need to be maintained or new experience models need to be created.

The QIP can be implemented on the project level and on the level of an organization. If the QIP is implemented on the organizational level, step 4 has one or more nested QIP cycles for piloting the improvement on a small scale. Figure 5.9 displays the integration of a *project* feedback/learning QIP cycle (control cycle) and the *organization* feedback/learning QIP cycle (capitalization cycle).

5.4.9 The Experience Factory

The implementation and institutionalization of the QIP as an organizational structure is the Experience Factory (EF). The concept of the EF, which was proposed by Rombach and Basili [27], makes an explicit distinction between a project organization and an experience organization within the Experience Factory. The main reason for this is the fact that projects that are run within an organization usually aim at delivering specific results, which could be a product or a service, for instance. The success of such a project is measured based on the delivered result and, in consequence, as the capturing of project experience does not contribute directly to the project results, these activities are not regarded as important within

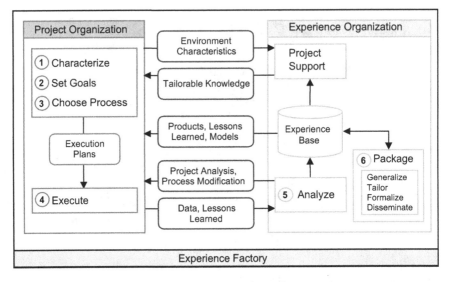

Fig. 5.10 Mapping of QIP steps onto the experience factory

the project organization. Therefore, an independent experience organization is suggested, whose primary goal is to capture experience from projects and transform this experience into reusable artifacts. The experience organization can be seen as an organizational unit that supports the project organization. The entire organizational setup of the Experience Factory is represented in Fig. 5.10 (adapted from [29]), where the steps of the QIP are mapped to the organizational units of the Experience Factory.

5.5 Process Improvement and Measurement: The GQM Approach

Measurement plays an important role in the context of process improvement and is, in fact, the core technique when it comes to the evaluation of the effects of process improvement. Only when the results of an improvement effort are measured and compared to the improvement goals is an evaluation of the success of the respective improvement effort possible. In consequence, measurement is at the very core of all improvement approaches. This section will briefly introduce a goal-oriented approach to measurement: the GQM method. GQM was developed by Basili and Weiss [30] and has evolved into a quasi-standard in the area of software development. GQM represents a systematic approach for tailoring and integrating measurement goals with models of the software processes, products, and quality perspectives of interest, based upon the specific needs of the project and the software domain of an organization.

GQM is explicitly goal-oriented, where goal-oriented means that measurement is not the purpose, but the tool to reach some superior goal. In practice, organizations often collect measurement data without knowing the purpose for which the data are collected. In such a situation of missing goal orientation, unnecessary measurement data are collected, which is a waste of valuable resources. On the other hand, there is often not enough appropriate data available to make definite statements with respect to organizational goals. In this situation, the organization or project acts based on insufficient information, which can lead to severe misjudgments. GQM can be used to resolve both situations and to provide the required information efficiently. Thus, GQM can be seen as a base technique for organizational measurement and improvement approaches.

The GQM approach ensures that measurement goals are defined explicitly by providing a formalization framework for the definition of measurement goals. This formalization framework basically consists of the following five questions that need to be answered [30]:

– What is the *object* that is being measured?
– What is the *purpose* of the measurement activities?
– Which *focus* of the object is of interest?
– Under which *viewpoint* is the object analyzed?
– What is the *context* in which the measurement activities happen?

Table 5.2 shows an example of possible GQM goal definitions:

Table 5.2 Example for GQM goal definition

	Examples	Example definition
Object	Process, product, other experience model, etc.	Analyze the system test process
Purpose	Characterize, evaluate, predict, motivate, improve, etc.	For the purpose of evaluation
Focus	Cost, correctness, defect removal, changes, reliability, user friendliness, etc.	With respect to defect slippage
Viewpoint	User, customer, manager, developer, corporation, etc.	From the point of view of the corporation
Context	Problem factors, people factors, resource factors, process factors, etc.	In the context of organization XY

After specification of the measurement goals, for every measurement goal, a set of quantifiable questions is derived. These questions are used to refine and operationalize the measurement goals. For every question, metrics are defined, and these metrics, in turn, specify the data that needs to be collected, which forms the basis of the measurement plan. Using the measurement plan, an organization can then collect measurement data. Finally, through the very nature of its structure, the GQM approach provides a framework for interpretation of the collected data. Thus, the GQM approach defines, top-down, what should be measured and provides, bottom-up, a way to interpret the measurement data (Fig. 5.11) [30]. In summary, the GQM approach ensures that, on the one hand,

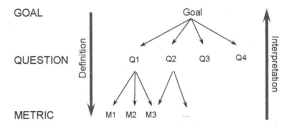

Fig. 5.11 The goal/question/metric paradigm

no unnecessary data are collected, and, on the other hand, that all required measurement data are available to make statements with respect to the defined questions and ultimately to reach the measurement goal (Fig. 5.11).

5.6 Aligning Improvement Goals and Strategies with Business

The previous sections discussed the two basic approaches to SPI, namely model-based and continuous improvement approaches. Both approaches represent different strategies for pursuing SPI within software organizations. One problematic aspect for both improvement strategies and associated goals is that they are usually not directly linked to business goals and thus to the contribution of business value. This does not mean that they have no value for a software organization, but rather that the characteristic of value contribution through improvement has an indirect nature and is difficult to show. In consequence, this value contribution might be questioned by management and software engineers may find themselves in a situation where they will need to advocate the value contribution of their improvement goals and strategies. This situation arises at the very beginning of an improvement endeavor, when stakeholders from management and engineering departments need to be convinced.

However, this situation might also occur in the course of or at certain milestones of an improvement endeavor, e.g., in the context of budget negotiations or during management reviews. In such situations, it is very important to be able to clearly show the value contribution of a specific improvement action. Thus, it is not sufficient to merely implement and follow an improvement strategy, but it is necessary to link the respective improvement strategy to the business goals of the organization. Linking the improvement strategy to business goals provides the necessary alignment of business goals and allows showing the direct value contribution. In order to quantify this value contribution, an approach to measurement is needed that explicitly integrates with high-level business goals and software measurement data.

In the area of strategic measurement systems, the concept of the BSC [31] is very popular. The BSC aims at aligning the organizational vision and strategies with its lower-level activities by defining a scoring-based measurement model that encompasses the most important organizational top-level dimensions. However, creating an effective measurement program is a very challenging task: It involves observation, experience facilitation, collaboration, decision making, analysis, and synthesis regarding goals and underlying context factors as well as assumptions. Furthermore, it assumes organizational learning and continuous evolvement of the measurement program. Thus, most organizations fall short of creating such an effective measurement program.

GQM⁺Strategies is a measurement approach that has its origins in software measurement and extends the established Goal Question Metric approach [32]. It adds the capability to create measurement programs that ensure alignment between business goals, strategies to reach these goals, associated software-specific (improvement) goals, and corresponding measurement goals.

This section will give a short introduction to the concept of the BSC and the GQM⁺Strategies approach. Furthermore, it will show how to align improvement goals and strategies with business goals within a software organization.

5.6.1 The Balanced Scorecard

The BSC [31] is a strategic management concept that aims at aligning a company's activities with its vision and strategy through the definition of a strategic measurement system. The BSC approach tries to measure whether the activities of a company are meeting its goals with respect to vision and strategy. BSC was initially developed by Robert S. Kaplan and David P. Norton and first published in 1992. Being a strategic management framework, the concept of the BSC originally aims at the top level of an organization [31]. At this level, the BSC helps to define and control organizational goals from the perspective of decision makers based on the definition of measures (called key performance indicators). The BSC framework differentiates four basic dimensions, which help to provide a holistic view of the organization. Figure 5.12 gives an overview of these dimensions, which are *financial, internal process, learning and growth*, as well as *customer perspectives* from an organizational point of view [33].

The *financial* dimension covers the financial aspects of the organization, e.g., revenues or costs. The *internal process* dimension describes the quality of internal processes, e.g., the time needed for product development. The *learning and growth* dimension covers aspects with respect to the organization's underlying capabilities for long-term development, e.g., the ratio of new vs. old products, or the rate with which high potentials leave the organization. Finally, the *customer* dimension investigates the organization's focus on its customers, e.g., customer satisfaction.

The operationalization of the BSC framework requires the definition of goals for the dimensions of the BSC, based on organizational characteristics. In order to derive goals and document relationships among them, the concept of the strategy map is used. A strategy map defines casual links between the four dimensions and goals and strategies that are related to them. For each goal of a BSC dimension, corresponding measures as well as target values are defined. The alignment of

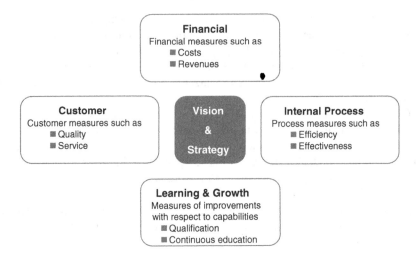

Fig. 5.12 The four BSC dimensions

different organizational levels or units is performed through the definition of corresponding measures that define objectives for lower levels. But the actual linkage and alignment of high-level measures to lower-level measures often remains implicit.

Nevertheless, the BSC is a widely adopted concept. It makes strategic goals explicit, defines measures for controlling the goals and sets target values, helps define causal chains for strategies in order to reach business goals, and is a widely adopted concept in the strategic management community. However, the definition of goals and measures is difficult and usually requires a lot of experience, and the goals and strategies on different organizational levels tend to be isolated from each other. In particular, there is no explicit linkage between measurements on the business level and on the project level; context and assumptions are missing, and typically, no interpretation models are defined.

5.6.2 GQM⁺Strategies

The GQM⁺Strategies[2] approach [32, 34, 35] addresses the need for a measurement-based approach that explicitly links goals and strategies through different organizational levels. Thus, it allows creating an alignment of business goals and strategies and lower-level (improvement) goals and strategies. Even though the development of the approach focused on software-related organizations, the basic

---

[2] GQM⁺Strategies is registered trademark no. 302008021763 at the German Patent and Trade Mark Office; international registration number IR992843.

Table 5.3 Terms used in GQM$^+$Strategies

Term	Definition
Business goal	Top-level goal an organization wishes to accomplish
Context factors	Environmental variables that represent the organizational environment and affect the kind of models and data that can be used
Assumptions	Estimated unknowns that can affect the interpretation of the data
Strategy	Planned and goal-oriented course of actions to achieve the defined goals at the respective organizational level
Lower-level goals	A set of goals inherited from upper-level goals as part of the upper-level goal strategy
GQM$^+$Strategies element	Conceptual element of the GQM$^+$Strategies grid that consists of a goal, strategies, context, and assumptions
GQM goal	Goal defined so that it can be measured using the GQM approach. A GQM goal is associated with goals at all levels and is used to measure the goal and strategy at the respective organizational level
Interpretation model	Model that helps interpret data to determine whether goals at all levels are achieved
GQM graph	Conceptual element of the GQM$^+$Strategies grid that consists of the GQM goal and associated questions and metrics as well as a corresponding interpretation model

concepts can be generalized to set up organization-wide measurement programs for controlling business goals and strategies as well as improvement goals and strategies on lower levels. GQM$^+$Strategies is based on the well-known GQM approach, which is in widespread use for creating and establishing measurement programs throughout the software industry. But the GQM approach never provided explicit support for integrating its software measurement model with elements of the larger organization, such as higher-level business goals and strategies.

GQM$^+$Strategies adds those needed extensions to GQM and thus, provides the capability to create measurement programs that provide alignment between business goals and strategies and lower-level goals and strategies. In particular, the approach can be used to define aligned (improvement) goals and strategies in a top-down or bottom-up fashion, based on the perspective and organizational role of the person applying the approach. In consequence, the GQM$^+$Strategies approach helps to clarify and harmonize goals and strategies across all levels of an organization, to communicate business goals throughout the whole organization, to align goals with strategies, to monitor the deployment strategy, and to obtain feedback about the success or failure of strategies and business goals.

Table 5.3 (adapted from [32]) provides an overview of terms that are frequently used in the GQM$^+$Strategies approach in order to support the understanding of the main concepts.

The definition of aligned goals and strategies across different organizational levels requires a structured way of modeling goals and strategies on the respective organizational levels. Furthermore, measurement models are needed to determine the success or failure of goals and strategies. Additionally, underlying assumptions and environmental factors need to be modeled in order to allow for informed

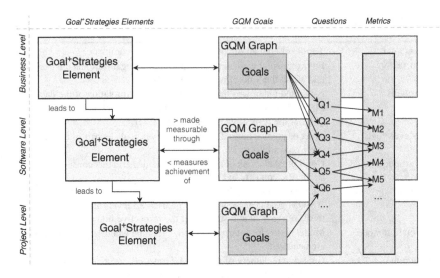

Fig. 5.13 Generic GQM+Strategies grid

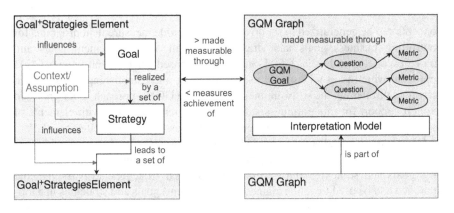

Fig. 5.14 GQM+Strategies conceptual model

decision making and interpretation, e.g., to determine the reasons why a specific strategy was not successful. The GQM⁺Strategies grid (Fig. 5.13) is the central component of the GQM⁺Strategies approach and addresses all these issues. The GQM⁺Strategies grid specifies goals and strategies across all organizational levels, including the measurement program needed for monitoring and controlling the respective goals and strategies and interpretation of results.

For modeling these grids, the GQM⁺Strategies approach provides the conceptual elements that are represented in Fig. 5.14 (adapted from [35]). Goal⁺Strategies elements (left side of Fig. 5.14) provide the capabilities to define linked sequences of goals and associated strategies.

The conceptual model [35] allows defining multiple goals for each organizational level, and for each goal, multiple strategies can be derived. Strategies describe a planned and goal-oriented course of actions to achieve the defined goals at the respective organizational level. A goal may be realized by a set of strategies, which may in turn lead to a sequence of goals. Additionally, Goal+Strategies elements provide the capabilities to capture the underlying rationales for the defined goals, strategies, and their linkages using context factors and assumptions. Context factors are environmental variables that represent the organizational environment. Assumptions are estimated aspects that can affect the interpretation of measurement data and, consequently, the interpretation of related goals and strategies. GQM+Strategies provides organizations not only with a mechanism for modeling goals and strategies, but also for defining measures consistent with larger, upper-level organizational objectives and for interpreting and rolling up the resulting measurement data at each level. For this purpose, GQM graphs (right side of Fig. 5.14) are defined at each goal level in order to measure the achievement of defined goals in combination with the chosen strategies. To this end, GQM measurement goals and derived questions and metrics, as well as an interpretation model, are defined. A GQM graph consists of a single GQM goal (which measures a Goal+Strategies element), corresponding questions, metrics, and interpretation models.

The conceptual model is supplemented by the GQM+Strategies derivation process (Fig. 5.15) for the definition of GQM+Strategies grids. The combination of the conceptual model and the derivation process provides a mechanism for organizations, not only for defining a GQM+Strategies grid, including measurement, consistent with upper-level organizational goals and strategies, but also for interpreting and

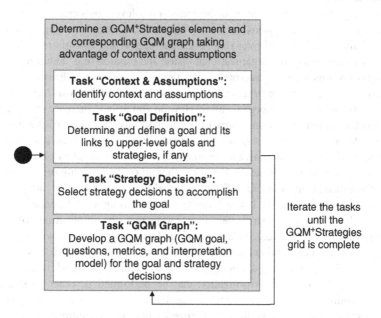

Fig. 5.15 GQM+Strategies grid derivation process

aggregating the resulting measurement data at each level. Figure 5.15 gives an overview of the GQM⁺Strategies grid derivation process and summarizes the tasks that need to be performed during the creation of a GQM⁺Strategies grid. As the process of creating the GQM⁺Strategies grid is usually iterative and based on strong interaction between different stakeholders, there is no fixed "best" order of performing these tasks. Moreover, this overview of tasks should help to define the respective levels within the GQM⁺Strategies grid.

It can be generally stated that the performance of these tasks can be divided into the definition of the GQM⁺Strategies elements, which constitute the basic structure of the to-be-defined GQM⁺Strategies grid, and the definition of the corresponding GQM measurement. The derivation process is iterated until all organizational levels (for which the measurement program is to be created) are defined. The following tasks are performed during the derivation process as described in [35].

- *Context and Assumptions:* Before defining the respective goals for an organization, the basic environment and motivation of the organization need to be determined and the rationales that lead to organizational goals need to be captured. Context factors explicitly characterize the organization and its environment and usually describe aspects like the organization's business model (i.e., products or services, customers, income sources), existing organizational processes and structures, as well as existing measurement programs. Assumptions document aspects which the stakeholders believe to be true but for which they have little or no empirical evidence. These aspects might include assumptions made about the technology, the market environment, future trends or organizational capabilities, and the workforce.
- *Goal Definition:* The definition of business or top-level goals can be supported by asking some basic questions, such as: What are the organizational principles upon which the organization thrives (e.g., organizational vision and mission)? What are the key elements of the organizational vision and mission (e.g., entrepreneurship, employee satisfaction, customer satisfaction, risk preference, learning environment)? Where does the organization want to be in 5 or 10 years? How do you define the success of the organization? How do you want to increase the success of the organization? What are current documented business goals of the organization? After compiling a list of top-level goals, conflicts and relationships between those goals should be analyzed. Furthermore, it is beneficial to prioritize these goals according to importance. Finally, either all or the most important goals can be formalized using the GQM⁺Strategies goal template (Table 5.4, adapted from [34]). The definition of lower-level goals has strong interdependencies with higher-level goals and strategies. In consequence, the implications of chosen upper-level strategies (e.g., strategies of the business level) on lower-level goals (e.g., software development-specific goals) have to be analyzed. Adequate lower-level goals need to be defined that help to achieve higher-level goals and strategies. Again, goal prioritization can be performed in order to select the most promising goals with respect to feasibility, cost, and benefit. These lower-level goals should then again be formalized using the goal template.

Table 5.4 GQM⁺Strategies goal formalization template

	Description	Examples
Activity	Activity that should be performed in order to accomplish the goal	Reducing, increasing, achieving, pursuing, or providing the main focus of the business goal
Focus	The main focus of the business goal	Cost, profit, turnover, market share, prestige, customer satisfaction
Object	The object of relevance	People, market, a project, collection of projects, customer
Magnitude (degree)	The quantification of the goal specified by a magnitude	X%, $YZ, A% increase
Timeframe	The timeframe in which the goal and the magnitude have to be achieved	X weeks, months or years, or permanently
Scope	The scope of the goal within the organization	The whole organization, a certain business unit, or a person
Constraints (limitations)	Basic constraints that may limit or interfere with accomplishing the goal	Limited influence on certain factors, laws, mission statement, and basic principles
Relations with other goals	Potential relations with other (complementary or competing) goals	Tradeoffs, conflicts, hierarchy, and ordering

– *Strategy Decisions:* Potential strategies for achieving the business goal need to be identified in this step. A strategy describes a planned and goal-oriented course of actions to achieve a defined goal at the respective organizational level. Multiple strategies may be defined and the most promising strategy has to be selected considering its costs and benefits, and taking into account context factors and assumptions that naturally restrict the feasibility of potential strategies.

– *GQM Graph:* Defining the GQM measurement plan for each GQM⁺Strategies grid level can be performed in parallel to the grid definition, but usually it is not an isolated task. Metrics derived across different levels of the GQM⁺Strategies grid can be reused and interpretation models for a higher-level goal may only be defined completely if the lower-level metrics and success criteria have already been modeled. The purpose of the GQM measurement plan is to evaluate the achievement of goals and strategies. Measurement goals need to be identified and the GQM goal template [32] (object, purpose, quality aspect, viewpoint, and context) is used for formalizing the chosen measurement goal. Based on the measurement goal, GQM questions and metrics as well as criteria for evaluating the achievement of the measurement goal are determined and the interpretation model is defined in order to aggregate and interpret the collected measurement data for decision making.

According to [35], there are three essential success factors for putting together an effective and sustainable measurement program:

Goal	Increase Customer Satisfaction						
Activity	Focus	Object	Magnitude	Timeframe	Scope	Constraints	Relations
Increase	Customer Satisfaction	Product "Mash"	Reduce number of customer complaints by 10%	12 weeks after release	Web Products Division	Mash price, functionality	Cost goals, schedule goals
Context	- Highly competitive market - Little control over development process - Limited budget			Assumptions	- Improving customer satisfaction will increase customer loyalty - Satisfaction can be measured by # of complaints - Many complaints are due to product reliability		

Strategy	Test reliability in		
Context		Assumptions	- Reducing defects by 20% reduces complaints by 10%

Fig. 5.16 Goal$^+$Strategies element

1. Definition of the right goals: Defining the right goals includes linking goals across all levels of the organization. Additionally, it is very important to identify the context and assumptions as well as the time frame and success criteria for each goal.
2. Collect the right data: Collecting the right data means quantifying and interpreting the goals at all levels. It is of particular importance to focus on maximizing the benefits as well as minimizing data collection and data analysis costs. This also includes taking maximum advantage of reusing and aggregating already existing data.
3. Define a sustainable measurement process: Defining a sustainable measurement process means institutionalizing measurement within your organization. This includes creating the right organizational structures for organizational learning, getting feedback to projects in a timely fashion, and maintaining commitment throughout all organizational levels.

The following example (adapted from [35]) will help to improve the understanding of the basic concepts of GQM$^+$Strategies:

Let us assume that company X builds a class of standard shrink-wrapped products for the general market. The products are sold directly to the customers and the organization has some measures in place to help manage the product lifecycle. The market for the kind of products that this company offers is very competitive. Customer satisfaction is seen as a major factor for securing market shares and remaining competitive, as satisfaction with the products implies customer loyalty. Management decides that in order to improve the current market position, an increase in customer satisfaction is required. Thus, the business level goal can be formalized as represented in the Goal$^+$Strategies element in Fig. 5.16:

Further assumptions for this goal are that the number of customer complaints is a feasible indicator for customer satisfaction. Additionally, it is assumed that many customer complaints are associated with reliability problems. Management concludes

GQM Goal	Object	Purpose	Focus	Viewpoint	Context
Customer Complaints Trend	Customer Complaints	Evaluation	Improvement in Customer Complaints	Quality Management	Web Products Division
Questions					
■ Q1: What is the trend in customer complaints? ■ Q1.1: How many customers complain 12 weeks after the Mash release? ■ Q1.2: How many customers complain for baseline products?					
Metrics					
CCR	CCM/CCB				Q1
CCM	Number of customer complaints in the first 12 weeks after release of Mash				Q1.1
CCB	Average number of customer complaints in the first 12 weeks after release of a set of baseline products				Q1.2
Decision criterion					
CCR <= 0.9 → Business Goal is achieved					

Fig. 5.17 GQM measurement model

that product reliability should be improved. In the following step, a strategic decision has to be made on how to achieve improvements in product reliability. Improvements in product reliability could be achieved by improving the development processes or by increasing testing capabilities. As budget and timeframe are important constraints, it becomes obvious that starting large process improvement initiatives is not a feasible strategy. Therefore, the organization decides to improve product reliability by increasing the testing capabilities. The assumption for this strategy is that reducing the number of defects by 20% will reduce customer complaints by 10% (Fig. 5.16).

In order to evaluate the success of the Goal$^+$Strategies element, a GQM measurement model has to be defined that analyzes the trend in customer complaints. Using the classic GQM approach, the measurement goal for the trend in customer complaints can be formalized:

Analyze the trend in *customer complaints* for the purpose of *evaluation* with respect to *improvement in customer complaints* from the point of view of *quality management* in the context of *Web Products Division*

For details of the GQM measurement model, see Fig. 5.17. From the measurement goal, questions can be refined and associated metrics can be derived. Thus, the trend in customer complaints is evaluated for the product Mash through an analysis of the ratio of customer complaints (CCR) that consists of customer complaints for Mash (CCM) and average customer complaints (measurement baseline CCB). The decision criterion describes the condition for success. Consequently, if CCR $\leq$ 0.9, the defined business goal is achieved within the defined timeframe.

Next, the business level strategy has to be refined to the next organizational level, which is the software level in our example. Based on the business level strategy of testing reliability in and the assumption that a defect reduction of 20% is required, the software level goal can be defined as "Improve system test effectiveness by 20%" (Fig. 5.16). The grid derivation process (Fig. 5.15) can now be

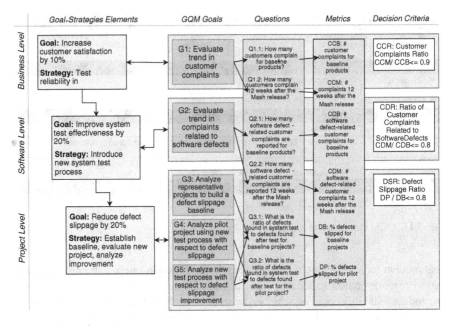

Fig. 5.18 GQM⁺Strategies grid example

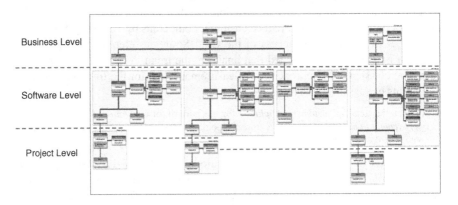

Fig. 5.19 Exemplary GQM⁺Strategies grid

performed on the software level and, in a subsequent iteration, also on the project level. A resulting GQM⁺Strategies grid is represented in Fig. 5.18.

In real life, GQM⁺Strategies grids may easily become very large, depending on the number of organizational levels, the goals on each level, and the strategies defined for each goal. Figure 5.19 shows a real-world GQM⁺Strategies grid that refines two organizational business-level goals to the software and project levels of an organization.

The GQM⁺Strategies approach strongly focuses on fulfilling specific business and measurement goals by creating explicit links from business goals all the way down to measures. It provides instructions on how to derive measures, yet is a generic approach that is widely applicable. However, stating (good) goals is not easy, but a necessary precondition. In general, the GQM⁺Strategies approach is an advanced approach that cannot be applied "out of the box," but must be tailored to an organization.

References

1. The Standish Group (2011) Welcome to the Standish Group International. http://www. standishgroup.com/. Accessed 11 Mar 2011
2. Humphrey WS (1989) Managing the software process. Addison-Wesley, Reading, MA
3. International Organization for Standardization (2006) ISO/IEC 15504:2004, 'Information technology—process assessment'. ISO/IEC, Geneva, Switzerland
4. Carnegie Mellon Software Engineering Institute (2010) Capability maturity model integration 1.3. http://www.sei.cmu.edu/cmmi/. Accessed 9 Jun 2011
5. International Organization for Standardization (2009) ISO/IEC ITC1 SC7 WG24, 'SLC profile and guidelines for VSE'. http://www.iso.org/iso/iso_technical_committee.html? commid=45086. Accessed 27 Jun 2011
6. Carnegie Mellon Software Engineering Institute (2002) Capability maturity model integration 1.2. http://www.sei.cmu.edu/cmmi/. Accessed 9 Jun 2011
7. Liggesmeyer P (2009) Software-Qualität: Testen, Analysieren und Verifizieren von Software. Spektrum Akademischer Verlag, Heidelberg
8. International Organization for Standardization (1995) ISO/IEC 12207:1995. ISO/IEC, Geneva, Switzerland
9. Automotive SIG (2007) Automotive SPICE process assessment model and SPICE process reference model
10. International Organization for Standardization (2008) ISO/IEC 15288, 'Systems and software engineering—system life cycle processes'. ISO, Geneva, Switzerland
11. Dale B (2003) Managing quality. Blackwell, Oxford
12. Moriguchi S (1997) Software excellence—a total quality management guide. Productivity Press, Portland, OR
13. Crosier T (1990) A guide for implementing total quality management, report SOAR-7. Reliability Analysis Center, Rome, NY
14. Kamiske GF, Brauer J (1999) Qualitätsmanagement von A bis Z. Carl Hanser Verlag, München Wien
15. Kanji KG, Asher M (1996) 100 Methods for total quality management. Sage, London
16. Feigenbaum AV (1951) Quality control: principles, practice, and administration. McGraw-Hill, New York
17. Liang Z (1991) Total quality control in education. In: Proceedings of the frontiers in education conference, September 1991, Purdue University, West Lafayette, IN, USA
18. Ishikawa K (1985) What is total quality control? The Japanese Way. Prentice Hall, Englewood Cliffs, NJ
19. Macedo J, Usano RR (1992) An expert system for conceiving company wide quality control strategies. In: Proceedings of 10th international conference of the system dynamics society, Utrecht, The Netherlands, 14–17 Jul 1992
20. Chu CH (1998) Topics in operations management quality and process reengineering, Pennsylvania state university course. http://net1.ist.psu.edu/chu/course/m428.htm#tqm1. Accessed 12 May 2011

21. Brunet AP, New S (2003) Kaizen in Japan: an empirical study. International Journal of Operations & Production Management 23(12):1426–1446
22. Brunet P (2000) Kaizen: from understanding to action. In: Seminar, Institution of Electrical Engineers (IEE), March 2000, pp 1/1–1/10
23. Crosby P (1979) Quality is free. McGraw-Hill, New York
24. Bellows WJ (2004) Conformance to specifications, zero defects, and six sigma quality—a closer look. International Journal of Internet and Enterprise Management 2(1)
25. Pan Z, Park H, Baik J, Choi H (2007) A Six Sigma framework for software process improvements and its implementation. In: Proceedings of the 14th Asia-Pacific software engineering conference, Nagoya, Japan, 5–7 Dec 2007
26. Tayntor CG (2003) Six Sigma software development. Auerbach Publications, Boca Raton, FL
27. Basili VR, Caldiera G, Rombach HD (1994) The experience factory. Wiley, New York
28. Althoff KD, Bomarius F, Tautz C (1998) Using case-based reasoning technology to build learning software organizations, IESE-Report No. 037.98/E, Fraunhofer IESE, Kaiserslautern, Germany
29. Bomarius F, Feldmann RL (2006) Get your experience factory ready for the next decade: ten years after 'How to build and run one', IESE-Report No. 075.06/E. Fraunhofer Institute for Experimental Software Engineering IESE, Kaiserslautern, Germany
30. Basili VR, Weiss DM (1984) A methodology for collecting valid software engineering data. IEEE Transactions on Software Engineering 10(6):728–738
31. Kaplan RS, Norton DP (1992) The balanced scorecard—measures that drive performance. Harvard Business Review (February) 1992:71–79
32. Basili V, Heidrich J, Lindvall M, Münch J, Regardie M, Rombach HD, Seaman C, Trendowicz A (2007) Bridging the gap between business strategy and software development. In: Proceedings of the international conference on information systems (ICIS), Montréal, Canada, 9–12 Dec 2007
33. Kaplan RS, Norton DP (1996) The balanced scorecard: translating strategy into action. Harvard Business School Press, Boston, MA
34. Basili V, Heidrich J, Lindvall M, Münch J, Regardie M, Rombach HD, Seaman C, Trendowicz A (2007) GQM+Strategies®: a comprehensive methodology for aligning business strategies with software measurement. In: Proceedings of the DASMA-Software-Metrik-Kongresses (MetriKon 2007), Kaiserslautern, Germany, 15–16 Nov 2007
35. Basili V, Heidrich J, Lindvall M, Münch J, Regardie M, Rombach HD, Seaman C, Trendowicz A (2009) Determining the impact of business strategies using principles from goal-oriented measurement. In: Proceedings of the 9th Internationale Tagung Wirtschaftsinformatik, Vienna, Austria, 25–27 Feb 2009

Chapter 6
Empirical Studies

This chapter introduces the role of empirical studies for software process engineering as an aid in determining the effects of a process model in a concrete environment. Such effects can be, for instance, the reliability of a developed code module, the defect detection rate of an inspection process, or the effort distribution of a lifecycle process model. Software processes are, to a large extent, human-based and consequently nondeterministic. In addition, they are heavily context dependent, i.e., their effects vary with the development environment. Therefore, empirical studies of different types are needed to understand and determine the effects of processes and to analyze risks when changing processes or introducing new ones. This chapter introduces controlled experiments as a means to evaluate process effects in a tightly controlled environment, case studies as a means to evaluate such effects in a typical environment, and surveys as a means to explore such effects on a large scale, with very little control over the context. Finally, experiment sequences as a means to learn from a number of (related or unrelated) empirical studies are described. Figure 6.1 displays the chapter structure.

Fig. 6.1 Chapter structure

6.1 Objectives of This Chapter

After reading this chapter, you should be able to:

- Distinguish and explain different experiment types
- Know when to select which type
- Know the benefits of conducting empirical studies

J. Münch et al., *Software Process Definition and Management*,
The Fraunhofer Series on Software and Systems Engineering,
DOI 10.1007/978-3-642-24291-5_6, © Springer-Verlag Berlin Heidelberg 2012

6.2 Experiments

Due to the ever-increasing demands on software (better, faster, cheaper), software development has changed a lot during the past 50 years. On the one hand, small programs written by single persons have evolved into gigantic "code monsters" developed and maintained by hundreds or thousands of people. In addition, software fulfills more functions every day, particularly critical ones, thus increasing complexity even more. On the other hand, business and technological environments change so fast that innovative software needs to be developed in a rapid and flexible way at acceptable quality levels. To cope with this, new techniques, methods, and tools are being developed constantly. New programming paradigms and languages are being introduced to improve the quality of software development and the resulting products.

There is, however, no silver bullet for software development. Each tool or programming paradigm has its own benefits and disadvantages. The hugely popular object-oriented programming, for example, makes construction of large systems possible in the first place and improves product quality in most cases. Nevertheless, engine control software is still being developed mostly in a functional manner, because using object-oriented technology would make the system more complex and slower.

This example makes it clear that there must be some kind of evaluation for new processes. No engineer would build a bridge with new and untested material. The same applies to software engineers: Using a new process without testing it properly may result in a disaster, namely low product quality and time/cost overruns.

One of the key elements of software process engineering is the proposal of new or the modification of existing process models, e.g., for reducing costs or improving product quality. For example, implementing a new inspection technique will most probably influence the time needed for defect detection and possibly correction, as well as the costs for these activities. To reflect this in an appropriate model, three possible ways to arrive at a new model can be distinguished. Either an existing model can be adapted, or a new model is introduced based on theoretical considerations, or a new model may be derived from observation. There are also combinations of two or all three ways.

When a new process model is introduced, adequate measures must be formulated so that the behavior of the model (compared to reality) can be evaluated. Often, this would be efficiency (e.g., the number of defects found per hour) and effectiveness (e.g., the total number of defects found). When evaluating a process model for the first time, this can be done through experiments.

Experiments are called "real" (as opposed to "virtual") if they feature real people spending real time on solving (possibly constructed) problems in a real-world environment. This costs time and money, because the people taking part in the experiment cannot do their normal work. This illustrates one characteristic feature of software (process) engineering: human involvement. Unlike other sciences such as chemistry or physics, software (process) engineering experiments heavily involve

Table 6.1 Classification by number of treatments and teams

Number of teams per treatment	Number of treatments	
	1	m
1	1:1 (case study)	1:m
n	n:1 (replicated experiment)	n:m (controlled experiment)

humans, and are in turn heavily influenced by human behavior. The psychological aspect is similarly important in software (process) engineering as in typical social sciences like anthropology, political science, psychology, and sociology.

The purpose of an experiment is usually to prove a hypothesis. A hypothesis is a supposed connection between a number of (controlled) input variables and a certain result. The experiment should either prove the correctness of the hypothesis or show that it is wrong. A null hypothesis symbolizes the opposite state to that suggested in a hypothesis, postulated in the hope of rejecting it and therefore proving the hypothesis. For example, if the hypothesis states "Reading technique A is more efficient than reading technique B," then the null hypothesis would be "Reading technique B is more efficient or equal to reading technique A."

An experimental *treatment* defines all kinds of measures a team is exposed to in an experiment in order to make statements after the treatment about a hypothesis defined prior to the treatment. One commonly used classification distinguishes the number of experimental treatments and teams. Table 6.1 gives an overview of the possible combinations [1].

A 1:1 situation does not provide reliable information for comparisons. The results may completely depend on the team members who were assigned to the experiment (experimental subjects), or on the task the team was supposed to deal with (experimental object). There is no way to know how much each of the two extremes influenced the result.

For example, if a team performs very badly in a defect detection experiment, this may be because team competence in this specific area is low, or because the reading technique used was not appropriate, or a combination of both. Without further information, there is no way to tell. 1:1 settings may be used as a proof of concept, though, or to check in which areas current processes may be improved. Case studies usually are conducted as a 1:1 experiment type.

A 1:m situation already enables the experimenter to have one team solve several problems. This enables him/her to evaluate whether team performance is caused by a certain method (the team performs poorly using one method, but well using another) or by the team itself (the team performs poorly using any method). Still, the methods may all be bad, thus making the team perform badly although it is not a bad team per se. Additionally, it is difficult to exclude learning effects throughout the treatments.

Using more than one team makes experiments more expensive. Having n teams replicate a single experiment (n:1 setting) enables the experimenter to assess team performance as well as an average for the method examined in the treatment. Still,

Table 6.2 Characteristic factors of real experiments

Factor	Survey	Case study	Controlled experiment
Execution control	None	Low	High
Investigation cost	Low	Medium	High
Ease of replication	High	High	High

this does not allow for comparing different approaches. This approach is often chosen to prove the validity of findings or to examine the benefits of a new method or technique in greater detail. The experiment is set up and conducted by one team and is replicated by other teams to validate the results.

The only approach for comparing different solutions for a problem in one experiment is the laboratory experiment, also referred to as controlled or formal experiment. Using an *n:m* setting, several teams perform several tasks. This provides information about how the methods compare (relatively) and how the respective team influenced the results. Unfortunately, this type of experiment is the most expensive one.

An *n:m* setting requires an amount of control that can typically only be achieved in laboratory environments. Conducting an *n:m* experiment in an industrial setting would increase project costs extremely, so most controlled experiments can be found in facilities such as universities or research institutes. Because of the high costs and the number of variables monitored, controlled experiments mostly have a very narrow focus. Table 6.2 gives an overview of the experiments described in this chapter and some of their characteristic factors.

Three of the most commonly used experiment types will be introduced briefly: controlled experiments, case studies, and surveys. Controlled experiments and case studies may be used to verify a newly introduced model very well, whereas surveys usually help in determining the current state of the practice and major causes of undesired effects.

The three experiment types differ in the types of variables that are considered. An overview is given in Fig. 6.2. Dependent variables are influenced by independent variables and therefore not considered separately. There are two types of independent variables: controlled ones and not controlled ones. Typically, the experimenter aims at lowering the number of controlled variables to save effort, and to choose the "right" ones for the respective context. The uncontrolled variables are to be kept as constant as possible, and also as representative for the respective context as possible. This prevents uneven influence on the experiment and describes the context well.

6.2.1 Controlled Experiments: Research in the Small

A controlled experiment aims at completely controlling the experimental environment. In the field of software engineering, this includes the number and expertise of

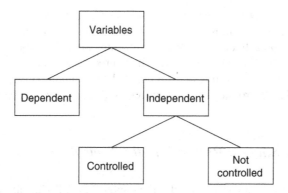

Fig. 6.2 Variable types in experiments

the test persons, the tasks they are given, but also variables like the time of the day at which the experiment takes place, or the room temperature. Because of this high level of control, controlled experiments are also called laboratory experiments. The tasks examined in the experiment vary from real problems taken from earlier software projects to completely imagined situations.

If a new defect detection method were being checked for efficiency, for example, it would be a good idea to use real documents from an older project. By doing so, two benefits can be achieved: First, an average real-world problem is present. This ensures that the results are not only some academic insights, but do help with everyday work. Second, comparing the new method against the currently used one is easy. The number and severity of errors remaining in the documents after defect detection with the new method may be weighed against the time consumed, and so the method may be compared against the "traditional" one. Of course, this only works if the test persons do not know the test data; in other words, if they were not part of the project, because in this case, they might not really detect the defects, but rather remember them.

If test subject knowledge or project confidentiality prevents the usage of real data as experimental material, then artificial data must be used. This could be specially created documents or a complete training system, which is developed and maintained exclusively for experimentation purposes. Still, help with a problem that really exists is the purpose of the experiment, so there should at least be some relationship to actual development in order to ensure that the results are not purely academic.

Made-up problems may also be used for comparing several new methods. Here, the problem may be specially tailored to the methods, focusing on areas with special interest. In our example, if project experience has shown a great density of interface problems, documents with a complex interface structure could be artificially created to test the new methods very intensively in this area. Creating a new scenario that has never happened before, but might happen someday and possibly have very severe consequences, could be a third area where this kind of experiment could be used.

Conducting a controlled experiment, however, requires significant amounts of both time and money. In most cases, an $n{:}m$ setting as described above is used. Due to this costly approach and the amount and complexity of the data acquired, only small portions of the software development process are analyzed in this way. Examples might include testing of different reading techniques in a defect detection process or different programming languages for solving specific problems.

6.2.2   Case Studies: Research in the Typical

A case study does not try to control all variables, but still aims at identifying the significant ones before the project starts. Once this is done, their status is recorded and monitored throughout the study in order to identify their influence on the results. This makes case studies suitable for industrial use because projects are only influenced on a minor scale: The number of values measured as well as project documentation (other than product documentation) may increase slightly, but this is only a minor "add-on" and does not require enormous amounts of extra time and money.

The most commonly recorded variables are inputs, constraints, and resources (technical and human). Most of the time, a single current software project is examined. Usually, only one team per task is scheduled, so the 1:1 setting is typical for a case study.

The case study approach can be found far more often in industry than the controlled experiment. This is because case studies can be conducted concurrent to the real project without enormous extra expenses. A sensible approach for process changes would be to alter a small part of the development process, small enough to prevent great problems for the overall process, but large enough to notice possible time and money savings, and then conduct a case study for a project with the new process. There is still a risk of confusing team influence and process influence, but in a software organization, it is possible to estimate team performance from other projects, thus making the extraction of process influence fairly accurate.

Because case studies only pay special attention to factors that are typical for the current situation, instead of controlling the complete environment, they are quite popular. Plenty of knowledge about project progression may be achieved at relatively low costs in a realistic setting.

6.2.3   Surveys: Research in the Large

In contrast to case studies where monitored variables are defined before the project starts, surveys are retrospective studies: The occurrence that is to be examined has already taken place. This means that typically, the survey is planned and conducted after the project is finished [2]. The focus of surveys is on larger-scale relationships and not so much on details. The experimenter tries to collect as much data as can be found, evaluate it, and determine connections between the discovered factors and the results. An analogy would be an assessment in a company: There is no influence of the survey on the project and the data available. The experimenter can only use whatever data were recorded throughout the project. Examples of surveys can be found in [3] and [4].

This shows one great risk of surveys: If, from comparison to past projects, a survey states that a certain factor combination has a significant effect on the project outcome, this may be an incorrect assumption. The observed effect might not have been caused by the formulated factor combination, but by another reason that was not discovered because it was not recorded during the project.

Of course, this risk does not only exist in surveys, but also in laboratory experiments and case studies, where the researcher has the possibility to set the monitored variables. The difference is that in laboratory experiments and case studies, the experimenter can use his/her experience to minimize the risks of mistakes such as not measuring important variables. A normal project usually is not explicitly set up to later support a survey, but rather to achieve the desired goals at minimum costs. Hence, the risk that important variable data is missing is greater in surveys than in laboratory experiments and case studies.

The results of a survey are usually not as detailed and "hard" as results from a case study or a controlled experiment. If a significant cause for a certain undesired effect was (supposedly) detected, a more thorough investigation may need to be undertaken to refine the findings. This may be done in the form of a case study or a formal experiment, depending on the situation. A case study may be conducted if a strong indication exists that a certain factor influences the result significantly, and there is a proposal to improve that factor with only a limited risk of failure. If there are several improvement proposals, or if it is not even sure which factor(s) are to be altered, a formal experiment may help to reduce the risk for everyday business, at higher experimentation costs.

6.2.4 Experiment Sequences

One of the biggest problems with experiments is comparing and evaluating the results. This is easy to understand when we look at surveys or case studies, because here, the context can only be described, and typically not changed. Nevertheless, why is this also difficult with controlled experiments? Was not one of their advantages the complete control of all variables, including the context?

Controlling all variables makes the results very valid—in the respective context. For example, Fagan argues that most defects would be detected during team meetings [5], whereas McCarthy et al. [6] and Votta [7] come to the opposite

Table 6.3 Exemplary setup for a planned experiment sequence

Team	Thesis	Task report	Application
1	X	X	
2	X		X
3		X	X

conclusion. The context is very different in all three cases. So which study is "correct" and which one is not? This question cannot be answered, because in their respective contexts, all three are correct.

Recording the context with every study is very important to evaluate the outcome. However, to arrive at a more comprehensive view of the software development process, all the different studies must be combined somehow. Their "essence" must be extracted and combined. This can be done by looking at all experiments in one process area (e.g., requirements specification, defect detection) as a sequence of experiments. Common variables and phenomena may then be detected and included in the global model.

Experiment sequences may be planned or unplanned. A planned experiment sequence usually consists of a number of teams conducting a number of experiments. An unplanned sequence collects experimental data from many experiments and extracts commonalities and differences. In most cases, the majority of the teams will take part only in one experiment, and the experiments usually examine similar phenomena.

An example of an unplanned experiment sequence can be found in [8]. Here, the author examined a large number of experiments (surveys, case studies, and laboratory experiments) and extracted factors that influence the progression and results of software inspections. The factors form a complex network of interrelations. Only very few common factors were found in every experiment that was reviewed. The combination of the experiments showed new correlations that would not have been obvious when regarding every experiment individually.

The question of context, however, still has not been answered satisfactorily. How can factors be included that significantly influence the process only sometimes? Here, for example, a model of the software development process would need to be tailored to the specific situation. Context information is mandatory and must be individually determined for each situation. Depending on the context, some factors may be left out at some point, while others are added. More research is needed here to determine when to include what.

A planned experiment sequence, on the other hand, might consist of several teams carrying out several tasks. For the purpose of evaluating a word processor, these tasks might be writing a 50-page thesis with few figures, writing a five-page report with lots of formulae, and writing a one-page application for a scholarship. One possible experimental setup is depicted in Table 6.3. By shuffling teams and tasks, both team performance and tool capability can be evaluated.

Unplanned experiment sequences may be used when findings from isolated experiments are to be generalized and supported by a broader foundation.

Analyzing many experiments concerning similar phenomena can lead to new conclusions and explanations, better than a single experiment would. In addition, case studies and surveys are often too hard to coordinate with each other to form a planned experiment sequence.

Planned experiment sequences may be used to break up tasks too complex to be investigated in a single *n:m* laboratory approach. By conducting an experiment sequence, the researcher may examine a complex phenomenon over several years without losing his/her focus.

6.3 Benefits

Following Basili et al. [9], benefits in the following areas can be expected from experiments in software engineering:

- *Basis.* Experiments provide a basis for the needed advancement in knowledge and understanding. Through experiments, the nature of the software development process can be assessed and evaluated.
- *Process and product effects.* Experiments help to evaluate, predict, understand, control, and improve both the software development process and the product.
- *Model and hypothesis development and refinement.* In iterations, models are built and hypotheses about the models are postulated. These hypotheses can be tested by experiments and then be refined, or new models can be constructed.
- *Systematic learning.* In a rather young profession such as software engineering, where there is still very much to learn, it is important to follow a systematic approach rather than intuition.

References

1. Rombach HD, Basili VR, Selby RW (1993) Experimental software engineering issues: a critical assessment and future directions. Proceedings of the International Workshop, Dagstuhl Castle, Germany. Lecture Notes in Computer Science 706, Springer, Heidelberg, 14–18 Sept 1992
2. Wohlin C, Suneson P, Höst M, Ohlsson MC, Regnell B, Wesslén A (2000) Experimentation in software engineering: an introduction. Kluwer Academic, Boston, MA
3. Meyer A (2002) Wer verdient wie viel? http://www.heise.de/artikel-archiv/ct/2002/06/110. Accessed 27 June 2011
4. Lurie M (2002) Winning database configurations: an IBM Informix Database survey. http://www7b.software.ibm.com/dmdd/zones/informix/library/techarticle/lurie/0201lurie.html. Accessed 27 June 2011
5. Fagan ME (1976) Design and code inspections to reduce errors in program development. IBM Syst J 15(3):182–211
6. McCarthy P, Porter AA, Siy HP, Votta LG (1996) An experiment to assess cost-benefits of inspection meetings and their alternatives: a pilot study. In: Proceedings of the 3rd international software metrics symposium (METRICS), Berlin, Germany, pp 100–111

7. Votta LG (1998) Does every inspection really need a meeting? Empirical Software Eng 3(1):9–35
8. Armbrust O (2002) Developing a characterization scheme for inspection experiments
9. Basili VR, Selby RW, Hutchens DH (1986) Experimentation in software engineering. IEEE T Software Eng 12(7):733–743

Chapter 7
Software Process Simulation

This chapter introduces software process simulation as a means to amend and complement empirical studies, for example, to evaluate changing contexts and to analyze process dynamics. It introduces two types of simulation models, namely continuous and discrete-event models, as well as their combination in hybrid models. In addition, this chapter describes a systematic method for the creation of simulation models and introduces an existing library of simulation model components that can be easily reused. Finally, it explains how process simulation can be combined with empirical studies to accelerate process understanding and improvement. Figure 7.1 displays the chapter structure.

Fig. 7.1 Chapter structure

7.1 Objectives of This Chapter

After reading this chapter, you should be able to:

– Explain the role of simulation in software process engineering
– Name and explain the two major types of software process simulation
– Explain their combination into hybrid simulation
– Understand the development of a simulation model

J. Münch et al., *Software Process Definition and Management*,
The Fraunhofer Series on Software and Systems Engineering,
DOI 10.1007/978-3-642-24291-5_7, © Springer-Verlag Berlin Heidelberg 2012

7.2 Software Process Simulation

While experiments are a valuable tool for evaluating the effects of a specific process (change), it may not always be possible to perform such experiments. In this case, simulations may help.

Software process engineering has only recently started to discover the possibilities of simulation. In this section, the benefits of process simulations will be discussed, as well as the question of what to simulate. Two different simulation approaches will be introduced later in this chapter, as will their combination.

Three main improvement classes benefitting from software development process simulation can be identified: cost, time, and knowledge improvements. Cost improvements originate from the fact that conventional experiments are very costly. The people needed as experimental subjects are usually employees. This makes every experimentation hour expensive, since the subjects get paid while not immediately contributing to the company's earnings. Conducting a simulation instead of a real experiment saves the expenses for experimental subjects.

Time benefits can be expected from the fact that simulations can be run at (almost) any desired speed. While an experiment with a new project management technique may take months, the simulation may be sped up almost arbitrarily by simply having simulation time pass faster than real time. On the other hand, simulation time may be slowed down arbitrarily. This is done when simulating biological processes, for example. It might be useful in a software engineering context when too much data is accumulated within too little time and therefore cannot be analyzed properly. While in the real world, decisions would have to be based on partial information, the simulation can be stopped and the data analyzed. When the analysis is complete, the simulation can be continued with a decision based on the completely analyzed data.

Knowledge improvements stem mainly from two areas: Simulation can be used for training purposes and experiments can be replicated in different contexts. Training software engineers in project management, for example, requires a lot of time. The trainee needs to make mistakes to learn from, which in turn cost time and money in the project, and has to be instructed to prevent him from making really bad mistakes that would cost even more time and money. Training people in a laboratory setting might be even worse. Using a simulation environment such as the one introduced in [1] enables the trainee to experience immediate feedback to his decisions. The consequences of choosing a certain reading technique, for example, do not occur months after the decision, but minutes. In this way, the complex feedback loops can be better understood and mistakes can be made without endangering everyday business.

Simulations can also be used to replicate an experiment in a different context, for example with less experienced subjects. If the properties of the experimental objects are sufficiently explored, the consequences of such changes can be examined in simulations instead of costly experiment replications. Learning from simulations can save both time and money compared to real experiments.

Another useful application of simulation is high-risk process modifications. These may be (yet) uncommon processes or catastrophe simulations. An example of the former is Extreme Programming, which seemed to contradict many software engineering principles of documentation and planning at first, but has proved to be beneficial in certain situations after all. When high-risk process changes are to be examined, simulations can provide a sandbox in which the changes can be tried out without any consequences. If the results show the proposed changes to be a complete letdown, at least no money was spent on expensive experiments.

A catastrophe simulation can investigate extreme process changes, for example, the loss of key personnel in a project. While it is clear that this will influence the process and its outcome noticeably, determining quantitative effects can only be done in an experiment. Will a project be delayed by 20% or by 200%? What about product quality? Since this situation rarely occurs, this kind of real experiment is not conducted because of the high costs associated with it. A simulation does not have such high costs. It probably also does not forecast the exact numbers, but nevertheless, it shows their magnitude and, as its main benefit, helps to better understand the situation and problem/challenge at hand. It may also show key problem areas, which may then be addressed in real life in order to absorb the worst consequences of the hypothetical catastrophe.

The following classification of simulations follows Kellner et al. [2]. Kellner et al. have determined relationships between a model's purpose and what has to be modeled, and have classified approaches on how to simulate.

When a simulation is to be set up, the first question to be answered is about the *purpose*. What is the simulation to be used for? Is it for strategic planning, or for training, or for operational process improvement? After having answered this question, it is possible to determine *what to include* in the simulation and *what to leave out*. To structure this decision, the *model scope, result variables, process abstraction,* and *input parameters* can be distinguished.

The *model scope* must be adapted to the model purpose. Let us say a software company wants to test a new reading technique for defect detection. Clearly, the inspection process must be modeled, but changes to the reading technique will most likely have other effects later in the development process. The defect density might be higher, therefore lowering product quality and increasing rework time. This must be considered in the model because, otherwise, the impact of the process change will not be reflected correctly in the model.

According to Kellner et al. [2], the model scope usually ranges from a part of the lifecycle of a single product to long-term organizational considerations. They introduced two subcategories: *time span* and *organizational breadth*. *Time span* is proposed to be divided into three subcategories: less than 12 months, 12–24 months, and more than 24 months. *Organizational breadth* considers the number of product/project teams: less than one, exactly one, or multiple teams involved.

The *result variables* are mandatory for answering the questions posed when determining the model purpose. Variables can be thought of as information sources in an abstract sense here; however, most models include variables such as costs, effort, time consumption, staffing needs, or throughputs. The choice of variables once again depends on the purpose of the model. If the purpose is to predict overall end-of-project effort, different variables must be measured than the ones needed for predictions at the end of every major development step.

Questions like these also influence the *level of abstraction* at which the model is settled. If effort at every major development step is to be determined, the model probably needs finer granularity than if only overall end-of-project effort is the focus. In any case, it is important to identify key activities and objects (documents) as well as their relationships and feedback loops. In addition, other resources such as staff and hardware must be considered. Depending on the level of abstraction, this list will get more or less detailed.

Finally, *input parameters* must be determined. They depend largely on the desired output variables and the process abstraction. In general, many parameters are needed for software process simulation; the model by Abdel-Hamid and Madnick [3] requires several hundreds. Kellner et al. [2] provide some examples: effort for design and code rework, defect detection efficiency, personnel capabilities, etc. Figure 7.2 illustrates the relationships among the aspects described above according to [2].

After determining the purpose of the model and what to include, the *choice of a simulation technique* is next. The continuous and the discrete simulation approaches will be introduced in Sects. 7.2.1 and 7.2.2, as will their combination (Sect. 7.2.3). In addition to that, there are several state- and rule-based approaches as well as queuing models [4].

Simulation techniques may be distinguished into *visual* and *textual models*. Most models support some kind of visual modeling today in order to facilitate

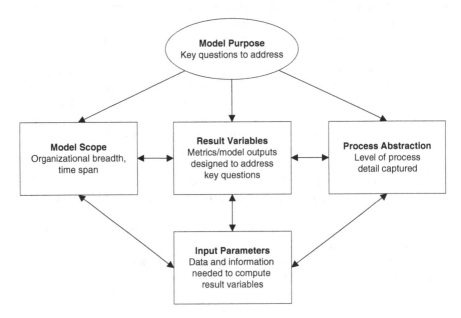

Fig. 7.2 Relationships among model aspects

development of the models. Some modeling tools support a semiautomatic validation functionality, e.g., Fraunhofer IESE's Spearmint [5]. Appropriate possibilities for specifying interrelationships among entities of the model enable accurate modeling of the real world. Continuous output of result variables as opposed to only presenting the results allows monitoring the simulation run and providing early intervention. Interactive simulations allow for altering input variables during execution.

Simulations can be entirely deterministic, entirely stochastic, or a mix of both. Entirely deterministic models use input parameters as single values without variation. The simulation needs to be run only once to determine its results. A stochastic simulation assumes random numbers out of a given probability distribution as input parameters. This recognizes the inherent uncertainty in software development, especially when evaluating human performance. Consequentially, several runs are needed to achieve a stable result. Batch runs of simulations with changed input parameters simplify this approach significantly.

A sensitivity analysis explores the effects of input variable variations on the result variables. This has two advantages: First, the researcher knows how much variation in the results has to be expected due to variations in input parameters, and second, he/she can identify the parameters with the biggest influence on the result. These should be handled and examined with special care.

Finally, to obtain valid results from the simulation, calibrating the simulation model against the real world is necessary. This should be done by integrating actually measured data into the model and comparing the results of simulations of real processes with the respective real-world values. Accurate measuring of input parameters and result variables is mandatory here. In many cases, however, no suitable real-world data is available. In this case, Kellner et al. [2] suggest trying to construct the data needed from available data (e.g., constructing cost data from effort data) or retrieving it from original documents, rather than final reports, or obtaining estimates from the staff or from published values.

7.2.1   Continuous Simulation

In 1972, the Club of Rome started an initiative to study the future of human activities on our planet. The initiative focused on five physical and easily measurable quantities: population, food production, industrial capital, production, and nonrenewable natural resources [6]. A research group at the Massachusetts Institute of Technology (MIT) developed a societal model of the world. This was the first continuous simulation model: the World Model [7].

Today, most continuous models are based on differential equations and/or iterations, which use several input variables for calculation and in turn supply output variables. The model itself consists of nodes connected through variables. The nodes may be instantaneous or noninstantaneous functions. Instantaneous functions present their output at the same time the input is available. Noninstantaneous functions, also called memory functions, take some time for their output to change.

This approach of a network of functions allows simulating real processes continuously. An analogy would be the construction of mathematical functions (add, subtract, multiply, integrate) with analog components like resistors, spools, or condensers. Even complex functions containing partial differential equations that would be difficult or impossible to solve analytically or numerically may be modeled using the three basic components mentioned above. Before computers became as powerful as they are today, the analog approach was the only way to solve this kind of equations within a reasonable amount of time. Due to the continuous nature of the "solver," the result could be measured instantly.

Of course, simulating this continuous system on a computer is not possible due to the digital technology used. To cope with this, the state of the system is computed at very short intervals, thereby forming a sufficiently correct illusion of continuity. This iterative recalculating makes continuous models simulated on digital systems grow complex very fast.

In software engineering contexts, continuous simulation is used primarily for large-scale views of processes, like the management of a complete development project or strategic company management. Dynamic modeling enables us to model feedback loops, which are very numerous and complex in software projects. The-well-known System Dynamics framework for continuous simulation models is described in great detail in [8].

7.2.2   Discrete-Event Simulation

The discrete approach shows parallels to clocked operations like those used by car manufacturers in production. The basic assumption is that the modeled system changes its state only at discrete moments of time, as opposed to the continuous model. So, every discrete state of the model is characterized by a vector containing all variables, and each step corresponds to a change in the vector.

Example. Let us consider a production line at a car manufacturer. Simplified, there are parts going in on one side and cars coming out on the other side. The production itself is clocked: Each work unit has to be completed within a certain amount of time. When that time is over, the car-to-be is moved to the next position, where another work unit is applied. (In reality, the work objects move constantly at a very low speed. This is done for commodity reasons and to realize minimal time buffer. Logically, it is a clocked sequence.) This way, the car moves through the complete factory in discrete steps.

Simulating this behavior is easy with the discrete approach. Each time a move is completed, a snapshot is taken of all production units. In this snapshot, the state of all work units and products (cars) is recorded. At the next snapshot, all cars have moved to the next position. The real time that passes between two snapshots or simulation steps can be arbitrary. Usually the next snapshot of all variables is calculated and then the simulation assigns the respective values. Since the time needed in the factory to complete a production step is known, the model appropriately describes reality.

A finer time grid is certainly possible: Instead of viewing every clock step as one simulation step, arrival at and departure from a work position can be used, thereby capturing work and transport time independently.

The discrete approach is used in software engineering as well. One important area is experimental software engineering, e.g., regarding inspection processes. Here, a discrete simulation can be used to describe the process flow. Possible simulation steps might be the start and completion of activities and lags, together with special events like (late) design changes. This enables discrete models to represent queues.

7.2.3   Hybrid Simulation

Continuous simulation models describe the interaction between project factors well, but suffer from a lack of detail when it comes to representing discrete system steps. Discrete simulation models perform well in the case of discrete system steps, but make it difficult to describe feedback loops in the system.

To overcome the disadvantages of the two approaches, a hybrid approach as described by Martin and Raffo [9] can be used. In a software development project, information about available and used manpower is very important. While a continuous model can show how manpower usage levels vary over time, a discrete model can point out bottlenecks, such as inspections. Because of insufficient manpower, documents are not inspected near-time, so consumers of those documents have to wait idly, which wastes manpower.

In a purely discrete approach, the number of inspection steps might be decreased to speed up the inspection process. While possibly eliminating the bottleneck, this might introduce more defects. The discrete model would not notice this until late in the project because continually changing numbers are not supported. The hybrid approach, however, would instantly notice the increase, and—depending on how the model is used for steering the project—more time would be allocated for rework, possibly to the extent that the savings in inspection are overcompensated. Thus, the hybrid approach helps in simulating the consequences of decisions more accurately than each of the two single approaches does individually.

7.2.4   Benefits

Following Kellner et al. [2], benefits in the following areas can be expected from simulation in software engineering:

- Strategic management issues. These may be questions such as whether to distribute work or concentrate it in one spot, or whether development should be done in-house or be outsourced, or whether to follow a product-line approach or not.
- Planning. Planning includes forecasting schedule, costs, product quality, and staffing needs, as well as considering resource constraints and risk analysis.
- Control and operational management. Operational management comprises project tracking, an overview of key project parameters such as project status and resource consumption, comparison of actual to planned values, as well as operational decisions such as whether to commence the next major phase (e.g., coding, integration testing).
- Process improvement and technology adoption. This includes evaluating and prioritizing suggested improvements before they are implemented as well as expost comparisons of process changes against simulations of the unchanged process with actually observed data.
- Understanding. Simulation models can help process members to better understand process flow and the complex feedback loops usually found in software development processes. Also, properties pervading many processes can be identified.
- Training and learning. Similar to pilots training in flight simulators, trainees can learn project management with the help of simulations. The consequences of mistakes can be explored in a safe environment and experience can be collected that is equivalent to years of real-world experience.

7.3 A Method for Developing Simulation Models

This section summarizes a method for systematically developing discrete-event software process simulation models, which was previously published in [10]. However, even though used for developing a discrete-event model, it can also be used to develop continuous simulation models. The method considers the development of a new simulation model without reusing or incorporating existing components. If reuse is considered (by either incorporating existing components or developing for reuse), the method has to be changed to address possible reuse of simulation model elements.

The lifecycle of a simulation model for long-term use is similar to that of software and consists of three main phases: *development, deployment,* and *operation,* including *maintenance and evolution.* The activities within these phases can have different temporal orders and dependencies; therefore, the resulting lifecycle can take on different forms, such as waterfall, iterative, or even agile.

The activities throughout the lifecycle can be divided into two categories: *engineering* and *management* activities.

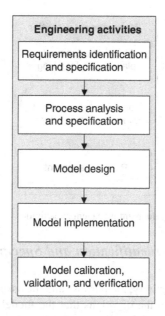

Fig. 7.3 Simulation model development engineering activities

The engineering activities for model development are (Fig. 7.3):

- Requirements identification and specification for the model to be built
- Analysis and specification of the modeled process
- Design of the model
- Implementation of the model
- Verification and validation throughout development

The management activities are (Fig. 7.4):

- Model development planning and tracking
- Measurement of the model and of the model development process
- Risk management (this refers to identifying and tracking risk factors and mitigating their effects. Some of the risk factors are: changes in customer requirements, changes in the description of the modeled process, and nonavailability of data for the quantitative part of the model.)

During the lifecycle of a simulation model, different roles are involved. In the development phase, mainly the model developer and the customer are involved. A "pair modeling" approach for creating the first version of the static process model and influence diagram can be very useful during this phase, because the discussion about the model and the influences is very inspiring. The following sections introduce the engineering activities in more detail.

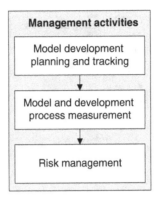

Fig. 7.4 Simulation model development management activities

7.3.1 Requirements Identification and Specification

During the requirements activity, the purpose and the usage of the model have to be defined. According to this, the questions that the model will have to answer are determined and so is the data that will be needed in order to answer these questions. The steps of the requirements specification are:

7.3.1.1 Definition of the Goals, Questions, and the Necessary Metrics

A goal-question-metrics-based approach like GQM can be used for defining the goal and the needed measures [11]. GQM can also be used to define and start an initial measurement program if needed. Purpose, scope, and level of detail for the model are described by the *goal*. The *questions* that the model should help to answer are formulated next. Afterward, parameters (*metrics*) of the model (outputs) have to be defined that (once their value is known) will answer the questions. Then those model input parameters have to be defined that are necessary for determining the output values. The input parameters should not be considered as final after the requirements phase; during the analysis phase, they will usually change.

7.3.1.2 Definition of Usage Scenarios

Define scenarios ("use cases") for using the model. For example, for answering the question: "How does the effectiveness of inspections affect the cost and schedule of the project?," a corresponding scenario would be: "All input parameters are kept constant and the parameter *inspection effectiveness* is given x different values between (min, max). The simulator is executed until a certain value for the number of defects per KLOC is achieved, and the values for *cost* and *duration* are examined for each of the cases." For traceability purposes, scenarios should be tracked to the questions they answer (for example, by using a matrix).

7.3.1.3   Development of Test Cases

Test cases can be developed in the requirements phase. They help to verify and validate the model and the resulting simulation.

7.3.1.4   Validation of Requirements

The customer (i.e., the organization that is going to use the simulation model) has to be involved in this activity and must agree with the content of the resulting model specification document. Changes can be made, but they have to be documented.

Throughout this section, we will illustrate the outputs of the activities by using some excerpts from a discrete-event simulator. This model and simulator support managerial decision making for planning the system testing phase of software development. The simulator offers the possibility of executing *what-if* scenarios with different values for the parameters that characterize the system testing process and the specific project. By analyzing the outputs of the simulator, its user can visualize predictions of the effects of his/her planning decisions.

7.3.1.5   Examples for Step 1 and Step 2

Goal
- Develop a decision support model for the planning of the system testing phase in the context of organization x such that trade-offs between duration, cost, and quality (remaining defects) can be analyzed and the most suitable process planning alternative can be selected.

Questions to be answered
- Q1: When to stop testing in order to achieve a specified quality (number of defects expected to remain in the delivered software)?
- Q2: If the delivery date is fixed, what will be the quality of the product if delivered at that time, and what will be the cost of the project?
- Q3: If the cost is fixed, when will the product have to be delivered and what will be its quality at that point?
- Q4: Should regression testing be performed? To what extent?

Output parameters
- O1: Cost of testing (computed from the effort) [$] for cost or [staff hours] for effort
- O2: Duration of testing [hours] or [days]
- O3: Quality of delivered software [number of defects per K lines of code]

(Some of the) Input parameters
- I1: Number of requirements to be tested
- I2: Indicator of the "size" of each software requirement (in terms of software modules (components) that implement that requirement and their "complexity/difficulty" factor)
- I3: For each software module, its "complexity/difficulty" factor
- I4: Number of resources (test beds and people) needed
- I5: Number of resources (test beds and people) available
- I6: Effectiveness of test cases (historic parameter that gives an indication of how many defects are expected to be discovered by a test case)

Scenarios
- S1: For a chosen value of the desired quality parameter, and for the fixed values of the other inputs, the simulator is run once until it stops (i.e., the desired quality is achieved) and the values of the cost and duration outputs are examined.
- S2: The simulator is run for a simulation duration corresponding to the chosen value of the target duration parameter, and for the fixed values of the other inputs. The values of the cost and quality outputs are examined.
- S3: For a chosen value of the desired cost parameter, and for the fixed values of the other inputs, the simulator is run once until it stops (i.e., the cost limit is reached) and the values of the quality and duration outputs are examined.
- S4: For a chosen value of the desired quality parameter, and for the fixed values of the other inputs, the simulator is run once until it stops (i.e., the desired quality is achieved) and the values of the cost and duration outputs are examined according to the variation in the extent of regression testing.
- S5: The simulator is run for a simulation duration corresponding to the chosen value of the target duration parameter, and for the fixed values of the other inputs, and the values of the cost and quality outputs are examined according to the variation in the extent of regression testing.
- S6: For a chosen value of the desired cost parameter, and for the fixed values of the other inputs, the simulator is run once until it stops (i.e., the cost limit is reached) and the values of the quality and duration outputs are examined according to the variation in the extent of regression testing.

7.3.2 Process Analysis and Specification

The understanding, specification, and analysis of the process that is to be modeled is one of the most important activities during the development of a simulation model.

Process analysis and specification can be divided into four subactivities, as shown in Fig. 7.5:

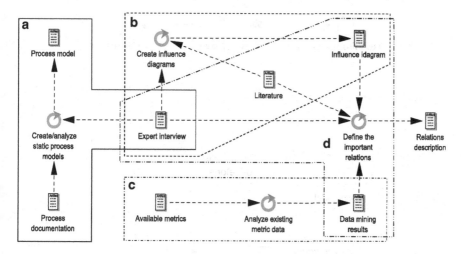

Fig. 7.5 Process analysis and specification

- Analysis and creation of a static process model ("a," straight line)
- Creation of the influence diagram for describing the relationships between parameters of the process ("b," dashed line)
- Collection and analysis of empirical data for deriving the quantitative relationships ("c," dash–dot line)
- Quantification of the relationships ("d," dash–dot–dot line)

Figure 7.5 sketches the product flow of this activity, i.e., it describes which artifacts (document symbol) are used or created by each task (arrowed circle symbol).

(a) *Analysis and creation of a static process model.* The software process to be modeled first needs to be understood and documented. This requires that the representations (abstractions) of the process should be intuitive enough to be understood by the customer and to constitute a communication vehicle between modeler and customer. These representations lead to a common definition and understanding of the object of modeling (i.e., the software process) and to a refinement of the problem to be modeled (initially formulated during the requirements specification activity). As input and sources of information for this activity, process documents are possibly supplemented with interviews with people involved in the process (or with the process "owner"). The created process model describes the artifacts used, the processes or activities performed, and the roles and tools involved. The process model shows which activities transform which artifacts and how information flows through the model.

(b) *Creation of the influence diagram for describing the relationships between parameters of the process.* For documenting the relationships between process parameters, influence diagrams can be used. Influence factors are typically

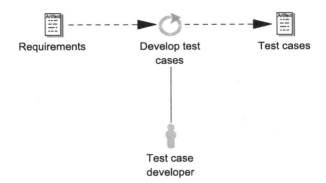

Fig. 7.6 Static process model

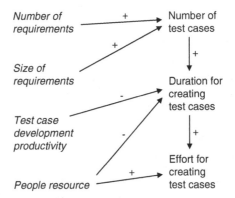

Fig. 7.7 Influence diagram

factors that change the result or behavior of other project parameters. The relationships between influencing and influenced parameters are represented in an influence diagram by arrows and + or −, depending on whether variation of the factors occurs in the same way or in opposite ways.

When the influence diagram is created, the inputs and outputs identified in the requirements phase should be considered. These inputs and, especially, the outputs have to be captured in the influence diagrams. Figure 7.6 presents a small excerpt of a static process model, Fig. 7.7 a corresponding influence diagram.

The influence diagrams that are developed in this step are later refined during design and especially during implementation, driven by a better understanding of what is really needed for implementation.

(c) *Collection and analysis of empirical data for deriving the quantitative relationships.* For identifying the quantitative relationships between process parameters, one needs to identify which data/metrics need to be collected and analyzed. Usually, not all required data is available, and additional metrics from the target organization should be collected. In this case, developing a process model can help to shape and focus the measurement program of a project.

(d) *Quantification of the relationships.* This is the task that is probably the hardest part of the analysis, because it requires quantifying the relations and distinguishing parameter types. The following parameter types can be distinguished:

- Calibration parameters: These parameters are used to calibrate the model according to the organization, such as productivity values, learning, skills, and number of developers.
- Project-specific input: These parameters are used to represent a specific project, such as number of test cases, modules, and size of tasks.
- Variable parameters: These are the parameters that are changed to analyze the results of the output variables. In general, these can be the same as the calibration parameters. The variable parameters during the model's lifecycle are determined either by the scenario from the requirements or by new requirements.

The distinction between these parameters is often not easy and shifts, especially for calibration and variable parameters, depending on the scenarios that are addressed by the model.

The mathematical quantification is done in this step. Depending on the availability of historical metric data, sophisticated data mining methods might be used to determine these relationships. Otherwise, interviews with customers or experts, or literature sources have to be used.

The outputs of the process analysis and specification phase are models (static model, influence diagrams, and relations) of the software development process and parameters that have to be simulated, measures (metrics) that need to be received from the real process, and a description of all the assumptions and decisions that are made during the analysis. The latter is useful for documenting the model for later maintenance and evolution.

The artifacts created during process analysis and specification have two distinct properties: the level of static or dynamic behavior they capture and the quantitative nature of the information they represent. Figure 7.8 shows the values for these properties for the static process model (which is static and qualitative), the influence diagram (static and qualitative), and the end product simulator, which is quantitative and dynamic.

Throughout this activity, several verification and validation steps must be performed:

- The static model has to be validated against the requirements (to make sure it is within the scope, and also that it is complete for the goal stated in the requirements) and against the real process (here the customer should be involved).
- The parameters in the influence diagram must be checked against the metrics (to ensure they are consistent) and against the input and output variables of the requirement specification.

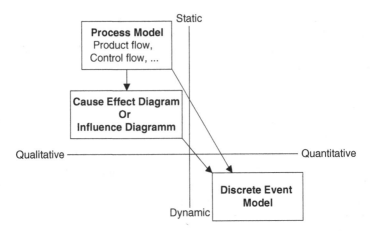

Fig. 7.8 Properties of different modeling artifacts

- The relations must be checked against the influence diagrams for completeness and consistency. All the factors of the influence diagram that influence the result have to be represented, for instance in the equation of the relation.
- The influence diagrams (possibly also the relations) must be validated by the customer with respect to their conformance to real influences.
- The units of measurement for all parameters should be checked.

7.3.3   Model Design

During this activity, the modeler develops the design of the model, which is independent of the implementation environment. The design is divided into different levels of detail, the high-level design and the detailed design.

7.3.3.1   High-Level Design

In the high-level design, the surrounding infrastructure is defined. Also, the basic mechanisms describing how the input and output data is managed and represented is defined, if necessary. Usually, a model's design comprises components such as a database or a spreadsheet, a visualization component, and the simulation model itself, together with the information flows between them.

Figure 7.9 shows the high-level design for a system testing simulation (STS) model. The model has two main modules, the *Development module,* which models the development of the software, and the *STS Testing module,* which models the system testing of the software. These two modules interact through the flow of items such as *Code, Resources,* and *Defects.* The whole model has graphical user

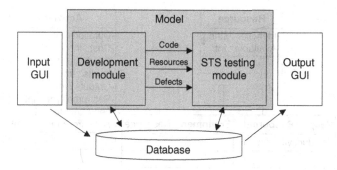

Fig. 7.9 High-level design (excerpt)

interfaces (GUI), both for input and for output. Through the input interface, the user of the simulator provides the values of the input parameters, which are saved in a database and then fed into the simulator. The outputs of the simulator are also saved in the database and then used by a visualization software, which displays them in a user-friendly format to the users of the model. The high-level design is the latest point in time for deciding which type of simulation approach to use (e.g., system dynamics, discrete event, or something else).

7.3.3.2   Detailed Design

In the detailed design, the "low-level design" of the simulation model is created. The designer has to make several decisions, such as:

- Which activities do we have to model? (i.e., what is the level of granularity for the model?)
- What items should be represented?
- What are the attributes of these items that should be captured?

Additionally, the designer has to define the flow of the different items (if more than one type of item is defined, also the combination of items). When creating the detailed design, the static process model can be used for identifying the activities and items, whereas the influence diagrams can be used for identifying the items' attributes.

The outcome of this activity is a detailed design of the model. Figure 7.10 shows such a design using a UML-like notation. The *Activity* object models an activity in a software process. Its attributes are: duration, cost, effort, inputs, outputs, resource type, and number (both people and equipment resources). The *Resource* object corresponds to the real-world resources needed to perform an activity. An example of instances of the *People_Resource* sub-class of *Resource* would be *Developer* or *Tester*. The human resources are characterized by their productivity, represented as the attribute *Productivity*. The object *Artifacts* captures the code (*SW_Artifacts*) and test cases (*Testing_Artifact*). The code has attributes such as its size, complexity,

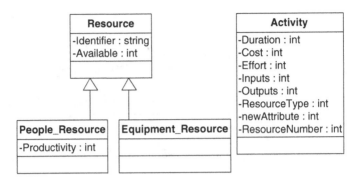

Fig. 7.10 Example of detailed design objects

and number of defects, while the test cases have an attribute related to their capability of detecting defects in code (*Effectiveness*).

In the design phase, verification and validation activities must be performed, for example to check the consistency between high- and low-level design as well as with the process description (static, influence diagrams, and relations) and the model requirements.

7.3.4 Model Implementation

During implementation, all of the information as well as the design decisions are transferred into the simulation model. The documents from the process specification and analysis and the design are necessary as inputs. This activity in the development process depends heavily on which simulation tool or language is used and is very similar to the implementation activity for a conventional software product. Figure 7.11 shows an excerpt of a discrete-event model developed in the commercial modeling tool *Extend*, using building blocks connected through inputs and outputs to determine model behavior.

7.3.5 Model Calibration, Validation, and Verification

Besides the validation and verification that occur throughout development, the implemented model and simulator must be checked to see whether they are suitable for the purpose and the problems they should address. Also, the model will be checked against reality (here the customer/user has to be involved). During such calibration runs, the model's parameters will be set. Figure 7.12 displays the results of one calibration run. It shows the mean deviation of the model outputs compared to the real experiment it is tested against for different parameter values. It can be

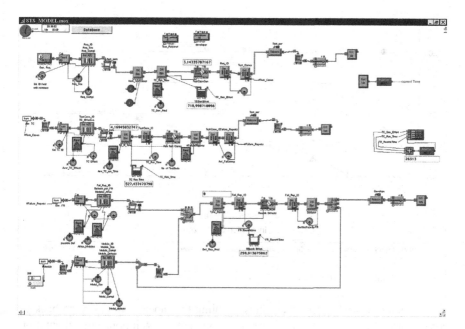

Fig. 7.11 Example simulation model

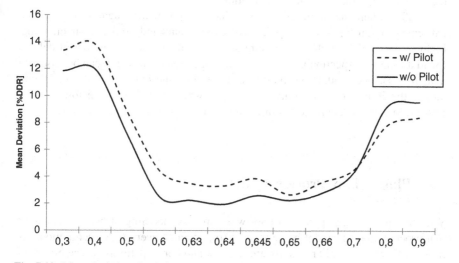

Fig. 7.12 Mean deviation simulation—experiment

observed that for the particular parameter displayed, model deviation from reality is lowest for a parameter value of 0.6–0.7.

Throughout the simulator development process, verification and validation (usually implemented by means of reviews) must be performed after each activity. Also, traceability between different products created during the simulator's

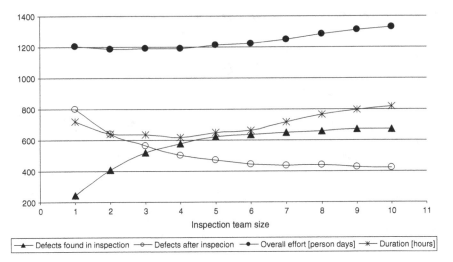

Fig. 7.13 Simulation model run results

development must be maintained, thus enabling the modeler to easily go back to correct or add elements during model development or evolution. Implementation decisions must be documented to allow future understanding of the current implementation and to facilitate model evolution.

Finally, when the simulation model has been validated against reality and calibrated, it can be used to replace real experiments and predict their outcome. Figure 7.13 displays a plot of one simulation run, depicting the number of defects found during an inspection in relation to the inspection team size. It can be observed that, for instance, with more than five inspectors, the number of defects found during the inspection rises only marginally, whereas the overall effort and the inspection duration continue to climb significantly [12].

7.4 Plug & Play Process Models

With the increasing popularity of software process modeling, it became apparent that process models cannot be developed from scratch every time such a model is needed. However, similar to software itself, a number of patterns can be observed within software processes, for example, a *work–test–rework* pattern that describes the common situation that some work is performed, its results are evaluated by a verification/validation step, and based on the evaluation results, some rework becomes necessary. Such generic patterns can be used for different processes (e.g., requirements elicitation, writing code) and in different domains (e.g., automotive, information systems). It is therefore feasible and recommendable to define such patterns for simulation models as well, forming "macroblocks" that can be used to quickly develop simulation models.

One such approach is the SimSWE library of reusable components for software process simulation [13]. The library provides (tool-independent) definitions of a multitude of components and, for each component, a Matlab®/Simulink® reference implementation under the LGPL license [14] for download [15]. The library contains components for both continuous and discrete-time simulation models. A basic set of components can be used with a standard Matlab/Simulink configuration without add-ons, supporting continuous simulation only. An extended set contains components that can also be used for discrete-event simulation, but requires Simulink addons (at present Stateflow® and SimEvent®). Each set is divided into six subcollections that represent different types of model components:

- Generators, e.g., for requirements
- Estimators, e.g., using cocomo ii [16]
- Generic activities, e.g., performing work
- Generic processes, e.g., the work–test–rework pattern mentioned earlier
- Management components, e.g., for employee training
- Utilities like conversions

The library is developed and shared as Open Source, yet the license allows for using components in a proprietary context without the need to publish modifications as Open Source as well. The library maintainers encourage users to apply the components and contribute additional components as well, in order to construct a set of standard software process simulation components that allow for the rapid development of software process simulation models and that make them easier to compare.

7.5 Combining Process Simulation and Empirical Studies

Even though discussed in separate chapters in this textbook, empirical studies and process simulation models can be combined to get additional benefits. For example, while in the 1960s or 1970s, nuclear weapon tests were a rather common phenomenon, this has ceased completely in the new millennium. In part, this reduction has been caused by increased knowledge about the harmful side effects of nuclear weapons (namely radiation and contamination of vast areas for many years), but not entirely.

Since the military has priorities other than preventing ecological damage, but an increasing fraction of human society was no longer willing to accept that, other ways for testing these weapons had to be found. Today, most nations have the ability to simulate nuclear explosions. This saves enormous expenses, because real testing is always destructive and nuclear weapons are not exactly cheap. In addition, simulations are not making people upset. Another great advantage is that simulations can be repeated as often as desired with any set of parameters, which is impossible with real tests.

Other areas where simulation is used amply are mechanical engineering and construction. Here, simulation helps to save cost and time. As a rather young profession, software engineering has only recently started to discover and use the benefits of simulation. Empirical software engineering is not very common yet in industry. Many decisions are still based on intuition rather than on measured data. This trial-and-error approach is very expensive and delivers lower-quality products than more systematic approaches would. When implemented, experiments already yield good results, for example in choosing a reading technique for inspections.

Still, the required experiments cost a lot of money, which companies naturally dislike, despite the benefits. But as in other professions, simulation can also help with this aspect in software engineering. A simulation is conducted in two basic parts: modeling the real-world situation, and afterwards simulating it on a computer. The model tries to reproduce some aspects of the real world as accurately as needed, in a representation that can be used in the simulation. The optimal model would contain exactly those entities and relations needed for the simulation, nothing more and nothing less.

An entity represents an element of the real world, e.g., a person or a document. Like their real counterparts, entities interact with each other; this is mapped to relations in the model. One problem in modeling is that it is usually not clear which entities and relations of the real world need to be modeled. This depends on the scope of the model: If the goal is to predict product quality, other factors must be included than when process optimization is aimed at. In any case, including too many factors increases model complexity unnecessarily and may even influence the results, whereas considering too few factors may render the results unreliable.

Working with simulations can be seen as research in a virtual lab (Fig. 7.14). Conventional software engineering laboratories explore the research object by using various empirical studies, e.g., controlled experiments or case studies. The virtual laboratory examines its research object with simulations. Transferring information from one to the other can help to improve research results on both sides.

Simulation supports any of the three types of experiments regarded earlier, each in a different way. Once the simulation model has been built and verified,

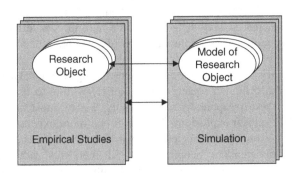

Fig. 7.14 Real and virtual laboratory approach

laboratory experiments can at least partially be replaced, for example to determine the consequences of (gentle) context changes. Case studies focus on monitoring real-life variables, so completely replacing them with simulations would not make sense. Simulations may still be useful for identifying variables that should be monitored. A simulation of an altered process can reveal variables that are likely to change significantly, so the case study can pay special attention to them. In terms of the other direction of the information flow, case studies can deliver valuable data for calibrating the simulation model. The authentic nature of the data (they are taken directly from a real project) also helps to refine the model.

Simulation does not seem very useful for replacing surveys, since surveys are optimized for finding relations in real-life processes. Replacing surveys of real processes with surveys of modeled processes would not save time or money. Actually, surveys can supply information for simulation models, just like case studies: In retrospective, problems often become obvious that were invisible during the project. A survey reveals them in many cases.

Let us say that a certain product was delivered significantly later than planned, and that this phenomenon did not occur for the first time. A survey reveals that the customer changed the initial specifications of the software several times in cooperation with customer service. However, it took customer service several weeks to communicate these changes to the development team, thus already delaying the necessary rework and, in addition, making it more complex by forcing the developers to change a more mature piece of software.

The survey reveals this lack of communication within the software development process, and modeling that part of the process could help to understand and solve the problem. Once the model has been built, the data from the survey can be used to calibrate it. Process changes can then be simulated before realizing them in the actual process. This indicates that surveys and simulation should be used as complements to each other, not as alternatives.

References

1. Navarro EO (2006) SimSE: a software engineering simulation environment for software process education. Dissertation, University of California, Irvine, CA
2. Kellner MI, Madachay RJ, Raffo DM (1999) Software process simulation modeling: why? what? how? J Syst Software 46(2–3):91–105
3. Abdel-Hamid T, Madnick SE (1991) Software project dynamics. Prentice Hall, Englewood Cliffs
4. Glass RL (1999) The journal of systems and software—special issue on process simulation modeling. Elsevier, New York
5. Fraunhofer Institute for Experimental Software Engineering IESE (1997–2011) Spearmint. http://www.iese.fraunhofer.de/competence/process/pmi/index.jsp. Accessed 27 Jun 2011
6. Pfahl D (2001) An integrated approach to simulation-based learning in support of strategic and project management in software organisations. Dissertation, University of Kaiserslautern, Germany
7. Meadows DH, Meadows DL, Randers J, Behrens WW III (1972) The limits to growth. Universe Books, New York

8. Madachy RJ (2008) Software process dynamics. Wiley, Hoboken, NJ
9. Martin RH, Raffo DA (2000) A model of the software development process using both continuous and discrete models. Software Process Improv Pract 5(2–3):147–157
10. Rus I, Neu H, Münch J (2003) A systematic methodology for developing discrete event simulation models of software development processes. In: Proceedings of the international workshop on software process simulation and modeling (ProSim), Portland, OR, USA, 3–4 May 2003
11. Basili VR, Caldiera G, Rombach HD (1994) Goal question metric paradigm. Wiley, New York
12. Neu H, Hanne T, Münch J, Nickel S, Wirsen A (2003) Creating a code inspection model for simulation-based decision support. In: Proceedings of the 4th international workshop on software process simulation and modeling (ProSim), Portland, OR, USA, 3–4 May 2003
13. Birkhölzer T, Madachy R, Pfahl D, Port D, Beitinger H, Schuster M, Olkov A (2010) SimSWE—a library of reusable components for software process simulation. In: Proceedings of the international conference on software process (ICSP 2010), Paderborn, Germany, 8–9 Jul 2010, pp 321–332
14. Free Software Foundation (2007) GNU lesser general public license. http://www.gnu.org/licenses/lgpl.html. Accessed 27 Jun 2011
15. Birkhölzer T, Madachy R, Pfahl D, Port D, Beitinger H, Schuster M, Olkov A (2010) SimSWE—library for software engineering simulation. http://simswe.ei.htwg-konstanz.de/wiki_simswe/index.php/Main_Page. Accessed 9 Jun 2011
16. Boehm BW, Harrowitz E (2000) Software cost estimation with Cocomo II. Prentice Hall, Englewood Cliffs, NJ

Chapter 8
Glossary

Atomic process	An atomic process (synonym: process step) is a process that does not allow further structuring in the form of sub-processes
Balanced Scorecard	The Balanced Scorecard (BSC) is a strategic management concept that aims at aligning a company's activities with its vision and strategy. The BSC approach tries to measure whether the activities of a company are meeting its goals with respect to vision and strategy
BSC	see Balanced Scorecard
CASE	Computer Aided Software Engineering
CMMI	CMMI is an approach that supports the evaluation and improvement of an organization's processes using a best-practice model
Continuous model	In a continuous (simulation) model, variables can change their value at any given moment. This means that model output is calculated continuously over time, not only at discrete points in time as it is done for discrete-event models
Continuous SPI	Continuous SPI focus on solutions for the most important challenges of a software development organization and usually involve improvement cycles based on an initial baseline
Control flow	The sequence of activities in a process (may be partially ordered)
Deming cycle	See plan, do, check, act
Discrete-event model	In a discrete-event (simulation) model, variables can change their value only at discrete moments of time. This means that between these times, all variables are constant, and the model state can be described as a vector of all variables at every such discrete point in time

J. Münch et al., *Software Process Definition and Management*,
The Fraunhofer Series on Software and Systems Engineering,
DOI 10.1007/978-3-642-24291-5_8, © Springer-Verlag Berlin Heidelberg 2012

ECMA	European Computer Manufacturers Association
Elicitation	See process elicitation
Engineering process model	A process model that describes (possibly in very much detail) a fraction of the complete software lifecycle process, for example, a specific type of inspection. Engineering process models can be very detailed, often not only describing "what" to do, but also explaining "how" to do it
EPF	Eclipse Process Framework
EPG	Electronic Process Guide, an electronic representation of a process description, e.g., a collection of linked web pages. An EPG typically contains links to additional information, e.g., document templates or work product examples
Experience Factory	The Experience Factory is an organizational structure that fits to the QIP
GQM	GQM is a systematic approach for tailoring and integrating measurement goals with models of the software processes, products, and quality perspectives of interest, based upon the specific needs of the project and the software domain of an organization
GQM⁺Strategies®	GQM⁺Strategies® is a strategic measurement approach that links higher-level goals of an organization, such as business goals, with software-related goals
ISO/IEC 15504	see SPICE
Lifecycle process model	A process model that captures the complete lifecycle of a software product. Typically, lifecycle process models abstract from a number of details, and instead provide a broader view on the process (focus on "what", not on "how")
Method content	Represents a library of descriptions of software engineering methods and best practices
Model	A model is an abstract and simplifying representation of an object or phenomenon of the real world
Model-based SPI	Model-based SPI approaches compare the current processes and practices of a development organization against a reference model or a benchmark
MVP-L	Multi-View Process Modeling Language
NIST	National Institute of Standards and Technology
PDCA	See plan, do, check, act
Plan, Do, Check, Act	Plan, do, check, act (PDCA) is an iterative four-step problem-solving process also known as Deming cycle
Practical Software and Systems Measurement	Practical Software and Systems Measurement (PSM) defines an information-driven measurement process that

	guides project managers in selecting, collecting, defining, analyzing, and reporting specific software issues
Principle	A principle is a policy or mode of action that describes important characteristics of a process model
Process	See software process
Process agent	See process performer
Process architecture	See process schema
Process definition	A process definition is a description of a process that can be enacted. Process scripts and process programs are specializations of process definitions
Process description	While a process is a vehicle for doing a job, a process description is a specification of how the job is to be done. Thus, cookbook recipes are process descriptions, while preparing a recipe is a process
Process elicitation	The discipline concerned with acquiring data from process participants in order to build a process model
Process enactment	Process enactment is the performance of process steps undertaken to reach a given goal. The performer (i.e., "agent") can be a human or a machine. In case of a machine, the term "process execution" is usually used
Process engineer	A process engineer is a person who pursues one or several goals of process modeling (e.g., defining, extending, maintaining, improving process models)
Process handbook	A description of the process that is intended to assist process performers with their daily work, i.e., tells them when to do what
Process manual	See process handbook
Process meta-model	See process schema
Process model	See software process model
Process notation	A formal language, i.e., a well-defined set of syntactical conventions, used to describe a process
Process owner	A process owner is a human or organizational entity that sets the goals of a process and is responsible for its achievement
Process performer	A process performer (synonym: agent) is a person or machine that enacts/executes the process in order to reach the process goal(s). Humans interpret process scripts, machines interpret process programs
Process program	A process program is a description of a process that can be interpreted by machines
Process schema	A process schema (synonym: process meta model, process architecture) is a conceptual framework for the consistent description of process models and their relations. A process schema describes, on the one hand, building blocks that form a process model, and, on the other hand, constraints on their composition

Process script	A process script is a description of a process that is suitable for interpretation by humans. A process script should be tailored to the needs of the process performer
Process stakeholder	A person or organizational entity that has an interest in the process, for example, because it is required to deliver specific input
Process step	See atomic process
Product	A product is each artifact that is consumed or produced in the context of engineering-style software development
Product flow	The product flow consists of the relationships between products and processes that describe the access mode to the products
Product model	A product model is a description of a product or a class of products
Project	A project is a unique endeavor, which is limited by a start date and an end date and should achieve a goal
Project phase	A project phase (short: phase) is a collection of logically separated project activities, usually culminating in the completion of a major deliverable or the achievement of a major milestone
Project plan	A project plan is a specification of the necessary resources for the execution of a process definition, the relations between these resources and processes, the produced products including the product flows, and restrictions of any type concerning the execution of the process
PSM	See practical software and systems measurement
QIP	The Quality Improvement Paradigm (QIP) is a six-step procedure for structuring software development and improvement activities. The QIP is based on PDCA and tailored to the specifics of software development
Real experiment	An experiment that takes place in the real world, with real experimental subjects
Role	A role is a set of processes belonging together that are assigned to one or several agents. A role combines the functional responsibility for the enactment of a process
SEE	Software Engineering Environment
Six Sigma	Six Sigma is a quality management framework that mainly aims at reducing variance in processes and preventing defects
Software process	A software process is a goal-oriented activity in the context of engineering-style software development
Software process model	A software process model (short: process model) is a model of a software process, i.e., an abstract and

	simplifying representation of a (class of) real-world software process(es)
SPEM	Software Process Engineering Metamodel, describing entities to be used for software process modeling
SPI	Software process improvement, i.e., activities targeted at improving the existing processes of an organization with respect to a certain goal, for example, for reducing the number of defects introduced in a product
SPICE	ISO/IEC 15504 (SPICE) is an international standard for evaluating and improving an organization's software processes
TQM	Total Quality Management (TQM) is a holistic management approach towards quality management and, in particular, continuous improvement within an organization
UML	Unified Modeling Language
Virtual experiment	A simulation of an experiment, typically on a computer, using a simulation model that describes some real-world phenomenon

Chapter 9
Authors

Jürgen Münch

Jürgen Münch is a Professor in the Department of Computer Science at the University of Helsinki. His research in software and systems engineering centers on the measurement and quantitative analysis of software processes and systems, software process modeling and management, cloud-based software engineering, global software development, and empirical software engineering. Prior to his current position, Prof. Dr. Münch was a division head at the Fraunhofer Institute for Experimental Software Engineering IESE in Kaiserslautern, Germany, where he was responsible for research and technology transfer in the area of software process and quality engineering. He was also an executive board member of the temporary research institute SFB 501 at the University of Kaiserslautern. Prof. Dr. Münch has been awarded the Distinguished Professor Award (FiDiPro), the IFIP TC2 Manfred Paul Award for Excellence in Software Theory and Practice, several best paper awards, and the technology innovation award from the Rhineland-Palatinate Lotto Foundation.

Ove Armbrust

Ove Armbrust is a Software Engineering Process Group Lead at Alpine Electronics Research of America. In this position, he is responsible for all software development processes of Alpine's U.S. R&D operations, including product development, customer interaction, and standards compliance. Prior to his current position, Dr. Armbrust was a researcher and senior engineer at the Fraunhofer Institute for Experimental Software Engineering IESE in Kaiserslautern, Germany. In its Processes and Measurement department, he focused his research activities on context-specific process adaptation, process compliance, and process scoping. In 2010, he received his Ph.D. in Computer Science from the University of Kaiserslautern, Germany. Besides his academic work, Dr. Armbrust has provided consultation services to a wide range of organizations from the automotive, aerospace, and finance domains regarding process improvement issues.

Martin Kowalczyk

Martin Kowalczyk graduated from the University of Karlsruhe, Germany, with a Diplom degree in Industrial Engineering in 2009 and started working at the

J. Münch et al., *Software Process Definition and Management*,
The Fraunhofer Series on Software and Systems Engineering,
DOI 10.1007/978-3-642-24291-5_9, © Springer-Verlag Berlin Heidelberg 2012

Fraunhofer Institute for Experimental Software Engineering (IESE) thereafter. He is a member of the Processes and Measurement department and works on subjects concerning software development processes and goal-oriented measurement approaches such as GQM$^+$Strategies®. In the context of industrial projects, he has worked for several organizations from the aerospace, finance, and services domains on topics from the area of process improvement and measurement. His current research interests focus on measurement-based alignment of goals and activities within software-based organizations.

Martín Soto
Martín Soto was born in Bogotá, Colombia, where he received his master's degree in Computer Science in 1995 from the Universidad de los Andes. In 2009, he received his Ph.D. in Computer Science from the University of Kaiserslautern, Germany. From 2000 to 2010, he was a researcher at the Fraunhofer Institute for Experimental Software Engineering (IESE) in the Processes and Measurement department, where he was working on process modeling for industrial and research purposes. His research interests concentrate on change management for process models. Since 2010, Dr. Soto has been Senior Developer at eleven GmbH.

Appendix

Problems for Chapter 1

Problem 1.1

What are the differences between a process and a project phase? It can often be observed when reading process standards or books about development processes that a phase is refined into process models. As an example, the requirements phase might be refined by the process models "Define and Describe Software Requirements," "Define Interface Requirements," and "Prioritize and Integrate Software Requirements." What might be problems with such a modeling approach and why should this be avoided?

Problem 1.2

Some process quality standards require that all processes of an organization need to be documented systematically. Discuss whether this is sufficient for assessing the quality of the processes performed in an organization or for improving processes.

Problem 1.3

Assume that a project consists of ten tasks that may be distributed across three different development sites in different countries. How many combinations of assigning these tasks to the different sites exist? What could be criteria for assigning specific tasks to sites?

J. Münch et al., *Software Process Definition and Management*,
The Fraunhofer Series on Software and Systems Engineering,
DOI 10.1007/978-3-642-24291-5, © Springer-Verlag Berlin Heidelberg 2012

Solutions to the Problems for Chapter 1

Solution for Problem 1.1

One main difference is that the project phase has a defined start and end date, whereas a process can be enacted several times depending on the conditions under which it can be enacted. For instance, the process "Define Interface Requirements" could also be enacted in the design phase if defects are detected in the interface specification. The requirements phase has already terminated at this point in time.

Therefore, refining phases by processes (or vice versa) often leads to inconsistent models and can cause significant problems during project execution.

Solution for Problem 1.2

Having all processes documented is not sufficient. It is important that the documented processes reflect the current practices of an organization.

Solution for Problem 1.3

If a software development project consists of ten independent development tasks that may be distributed across three development sites, theoretically $3^{10} = 59,049$ different combinations of allocating tasks to sites exist.

Typical criteria for allocating tasks to sites in global software development are:

- Cost
- Availability of resources (such as developers)
- Expertise
- Proximity to markets (this is especially relevant for requirements engineering tasks)
- Development quality
- Personal trust
- Time differences
- Cultural differences
- Willingness at site
- Established relationships

In addition, political or strategic decisions as well as contractual issues and the collaboration history between sites might have an influence.

Problems for Chapter 2

Problem 2.1

Explain the difference between a descriptive and a prescriptive process model.

Problem 2.2

What is the difference between a lifecycle model and an engineering model? Name two examples each and explain why they fit into their corresponding category.

Problem 2.3

Describe two typical problems that may occur while deploying a prescriptive process model. For each of these problems, discuss potential strategies for overcoming it.

Solutions to the Problems for Chapter 2

Solution for Problem 2.1

The difference between the two lies in purpose, not necessarily in content.

Prescriptive models tell people what to do in projects and are intended to be used as guidance or handbooks during daily work. However, they are often used to publish a specific (mandatory) process, the application of which is expected.

Descriptive models are normally a description of the actual, currently used real-world process. They are typically used for evaluation and improvement of the current work procedures, in particular to pin down (unspecific) problems experienced during daily business.

A prescriptive model and a descriptive model may be 100% identical in contents and presentation—yet one may be used to mandate a specific process ("you must follow what is written here"), and the other may describe the current processes ("so this is how we are doing our projects").

Solution for Problem 2.2

Lifecycle models describe activities of a product development lifecycle at a high level of abstraction. Engineering process models describe the same object as lifecycle models, but they differ in the level of abstraction and the focus on specific roles and aspects. In particular, engineering models are usually more detailed and highlight certain aspects. As a (very simple) rule of thumb, an engineering model would enable a new employee to start working, while a lifecycle model would leave the same employee asking "ok, but what am I supposed to do *concretely?*"

Examples of lifecycle models:

- Waterfall model: Very generic, covers only major processes.
- Iterative enhancement model: Describes a number of processes and the general sequence to execute them. Not tied to particular practices or techniques.
- Unified process: Covers a large fraction of the lifecycle including requirements elicitation and testing.

Examples of engineering models:

- Checklist-based design inspections: Describe a specific technique for defect detection.
- Model-based statistical testing: Describes specific testing techniques (model-based).
- Hybrid cost estimation (CoBRA): Is relevant in a single phase (project planning) and describes a specific estimation technique.

Solution for Problem 2.3

Resistance to change: People can resist change and insist on doing their work as they are used to. They may fail to see the point of introducing a new process, feel that the changes may make their existing knowledge irrelevant, etc.

Counter-strategies:

1. Consider a more gradual process deployment strategy so that people have more time to adapt to change and can learn the new procedures in a step-wise fashion.
2. Sell the new process, for example, by making sure that people are well informed about the potential advantages of the new process.
3. Involve affected people in process improvement efforts, for example, by giving them the opportunity to provide feedback (and by seriously taking this feedback into account).

Inappropriate process: The deployed process is not appropriate for the organization/unit or its effects and risks are not sufficiently understood. For example, the process may be intended for an application domain that does not match the organization. Also, necessary tailoring such as changing, for instance, a test process, might lead to lower test efficiency/effectiveness and bear unknown risks with respect to the reliability of the tested product.

Counter-strategies:

1. Perform case studies to determine how appropriate the process is for the organization.
2. Use feedback from process performers to tailor the process.
3. Analyze process traces to identify potential inefficiencies and use that information to improve the process definition.

Missing tailoring support: No or insufficient guidelines are provided to customize the process to its context.

Counter-strategies:

1. Analyze potential variations by looking at specific project needs.
2. Define tailoring guidelines.
3. Validate the guidelines by tailoring the process for specific project contexts and analyze process performance after project completion.

Problems for Chapter 3

Problem 3.1

Looking at the eight-step approach: Suppose that for a certain process modeling effort, the goal "process automation" was chosen in step 1. What would be the consequences for step 3?

Problem 3.2

Suppose now that the selected goal was "process guidance." What would be the consequences for step 3 in this case?

Problem 3.3

Steps 7 and 8 of the presented descriptive process modeling approach are concerned with analyses. What are the differences between these two steps? Why are they separate from each other?

Problem 3.4

You have just finished creating a detailed model for the development processes of a medium-sized software company. One aspect of the process you have learned about during your process modeling work is that the company uses a version management system to store the source code of all of their products, as well as many documents related to said products. You know that most people in development-related roles rely quite strongly on this system for their daily work. Indeed, people in the company normally collaborate around products by storing them in this system, so that other people have access to them and can change them if necessary.

How could you use the version management system data (content, logs, etc.) to determine whether your process model reflects your real software processes? Suggest concrete ways in which data stored in the version management system could be used to check the accuracy of your new process model.

Solutions to the Problems for Chapter 3

Solution for Problem 3.1

In general, the selected notation would have to be interpretable by a machine, so that it can be used as a basis for supporting execution through an automated system. This requires a notation with a high level of formality.

Solution for Problem 3.2

The selected notation would have to be human-readable, or at least, it should be able to produce human-readable documentation, for example, by automatically generating it using a documentation generator.

Solution for Problem 3.3

Step 7 analyzes the process model with respect to internal properties such as consistency. This is basically a quality assurance step regarding the created process model; it normally contributes only little to the goals of the process-modeling effort. In step 7, the process model is the object of interest, and a set of (external) tools is used to analyze it.

Step 8 uses the model to analyze the process itself, i.e., to achieve the goals of the modeling effort. In step 8, the process itself is the object of interest, and the process model is used as a tool to identify bottlenecks, for example.

The two steps are separate because without being sure that the model has sufficient quality, it is very hard to make any statements with respect to the underlying process. In particular, with an unchecked model, if a shortcoming is detected (such as, for example, a missing input our output product), one cannot be sure whether it is because the model is faulty or because the process itself is faulty.

Solution for Problem 3.4

Since the version management system logs every checking and update of all documents, it is possible to create a timeline, with the documents' lifecycle in (partial) order. This order can be used to check whether the actual process that people are following is represented accurately in your process model. For instance, if the process model states that document A is used as input for an activity that produces document B, you could check whether document A exists before document B is checked in for the first time, and in which state document A is when B is checked in. Similarly, you can check which people read and write which documents, which in turn allows for checking your process model's role assignments.

Problems for Chapter 4

Problem 4.1

The development process for a certain company involves the following products:

- Problem Description (PD)
- Requirements (Req)
- Design (Des)
- Component Requirements (CReq)
- Component Test Cases (CTC)
- Components Code (Co)
- Component Test Results (CTR)

Your task is to create an MVP-L graphical process model for this company. Start by defining process steps for producing the products listed above (with the exception of the Problem Description, which is provided at the start of the process). In order to make sure that the test cases for each component properly match the requirements specified for the component, the Component Requirements and the

Component Tests Cases products must be produced by a single process step. Also, in order to test the components, not only the Components Code product, but also the Component Test Cases are necessary as input. Create a process model that produces the products in a simple waterfall. Use the following template.

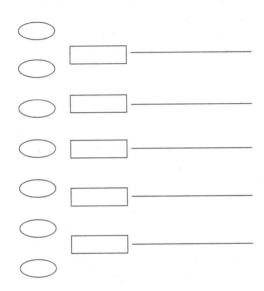

Problem 4.2

Draw the MVP-L state diagram for processes. Make sure that you include all possible transitions and label them properly.

Problem 4.3

Suppose you want to create an MVP-L process model that is able to limit the maximum effort invested into a development task. Why is it inadequate to include this limit in the task exit criteria? What would be the appropriate place for making sure that effort limits are not surpassed?

Solutions to the Problems for Chapter 4

Solution for Problem 4.1

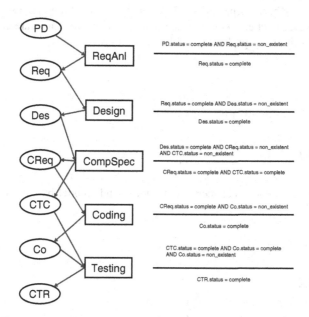

Solution for Problem 4.2

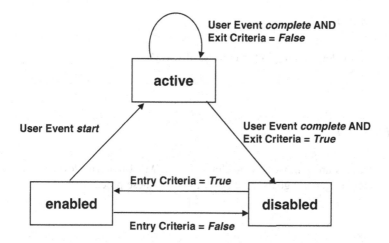

Solution for Problem 4.3

Using the exit criteria is inadequate because they are checked only after the process is marked as "complete" by the user. This could be too late, because the effort limit may have already been surpassed—so you cannot do anything about it anymore.

The right place to check would be an invariant. Since invariants are checked in a continuous fashion, any problems will be noticed immediately.

Problems for Chapter 5

Problem 5.1

Explain the difference between continuous and model-based improvement approaches.

Problem 5.2

What is the difference between the staged and continuous representations of CMMI?

Problem 5.3

What is equivalent staging in the context of CMMI?

Problem 5.4

Which process areas must be considered for a CMMI maturity level 3 appraisal? Which specific/generic goals must be fulfilled by these processes?

Solutions to the Problems for Chapter 5

Solution for Problem 5.1

Model-based improvement approaches compare an organization's processes with a predefined model (assessment/appraisal). From the comparison results, conclusions are drawn on the quality of the organization's processes, and improvement actions are derived that are supposed to make the organization's processes more similar to the model, assuming that this improves the processes.

Continuous improvement approaches focus on specific areas where problems are detected, or where huge benefits are expected from improvement. For these areas, specific improvement actions are determined. This is assumed to provide a more context- and organization-specific path to improvement than model-based approaches, but it also requires more skills, for example, in determining the weaknesses in the first place.

Solution for Problem 5.2

Continuous representation allows for appraising any selection of process areas. For every process area, a capability level (CL) is determined, which symbolizes the organization's process capabilities with respect to this process area.

Originally taken from CMMI's predecessor CMM, staged representation assigns a single maturity level (ML) to an organization, based on a specific selection of process areas.

Solution for Problem 5.3

Maturity levels are associated with particular capability levels of specific process areas. An organization has reached a particular maturity level when it has reached the corresponding capability levels in all relevant process areas. Equivalent staging is the process of deriving a maturity level from the determined capability levels.

Solution for Problem 5.4

Process areas to be considered:

– Requirements Management (REQM)
– Project Planning (PP)

- Project Monitoring and Control (PMC)
- Supplier Agreement Management (SAM)
- Measurement and Analysis (MA)
- Process and Product Quality Assurance (PPQA)
- Configuration Management (CM)
- Technical Solution (TS)
- Product Integration (PI)
- Validation (VAL)
- Verification (VER)
- Organizational Process Focus (OPF)
- Organizational Process Definition (OPD)
- Organizational Training (OT)
- Requirements Development (RD)
- Decision Analysis and Resolution (DAR)
- Integrated Project Management (IPM)
- Risk Management (RSKM)

For a maturity level 3 appraisal, generic goals 1, 2, and 3 must be fulfilled by these process areas.

Problems for Chapter 6

Problem 6.1

The traditional test method in a large development organization involves producing test cases in a primarily manual way. These test cases are then reviewed and collected into a test suite, which, in turn, is used to test every product release. The organization is considering the gradual introduction of a new model-based test method. In this method, a set of models is created that describe the tested system and its environment. Using these models as a basis, a test suite generation system produces a large number of test cases in a completely automated fashion.

Although this new method has the potential of saving a significant amount of work, its introduction would also involve significant risk. For this reason, the organization wants to empirically study its viability and effectiveness. Concretely, the following questions should be addressed:

1. Are the Quality Assurance (QA) people satisfied with the current method? (There are around 100 people in the QA department).
2. Does the new method reduce Quality Assurance costs (with respect to the current method) when applied to small systems?
3. Will the application of the new method reduce overall project costs when used in the (rather large) projects that are common in the organization?

Which types of empirical studies (controlled experiment, case study, survey) would you use to address each of these questions? Explain why your type of choice for each question would be appropriate and why it would be better than other study types in that particular case.

Solutions to the Problems for Chapter 6

Solution for Problem 6.1

1. Survey. Other methods would not address the existing experience, but new experiences happening during the execution of the experiment or case study. A survey would also make it possible to maximize the number of QA members that are reached. Other methods would normally reach fewer participants and usually involve much higher costs. Also, since members are already familiar with the current method, a survey is convenient because it collects data about their existing experience and perception in a systematic fashion.
2. Controlled experiment. A controlled experiment can be used here because of the small size of the tested system. It provides a higher level of control over the influence factors than a case study, so it is preferable.
3. Case study. Given the project size, it is probably impossible to use controlled experiments in this case because the influence factors cannot be properly controlled during the long time frame necessary for completing a whole project.

Problems for Chapter 7

Problem 7.1

When would you use a continuous simulation approach, and when would you prefer a discrete-event approach? Give an example for each preference and explain your decision.

Solutions to the Problems for Chapter 7

Solution for Problem 7.1

A continuous simulation approach is beneficial for large-scale processes, for example, when modeling an entire organization. Since a continuous simulation model immediately reacts to changes in its variables, it provides an adequate representation of the complex feedback loops found in (software) organizations.

When analyzing a specific portion of the organization's processes, however, a discrete-event provides more detailed insight into the process. Since the simulation is clocked, it can be run at any speed and stopped at any time, so causes and effects can be analyzed in great detail. It also provides the means to model the activities of interest in very fine detail, and to identify different states such as the start of an activity or the creation of a document. This helps to understand the simulation results.

Both forms can be combined, of course: The continuous model can be used for the "big picture," i.e., the overall organization with all feedback loops. Discrete-event models can be used within the continuous model to describe those parts of the process that are of particular interest, and thus contributing the necessary level of detail.

Index

J. Münch et al., *Software Process Definition and Management*,
The Fraunhofer Series on Software and Systems Engineering,
DOI 10.1007/978-3-642-24291-5, © Springer-Verlag Berlin Heidelberg 2012